THE EPISTLE TO THE EPHESIANS.

THE
EPISTLE TO THE EPHESIANS:

ITS DOCTRINE AND ETHICS.

BY

R. W. DALE, M.A.,

BIRMINGHAM.

SECOND THOUSAND.

Wipf and Stock Publishers
199 W 8th Ave, Suite 3
Eugene, OR 97401

The Epistle to the Ephesians
Its Doctrine and Ethics
By Dale, R. W.
ISBN: 1-59752-600-2
Publication date 3/17/2006
Previously published by Hodder and Stoughton, 1882

PREFACE.

THESE Lectures were intended to illustrate to a popular audience the Doctrine and the Ethics of Paul's Epistle to the Ephesians. As they were delivered on Sunday mornings, in the ordinary course of my ministry, it was necessary for the sake of "edification" to dwell on some topics at greater length and with greater urgency than would have been necessary for purposes of exposition; and for the sake of "practice" it was necessary to apply the precepts of the Epistle to the details of conduct. Some passages which were suggested by the obligations of the pastor rather than of the expositor I have omitted; others I have condensed; and to many passages I have given a less free and familiar form than that in which they were delivered. One or two of the Lectures, as they appear in this volume, were obviously too long for endurance in these times, though they would have been regarded as abnormally brief by the robust ecclesiastical ancestors of the congregation of which I am the minister; in delivery these Lectures had to be divided.

But both in substance and in style the Lectures still retain clear traces of their original character. They were written for a popular congregation, not for the solitary student. And I do not know that I should have had the courage to publish them but for the very kind and hearty reception which has been given both in England and America to a similar series of Lectures which I published some years ago on the Epistle to the Hebrews. I have learnt that there are large numbers of Christian people to whom expository lectures of this popular kind are of more service than ordinary commentaries.

My obligations to Meyer are too numerous to admit of recognition in detail. Throughout my study of the Epistle his commentary was always at my side; whenever I have differed from him it has been with the greatest hesitation, and with the uncomfortable apprehension that, after all, he was probably in the right and I in the wrong. I ought also to express my obligations to Bishop Ellicott. In my early ministry I found his commentaries of great value; and in the preparation of these Lectures my sense of their excellence has been confirmed and renewed.

R. W. DALE.

[ERRATUM.—In second line of note, on page 1, *for* "influences" *read* "tendencies."]

CONTENTS.

	PAGE
INTRODUCTORY	1

LECT.
- I. PAUL'S APOSTLESHIP—THE SAINTS AT EPHESUS—PAUL'S BENEDICTION. (Eph. i. 1, 2) . . . 11
- II. ELECTION IN CHRIST. (Chap. i. 3, 4) . . . 25
- III. REGENERATION AND SONSHIP IN CHRIST. (Chap. i. 5, 6) 40
- IV. THE FORGIVENESS OF SINS. (Chap. i. 7) . . . 53
- V. THE FORGIVENESS OF SINS AND THE DEATH OF CHRIST. (Chap. i. 7). 68
- VI. THE FINAL RESTORATION OF ALL THINGS. (Chap. i. 8–10) 90
- VII. THE HOLY SPIRIT THE SEAL OF GOD'S HERITAGE AND THE EARNEST OF OUR INHERITANCE. (Chap. i. 11–14) 109
- VIII. THE ILLUMINATION OF THE SPIRIT. (Chap. i. 15–17) 128
- IX. THE RESURRECTION AND GLORY OF CHRIST IN RELATION TO THE HOPE OF THE CHURCH. (Chap. i. 18–ii. 7) 144
- X. SALVATION BY GRACE. (Chap. ii. 8, 9) . . . 170
- XI. CHRISTIAN MEN GOD'S WORKMANSHIP. (Chap. ii. 10) 185
- XII. JUDAISM AND CHRISTIANITY. (Chap. ii. 11–22) . 201

CONTENTS.

LECT.		PAGE
XIII.	THE GRACE GIVEN TO PAUL. (Chap. iii. 1–13)	220
XIV.	FILLED UNTO ALL THE FULNESS OF GOD. (Chap. iii. 14–21)	242
XV.	THE UNITY OF THE CHURCH. (Chap. iv. 1–16)	260
XVI.	THE IMMORALITY OF THE HEATHEN. (Chap. iv. 17–19)	294
XVII.	THE CHRISTIAN METHOD OF MORAL REGENERATION. (Chap. iv. 20–24)	308
XVIII.	MISCELLANEOUS MORAL PRECEPTS. (Chap. iv. 25—v. 21)	323
XIX.	WIVES AND HUSBANDS. (Chap. v. 22–33)	349
XX.	CHILDREN AND PARENTS. (Chap. vi. 1–4)	378
XXI.	SERVANTS AND MASTERS. (Chap. vi. 5-9)	398
XXII.	THE WAR AGAINST PRINCIPALITIES AND POWERS. (Chap. vi. 10–12)	412
XXIII.	THE WHOLE ARMOUR OF GOD. (Chap. vi. 13–17)	426
XXIV.	PRAYER; INTERCESSORY PRAYER; CONCLUSION. (Chap. vi. 18–24)	435

INTRODUCTORY.

EPHESUS.

JERUSALEM, Antioch, Ephesus, Rome—these great cities represent the most considerable influences which determined the early fortunes and development of the Christian church.[1]

In Jerusalem the sacred traditions of sixteen centuries were too strong for the free and adventurous spirit of the new Faith. The Lord Jesus Christ Himself had observed the religious customs of the Jewish people, had worshipped in their synagogues and in their temple, had kept their feasts; and though He had disregarded, ostentatiously disregarded, some of the mechanical and technical precepts which had been deduced from the commandments of the Jewish law, He had acknowledged the authority of the law itself, and had never challenged the claims of the Jews to religious supremacy over the rest of mankind.

There were some of His words, indeed, which naturally created doubt, and even alarm, among those who regarded the institutions and prerogatives of

---

[1] In Alexandria, under the influence of a high culture, there was a blending and reconciliation of influences which were separately active elsewhere.

Judaism with blind and passionate veneration. What must have seemed the light audacity with which He spoke of the possible destruction of the temple, the very home of God, and of His raising it up in three days; His denial that the distinction between things clean and unclean had any real moral significance; His declaration to the Samaritan woman that the hour was coming when the sacredness both of mount Gerizim and of Jerusalem would have passed away; the startling warning in His conversation with Nicodemus that Jewish birth was not an adequate title to the blessedness of the Messianic age, and that "except a man be born anew he cannot see the kingdom of God": were all very perplexing and even ominous. But in the general current of our Lord's popular teaching there was little or nothing to suggest that a great religious catastrophe was impending.

Knowing who He was and what He accomplished for mankind by His incarnation, His death, and His resurrection, we see that it was inevitable that the ancient institutions of Judaism should lose their sanctity. Now that we have had time to consider "the grace and truth" which "came by Jesus Christ," we can see that there was a great contrast between the spiritual and ethical contents of the new Faith and the spiritual and ethical contents of the old Faith; a contrast so immense that the organisation which was a support and defence to the religious life of ancient saints would be a peril to the nobler life of the kingdom of heaven and a restraint upon its free and vigorous development. But the approaching change was not suspected by even the closest friends of Christ during His earthly ministry. That the dissolution of all things was at hand was an impression which they might naturally have received from some things that He said shortly before His crucifixion; but I suppose that they all believed that as long as the world lasted Judaism would last.

Even after His resurrection and ascension into heaven this seems to have been the common belief of the Jewish Christians that lived in Jerusalem and its neighbourhood. The temple was still standing; the priests still discharged their functions; morning and evening the sacrifices commanded by the ancient law were still offered; the sabbath was still honoured; at every great festival the city was still thronged by tens of thousands of Jews and proselytes from remote lands; the only sacred books which, as yet, God had given to men were the writings of Moses and the prophets; and these were still read, as they had been read for several centuries, in the synagogues every sabbath day. Those who believed that Jesus was the Christ had received some fresh and wonderful revelations of the righteousness and love of God; but while rejoicing in their new knowledge, their new religious life, and their new hopes, they saw no reason for suspecting that the ancient institutions of their race had passed away. The apostles themselves did not at once discover that Christ had made all things new; that the altars, the sacrifices, the sabbaths, the festivals, the priests of Judaism had given place to a more spiritual service; that the temple was no longer sacred; that the Jewish people were no longer the elect race, and that their prerogatives had disappeared in that Divine and eternal kingdom which acknowledged no distinction between Jew and Gentile, and conferred on all who are in Christ the same august titles, making them all the sons of God and the heirs of eternal glory.

At Antioch the church began to be conscious of a larger freedom. The church in that city was principally composed of Gentiles. To heathen men who had found God in Christ, the future was far greater and nobler than the past. They were not under the spell of ancient traditions, but were exulting in the inspiration of new and infinite hopes. They had received all things from Christ. They listened with interest to what they heard from their Jewish brethren about what God had done for the Jewish people in past centuries, and they listened with veneration to the words which had been spoken in God's name by Jewish prophets. But to them Christ was not only supreme: from Him, and from Him alone, had come their knowledge of the true God, their assurance of the remission of sins, and their hope of immortality. Their Jewish brethren might, if they pleased, continue to observe the customs of their ancestors; but, for themselves, they were Christians, not Jews; and the power and love of Christ were sufficient for them apart from the institutions of Judaism. We owe it to these generous and courageous men, and above all to the apostle Paul, their great leader, that Christianity disentangled itself from what would have been a disastrous alliance with the traditions, customs, prejudices, and fortunes of the Jewish race, and asserted its true character as the kingdom of God among men and not a new Jewish sect. "The disciples were called Christians first at Antioch."

When the new Faith had achieved its freedom from the control of the synagogue, and began to make its own way in the great heathen world, it was exposed to fresh perils. Many of its converts were men that had been corrupted by the gross licentiousness of heathen society, and they brought the vicious habits and the base ethical ideas of their former life into the church. Men who had acknowledged the authority of Christ, who had received Christian baptism, who sat at the Lord's supper, and who were rejoicing in the great hopes of the Christian life, had to be told that they must not be guilty of lying, theft, drunkenness, and the grossest sensual sins. Christian truth was in danger as well as Christian morality. The gospel, notwithstanding its wonderful discoveries concerning God and His relations to the human race, concerning the spiritual nature of man and the immortal life and blessedness conferred by Christ, left unsolved some of the philosophical questions in which the restless and subtle curiosity of the Greek intellect found an irresistible attraction; and it also appeared to leave unoccupied those vast regions of thought which had been the chosen field of very much of oriental speculation. Some Christian converts made a natural attempt to handle the facts and truths of the Christian faith according to the methods of the philosophical schools; they endeavoured to supplement what seemed to them the incompleteness of apostolic teaching by precarious inferences from Christian truths imperfectly apprehended, or by speculative theories which were altogether alien from the contents of the gospel. In some cases there was an attempt to blend with the historical manifestation of God in Christ one or other of those wild and elaborate schemes of the universe which were among the most audacious and the most worthless products of the oriental imagination.[1]

All these influences—the licentiousness, the excessive intellectual subtlety, the vague and reckless speculation—affected the development of Christian life and thought in those Asiatic Greek cities of which Ephesus was the largest, the richest, the most splendid, and the most corrupt.

Rome is the representative of influences of altogether a different kind. The traditions of universal sovereignty and the imperial temper of the masters of the world became the inheritance of the Roman church, and gradually created that immense authority which for good or for evil, but at last for

---

[1] See the striking account of "Le Syncrétisme Oriental," in chap. viii. of M. Renan's *Marc.-Aurèle*.

evil only, was exerted by the Bishop of Rome over all western Christendom.[1]

It was from Rome that Paul wrote this epistle to the church at Ephesus; he had been a prisoner there for about two years. There are indications in the earlier chapters of the epistle that the power of the empire of which Rome was the centre had touched his imagination, and perhaps had given a new and grander form to his conception of the future triumphs of the Divine kingdom. It is in the epistle to the church at Colosse, a city on the high road between Ephesus and the Euphrates, that he directly attacks the heresies which had been brought into the church by theosophic speculation, but in this epistle also Paul recognised and desired to satisfy the cravings of the Asiatic intellect for large and daring theories of the invisible and spiritual universe. A considerable part of the epistle is occupied with precepts directed against those moral corruptions from which the Ephesian Christians had not yet escaped.

Ephesus, as I have already said, was a rich and splendid city. It was the capital of the great Roman

---

[1] What Dr. Lightfoot justly describes as "the urgent and almost imperious tone which the Romans adopt in addressing their Corinthian brethren during the closing years of the first century" illustrates the origin of the Roman supremacy. It was the church however, not the bishop, that assumed this moral authority. See Dr. Lightfoot's most valuable dissertation prefixed to his edition of the newly recovered portions of the Epistle of Clement.

province of Asia. It had an extensive commerce. When the fertile countries of Asia Minor, now impoverished by the government of the Turk, were wealthiest, Ephesus was all that Smyrna now is to the diminished trade of the Levant. And it was famous throughout the world for the magnificence of the temple of Diana.

Paul knew the city well. As he was returning to Syria from Greece on his second missionary journey he called there with Aquila and Priscilla, stayed there a few days, discussed the claims of the Lord Jesus in the synagogue, and promised to return. On his third missionary journey, after visiting the churches in the interior of Asia Minor, he came down to the coast and remained in Ephesus and its neighbourhood for two or three years. For three months he went week after week to the synagogue, speaking boldly and reasoning with the Jews "concerning the kingdom of God." Then he separated his converts from the Jewish congregation and hired the school, the lecture hall, of Tyrannus, who was probably a Greek lecturer on rhetoric and philosophy. There he was able to meet day after day with all who cared to listen to his exposition and defence of the Christian gospel. His teaching seems to have made a great impression on the city, and at last provoked the alarm of the trades that depended on the reverence for Diana. There was a violent popular tumult, and Paul left Ephesus for Macedonia and Greece. On his way back from Greece to Jerusalem he called at Miletus, which was twenty or thirty miles from Ephesus, and sent a message to the elders of the Ephesian church to meet him ; the pathetic address which he delivered to them has been preserved by Luke, and is contained in the twentieth chapter of the Acts of the Apostles.

Considering the length of time that Paul had lived in Ephesus, it is remarkable that the epistle does not contain any of the kindly messages to personal friends which are so numerous in other epistles of his. The explanation seems to be that the epistle was intended for the use of more than one church. In some very early manuscripts there is a curious omission of the words "at Ephesus" in the first verse. I imagine that Paul left a blank to be filled up by the copyist, and that while one copy was meant for the saints "at Ephesus," another was probably meant for the saints "at Laodicea," and perhaps another for a third church in the same neighbourhood. Tychicus carried the copies with him to the churches for which they were intended, and was also entrusted with the personal messages and the account of himself which Paul wished to be given to his friends. "But that ye also may know my affairs, how I do, Tychicus, the beloved brother and faithful minister in the Lord, shall make known to you all things: whom I have sent to you for this very purpose, that ye may know our state, and that he may comfort your hearts."

NOTE.—Throughout these Lectures I have spoken of "*the church at Ephesus*," although this phrase does not occur in the Epistle itself. It was addressed to "*the saints*," not to "*the church*"; this may have been because copies of the letter were to be sent to cities in which there was more than one "church." When the Apocalypse was written there was only one church in Ephesus (Apoc. ii. 1), and there was only one when Paul met the Ephesian elders at Miletus; it is reasonable to conclude that there was only one when this Epistle was written. At an earlier time there may have been more than one. The subject is an old topic of controversy between the Presbyterians and the Independents. See Dr. Davidson's "Ecclesiastical Polity of the New Testament," pages 76-88.

I.

PAUL'S APOSTLESHIP—THE SAINTS AT EPHESUS—PAUL'S BENEDICTION.

"Paul, an apostle of Christ Jesus, through the will of God, to the saints which are at Ephesus, and the faithful in Christ Jesus: grace to you, and peace, from God our Father, and the Lord Jesus Christ."

—EPH. i. 1, 2.

IN these words we have :

I. Paul's description of himself: *"an apostle of Jesus Christ through the will of God."*

II. Paul's description of those to whom he is writing: *"the saints . . and the faithful in Christ Jesus."*

III. Paul's salutation or benediction: *"Grace to you, and peace, from God our Father, and the Lord Jesus Christ."*

I.

Paul describes himself as "an apostle of Jesus Christ *through the will of God.*" He was not appointed to his office through the intervention of the church,[1] or of those who had been apostles before him; his call came direct from Heaven. Much less

---

[1] The church at Antioch separated Paul for the work to which he had been called (Acts xiii. 1–3); but his original call and his apostolic authority came direct from Christ.

had he dared to undertake his great work at the impulse of his own zeal for the honour of Christ and the redemption of men. To the last he thought of himself as "less than the least of all saints," and had he chosen his own place it would have been among the obscurest of those who trusted in Christ for the pardon of sin and eternal life. He had been "a blasphemer and persecutor"; he was "the chief of sinners"; he was "not meet to be called an apostle because [he] persecuted the church of God." But God's grace to him had been very wonderful, and it was this grace which had appointed him to "preach unto the Gentiles the unsearchable riches of Christ."

In the depths of his humility were the foundations of his strength. His courage and confidence might have been shaken if he had ever had to consider his intellectual, his moral, or his spiritual qualifications for his work. If he had permitted himself to ask whether, after his violent hostility to Christ, it was fitting that he should be a preacher of the Christian gospel and a founder of Christian churches, he might have shrunk from the honour of his conspicuous service. But nothing came between him and the will of God. When he was giving an account to Agrippa of Christ's appearance to him on the Damascus road he said "I was not disobedient unto the heavenly vision"; but it does not seem to have been the habit of his mind to think of even his own consent to the Divine call. He says in one of his epistles that Christ's love—not his own gratitude for Christ's love, his own joy in it, but Christ's love—constrained him to live a life of incessant and laborious devotion to Christ's service. The love in Christ's heart was an energy acting immediately on all the faculties and powers of his own life. And when he describes himself as an apostle "*through the will of God*" he means that he felt that the Divine will was in immediate contact with him, was the strong yet gracious force which placed him in the apostleship, and which sustained him in all his apostolic labours and sufferings. He attributed nothing to the vigour of his faith, to the passion of his gratitude for the Divine goodness, to the completeness of his self-consecration to Christ's service; he was living and acting under the control of forces which had their origin beyond and above himself; his apostolic work was the effect and expression of a Divine volition.

The expression is characteristic of the Pauline theology; Paul believed that the Divine will is the root and origin of all Christian righteousness and blessedness. And this is the secret of a strong and calm and effective Christian life. The secret is hard to learn. We find it difficult not to interpose something between "the will of God" and our personal redemption; between "the will of God" and our obedience to the Divine law; between "the will of God" and the work which we are doing for God and for mankind; and so the direct action of the power and grace of God upon our life is deflected and impeded. Instead of welcoming the Divine

mercy with frank delight, we ask whether our own
faith is sufficiently simple and strong to warrant us
in accepting the great blessings of the Christian redemption. We should remember that whatever our
ill desert may be, it is "the will of God" that we
should receive "repentance and the remission of
sins," and we should say from our very heart "Thy
will be done." After we have endeavoured to serve
God for many years we miss the life and strength
which He has actually given us in Christ, and we
miss them because we are perplexed and uncertain
as to whether we have consented, without reserve
and qualification, to achieve a moral and spiritual
perfection which has its roots in Christ and not
in ourselves, the honour of which will be Christ's,
not ours. Again we should remember that it is "the
will of God" that this righteousness should be ours,
that it is the law of human nature to receive perpetual
accessions of strength from Divine fountains, and we
should say "Thy will be done." The vigour and
hopefulness of our work for others are lessened by the
uneasy consciousness that we are wanting in spiritual
fervour and force; by the fear that our motives are
not perfectly unselfish, that our consecration is not
complete, that our intellectual qualifications are
inadequate. Thoughts like these are sufficient to
paralyse the strength of the strongest and to quench
the fire of the most zealous. Whatever work lies
under our hand should be taken up in the spirit in
which Paul accepted his apostleship and discharged

its duties. Our election to a service to which we have no claim, and which is beyond our strength, is an illustration of God's wonderful grace, and an assurance that a power, not our own, will ally itself with our weakness; we should say again, "Thy will be done."

But has the human will no place or function in human redemption, and in the active service in which Christian men show their loyalty to Christ and their love for the race? Is "the will of God" the only force in the spiritual universe? Must there not be a real response on our part to the Divine mercy before the Divine mercy can pardon our sin? If Christ is to abide in us, must not we abide in Him? If we are to do any work worth doing for God or man, must not the fires of enthusiasm and charity be kindled in our own hearts, and must not those fires consume the cowardice, the selfishness, the vanity, and the personal ambition by which our work would be spoiled?

There are some of you, I hope, to whom these questions occasion no difficulty. When God comes into real and close contact with the soul, we can think only of Him, not of ourselves; of His mercy, not of our own faith; of His grace, not of our own consent to receive it; of His choice of us, not of our choice of Him; of His will, not of our own submission to it.

Paul was an apostle "*through the will of God.*" His own will consented, no doubt, to receive the apostleship; but it was the habit of his mind to refer his whole apostolic life and work directly to God. Our own spiritual activity reaches its greatest intensity when we are so filled with the glory of the Divine righteousness, the Divine love, and the Divine power, that we are conscious only of God, and all thought of ourselves is lost in Him.

II.

Having described himself, Paul goes on to describe those to whom the epistle is written. They are "*the saints which are at Ephesus, and the faithful in Christ Jesus.*"

They are "*saints.*" It is impossible, I fear, to restore this word to its ancient and noble uses. It has been tainted with superstition, which has limited its application to those who have exhibited an exceptional holiness; and for many centuries it has been restricted to men whose holiness has been of a very technical and artificial type. It has been degraded by unbelief, which, in bitter mockery of the contrast between lofty aims and ignoble achievement, has flung it as an epithet of scorn at all who have professed to make the Divine will, and not the laws and customs of human society, the rule of their conduct.

In the early days all Christians were "*saints.*" The title did not attribute any personal merit to them; it simply recalled their prerogatives and their obligations. Whenever they were so described they were reminded that God had made them His own.

They were "holy" because they belonged to Him. The temple had once been "holy," not because of its magnitude, its stateliness, and the costly materials of which it was built, but because it was the home of God; and the tabernacle which was erected in the wilderness, though a much meaner structure, was just as "holy" as the temple of Solomon, with its marble courts and its profusion of cedar and brass and silver and gold. The altars were "holy" because they were erected for the service of God. The sacrifices were "holy" because they were offered to Him. The priests were "holy" because they were divinely chosen to discharge the functions of the temple service. The sabbath was "holy" because God had placed His hand upon it and separated its hours from common uses. The whole Jewish people were "holy" because they were organised into a nation, not for the common purposes which have been the ends of the national existence of other races, but to receive in trust for all mankind exceptional revelations of the character and will of God. And now, according to Paul's conception, every Christian man was a temple, a sacrifice, a priest; his whole life was a sabbath; he belonged to an elect race; he was the subject of an invisible and Divine kingdom; he was a "saint."

The institutions of Judaism had given only a very rough and coarse representation of the idea of holiness; and there are passages in this epistle which will throw far more light upon what is really mean

by being a "saint" than we can derive from the
Jewish temple, the Jewish priests, the Jewish sacrifices,
and the Jewish sabbath; but the rudimentary
conception is to be found in the holy places, the
holy things, the holy times, and the holy persons of
the ancient Faith.

And there was one essential element in that
rudimentary conception which remains unchanged in
the new and higher form of sanctity which is presented
in the Christian church. Speaking broadly,
nothing became "holy" in Jewish times by any
human act consecrating it to God. No man could
erect a building and make it a temple. There was
only one temple, and this had been erected by
Divine appointment and on a Divine plan. When the
Jews began to build synagogues in different parts of
the country for religious instruction and worship it
was not supposed that the buildings had any sanctity.
A synagogue was not, like the temple, the home
and palace of God; it was erected for the convenience
of a congregation. Nor could any man,
at the impulse of his own devout zeal, make himself
a priest, or obtain admission into the priesthood
by the authority of those who were priests already.
No man took this honour to himself; it belonged
exclusively to the family on which God had conferred
it. Nor could any general consent to set
apart a day for religious uses make the day sacred as
the sabbath was sacred. No person, no place, no
time could be set apart for God by any human

appointment, and so made holy. Every consecrated person, place, and time was consecrated, not by the fervour of human devotion, but by the authority of the Divine will.

And a "saint," a consecrated man, according to the apostolic conception, is one whom God has set apart for Himself. The act of consecration is God's act, not ours. As I have said already, the title of "saint" implies no personal merit; it is the record of a great manifestation of God's condescension and love. Our part is subordinate and secondary. We have only to submit to the authority of the Divine claim, and to receive the dignity conferred by the Divine love.

The common conception is precisely the reverse of this, and precisely the reverse of the truth. It begins with a human volition instead of a Divine volition. It makes the act of consecration a human act instead of a Divine act. God's place becomes subordinate and secondary; He only accepts what we give. As the sanctity is supposed to originate in the voluntary surrender of the heart and life to God, the measure of the sanctity is determined by the extent of the surrender; and a man is more or less of a saint in the degree in which he makes himself over to God.

The apostolic idea was far more profound. It was an essential part of Paul's whole theory of man's relation to God. The theology of the Epistle to the Romans, the theology of this epistle, obliged him to rest the idea of sanctity, not on the shifting sands of human volition, but on the eternal foundations of the Divine love.

Those whom he describes as "saints" he also describes as "*the faithful in Christ Jesus.*" Scholars are divided as to whether Paul means that they have *faith* or whether he means that they have *fidelity.* The word which he uses may stand as well for the one idea as for the other. Had he been asked in which sense he employed it, I think he might have answered that Faith carries Fidelity with it. For to Paul faith was very much more than intellectual belief; it was an act in which the intellect, the heart, the conscience, and the will acknowledged Christ as the Redeemer and the Ruler of men. As long as faith of this kind exists in a man, Christ has sovereignty over his life; and the man's faith guarantees his fidelity.

They are the faithful "*in Christ Jesus.*" This is one of Paul's characteristic phrases. I shall not attempt to explain it in this lecture. The doctrinal teaching of this epistle is very little more than a development of this single expression. To explain what Paul meant by being "in Christ" would be to expound a great part of his theology.

III.

The closing words of the second verse, "*Grace to you and peace from God our Father and the Lord Jesus Christ,*" are commonly described as the salutation of the epistle; they take the place of the kindly words which were usual in the beginning of ancient letters. But "*Grace and peace from God our Father and the Lord Jesus Christ*" belong to too lofty a region for the words to be regarded as merely an expression of courtesy and good will. They are not a prayer, for they are not addressed to God but to men; and yet they are very much more than a wish. I think that we must call them a Benediction.

When our Lord sent out His twelve apostles on an evangelistic journey during His own ministry, He said to them: "Into whatsoever city or village ye shall enter, search out who in it is worthy, and there abide till ye go forth. And as ye enter into the house salute it. And if the house be worthy, let your peace come upon it: but if it be not worthy, let your peace return to you." The customary Jewish salutation, "Peace be with this house," when spoken by the apostles of Christ, was to be made real and effective by the concurrence of the Divine grace. It was really to bring peace to those whose hearts were simple, trustful and devout; the words of benediction were to be confirmed and fulfilled by God. And Paul had equal authority to speak in God's name. To those in the Ephesian church who were really "saints," and who were really "faithful in Christ Jesus," his words were to be more than a courteous and affectionate desire for their religious welfare. His words were "with power." They were a gospel, a message from God. They were to bring home to Christian hearts a fresh assurance of the "*grace*" of God the Father and of the Lord Jesus Christ, a fuller realization and a richer consciousness of the "*peace*," the infinite and eternal blessings, which that grace conferred.

It is the prerogative and function of priests to bless in God's name. This prerogative belonged to the apostle, and in this salutation he is discharging the function. The tradition of this august and benignant power has never disappeared from the church; but in the dark and evil days through which Christendom has passed it came to be restricted to those who claimed to be priests in a sense in which ordinary Christian men are not. But even in churches which have conceded to the priesthood an exclusive sanctity there survive traces of the original dignity of the people. The old form of the ancient liturgies is still retained, and when the priest says to the congregation " The Lord be with you," the congregation replies "And with thy spirit." The blessing of the priest bestowed on the people is answered by the blessing of the people bestowed on the priest.

The power of benediction, which belongs to the commonalty of the church and not to church officers only, is a beautiful illustration of the true ideal of the Christian life. We dwell in Christ and Christ dwells in us. It is a superstitious and most ruinous falsehood to tell men to reverence the Real Presence of Christ in the consecrated wafer with the lamp burning before it in the silent church. His Real

Presence, according to His own teaching, is to be found in the common life and activity of every Christian man. His Real Presence is to be found in the Christian tradesman at his counter, the Christian clerk at his desk, the Christian mechanic at his bench, the Christian mother among her children. Christ is really present in the Christian physician going through the wards of a hospital, in the Christian barrister pleading in court, in the Christian statesman contending in parliament for justice and peace. The service which, as Christian men, we render to our race is Christ's service rather than ours. When we pity human suffering our pity is made more tender by Christ's own compassion; when we struggle against injustice and tyranny the fires of our indignation are kindled and made more vehement by Christ's infinite hatred of unrighteousness.

And so, if the true ideal of the Christian life were fulfilled, men would be conscious that whenever we came near to them Christ came near, bringing with Him the rest of heart, the courage, and the hope which His presence always inspires. When we invoked on men the Divine favour and the Divine peace, the invocation would be His rather than ours; it would be spoken in His name, not in our own; and what we spoke on earth would be confirmed and made good in heaven. We have ceased to bless each other, because our consciousness of union with Him who alone can make the "blessing" effective has become faint and dim. When He was on earth those who touched the border of His garment were healed of physical sickness. Now that He is in heaven there streams from Him a mightier and more gracious power; and if our union with Christ and Christ's union with us were more complete, that power, working through us, would be a perpetual source of blessing to mankind.

II.

ELECTION IN CHRIST.

"*Blessed be the God and Father of our Lord Jesus Christ, who hath blessed us with every spiritual blessing in the heavenly places in Christ: even as He chose us in Him before the foundation of the world, that we should be holy and without blemish before Him in love.*"   EPH. i. 3, 4.

THE first three chapters of this epistle are a very striking example of Paul's manner. No one ever wrote in the same way before or since. I suppose indeed that he did not actually write the epistle himself, but dictated it, and as he spoke he was swept along by the impetuous rush of a fervent passion. One proposition melts into another. Thought flows into thought. No one sentence is complete, apart from the sentence which precedes it and the sentence which follows it. But if once we permit our mind to move from the words whose full meaning we are trying to discover, we shall drift away with the stream and shall soon find ourselves in remote provinces of truth.

The verses which we have now to consider can hardly be understood without looking forward to what Paul has written in the very heart of the epistle; and yet if we try to anticipate what occurs later on we shall be likely to miss what he has written here. But we must do our best, remembering however that it is necessary to be in possession of the whole movement of the apostle's thought, to grasp the real and complete meaning of any part of it.

"*Blessed be the God and Father of our Lord Jesus Christ.*" These words recall the joy and triumph of the ancient psalms. They read as if Paul was intending to write a song of happy thanksgiving. His heart is all a-flame. It is clear that he is not writing under the influence of any mere intellectual excitement created by the clearness of his vision of some great theory of God's relations to the human race or to the universe in general. Whatever doctrinal theory may be implied or explicitly asserted in the sentences which follow, he begins by thanking and praising God for the infinite and everlasting blessings which he himself and other Christian men had found in Christ.

"*Blessed be the God and Father of our Lord Jesus Christ, who hath blessed us with every spiritual blessing in the heavenly places in Christ.*" When Paul wrote this epistle, five-and-twenty or thirty years had passed by since Christ appeared to him near Damascus. They had been very wonderful years. None of them had been wasted. It is evident from his epistles that his religious thought was constantly extending its control from one region of truth to another, as well as constantly securing a firmer hold

of the truth which he had already mastered; and
with the growth of his religious knowledge there was
a corresponding growth of his religious life. It is
true, no doubt, that his conversion was followed by
an immediate and complete revolution both in his
belief and in his conduct. When he went into the
synagogues of Damascus and proclaimed that Jesus
was the Son of God all that heard him were amazed.
Only a few weeks ago he had been hunting the
disciples of Christ from house to house in Jerusalem,
dragging them from their hiding-places, and sending
them to prison; he had come to Damascus to carry
on the work of persecution. And now instead of
laying the church waste he was its champion and
defender. It was clear that a most extraordinary
change had passed upon him; but the change went
on; the power of his new faith was not exhausted
in the immense transformation which passed upon
him as soon as he received it; when he wrote
this epistle he was a very different man from what
he was when he began to preach the Christian
gospel.

And he attributes to Christ the whole development of his spiritual life. The larger knowledge
of God and of the ways of God, which came to
him from year to year, had come from Christ; and
he felt sure that whatever fresh discoveries of God
might come to him would also come from Christ.
Faith, hope, joy, peace, patience, courage, zeal, love
for God, love for men—he had found them all in

Christ. It was on the ground of his own personal experience that he was able to tell men that the "riches of Christ" are "unsearchable." And when he exclaims, "*Blessed be the God and Father of our Lord Jesus Christ, who hath blessed us with every spiritual blessing . . . in Christ,*" he is expressing the deep and passionate gratitude created by the happy and sacred memories of many years; he himself had found in Christ "*every spiritual blessing.*"

He defines the blessings with which God has blessed us in Christ as "*Spiritual*" blessings; he does not intend simply to distinguish them from material, physical, or intellectual blessings, he means to attribute them to the Spirit of God. Those who are "in Christ" receive the illumination and inspiration of the Holy Spirit. Whatever perfection of righteousness, whatever depth of peace, whatever intensity of joy, whatever fulness of Divine knowledge reveal the power of the Spirit of God in the spiritual life of man, "*every spiritual blessing,*" has been made ours in Christ.

Further, Paul describes these blessings as having been conferred upon us "*in heavenly places*" in Christ. To the apostle the visible order of human life was merely temporary, and was soon to pass away. Cities, empires, the solid earth itself, sun and stars, had for him no enduring reality. But the blessings which God has conferred upon us in Christ have their place among unseen and eternal things. He has "blessed us with every spiritual blessing in *heavenly places* in Christ."

And now the thought of the apostle has risen to its true home, among the sublimities of the life of God. It is there, and there alone, that he finds the fountain of those eternal blessings which are the glorious inheritance of the church. These blessings are not the natural reward and crown of human loyalty to the Divine throne. Nor are they blessings which were first thought of by saintly souls in hours of lofty and daring speculation on the immeasurable possibilities of the infinite future and which were conferred in answer to their prayers, and to satisfy the generous cravings of noble natures. Paul goes back to the silent ages "*before the foundation of the world*"; and he says that before the creation of the universe began it was the Divine purpose that all who are in Christ should be an elect race, separated from the rest of mankind, consecrated to God by His own act, delivered by His own power from every stain and imperfection, "*holy and without blemish before Him*," and dwelling for ever in the blessedness and security of His "*love*."

I need hardly remind you that Calvinism has derived its strongest scriptural support from the interpretation which has been placed upon certain passages in the writings of the apostle Paul. On the first few verses of this epistle the Calvinistic theory of election and predestination has been supposed to rest as on foundations of eternal granite.

According to this theory, as defined in the third chapter of the Westminster Confession of Faith, a certain number of men "are by the decree of God, for the manifestation of His glory," "predestinated unto everlasting life, and others foreordained to everlasting death"; the particular individuals thus predestinated and foreordained are unchangeably determined; "and their number is so certain and definite, that it cannot be either increased or diminished." The decree of God that some men shall be saved does not rest upon "any foresight of [their] faith"; the decree of God that others should be lost does not rest upon any foresight of their unbelief. Further, "as God hath appointed the elect unto glory, so hath He by the eternal and most free purpose of His will foreordained all the means thereunto. Wherefore they who are elected . . . are effectually called unto faith in Christ by His Spirit working in due season; are justified, adopted, sanctified, and kept by His power through faith unto salvation. . . . The rest of mankind God was pleased, according to the unsearchable counsel of His own will, whereby He extendeth or withholdeth mercy as He pleaseth, for the glory of His sovereign power over His creatures, to pass by and to ordain them to dishonour and wrath for their sin, to the praise of His glorious justice."

That is the theory of the Westminster divines; it is not the theory of the apostle Paul. It is true that the technical terms of the Calvinistic theology are to be found in his epistles, but they do not stand for the Calvinistic ideas. When Paul speaks of God as electing men, choosing them, foreordaining them, predestinating them, he means something very different from what Calvinism means when it uses the same words.

Calvinism teaches that by the decree of God some men are foreordained to everlasting death; Paul teaches that it is the will of God "that all men should be saved and come to the knowledge of the truth."[1] Calvinism teaches that "neither are any other redeemed by Christ . . . but the elect only"; Paul teaches that "Christ gave Himself a ransom for all."[2] Calvinism teaches that God's choice falls on men when they are not "in Christ," and brings them into union with Him that they may receive the forgiveness of sins and eternal life; Paul teaches that the elect are those who are "in Christ," and that being in Him they enter into the possession of those eternal blessings which before the foundation of the world it was God's purpose, His decree, to confer upon all Christians. According to the Calvinistic conception some men who are still "children of wrath, even as the rest," to use a phrase which occurs later in this epistle, are among the "elect" and will therefore some day become children of God. That is a mode of speech foreign to Paul's thought; according to Paul no man is elect except he is "in Christ." We are

---

[1] 1 Tim. ii. 3.   [2] 1 Tim. ii. 6.

all among the non-elect until we are in Him. But once in Christ we are caught in the currents of the eternal purposes of the Divine love; we belong to the elect race; all things are ours; we are the children of God and the heirs of His glory. God has "blessed us with every spiritual blessing . . . *in Christ.*" God "chose us *in Him* before the foundation of the world that we should be holy and without blame before Him in love."

It may be alleged that all that Paul has written on these high matters is mere speculation. God's eternal purposes lie beyond the farthest reach of human inquiry. What could the apostle know about them, unless indeed a revelation came to him in some Divine vision or by some Divine voice? and is it reasonable to suppose that God would make known to men by supernatural means what has so remote a connection with practical righteousness?

But criticism of this kind is rash and superficial. When Paul wrote these words about God's eternal choice or election of those that are in Christ, and about their being foreordained by God unto adoption as sons through Jesus Christ unto Himself, he was absolutely sure of his ground. There is not a touch of speculation in this glorious passage. It was not even necessary that he should appeal, as he appeals elsewhere, to "visions and revelations." He was only telling the Ephesian Christians what he had actually seen for himself, what was plainer and more real to him than earth and ocean. The Ephesians might see the truth for themselves, and just as Paul had seen it. We in these days may also see it for ourselves. There is a very just sense in which we may say that it had been revealed to the apostle, but once revealed it is an open secret for all devout Christian men. We need not quote texts in order to prove it; while we believe the truth on Paul's bare authority we do not really know it.

That God had blessed him with every spiritual blessing in heavenly places in Christ was with Paul not a matter of speculation; it was not even a matter of faith; it was a matter of experience. He knew it, just as he knew that the sun warmed him and that the water quenched his thirst. The blessings had actually become his. For five-and-twenty or thirty years he had been receiving them.

He knew that he was "in Christ." This too was not a matter of bare faith, but of experience. Long before he wrote this epistle he had said: "I have been crucified with Christ; yet I live; and yet no longer I, but Christ liveth in me."[1] A little later he had told his own story in the memorable words, "if any man is in Christ he is a new creature; the old things are passed away; behold they are become new."[2] And in this union with Christ he had found a freedom, a force, a fulness of life, which to him were the assurance that only "in Christ" could man fulfil

---

[1] Gal. ii. 20. [2] 2 Cor. v. 17.

the Divine idea of human perfection and blessedness. In Christ he had received the light of God and the strength of God and the joy of God. As a blind man whose sight has been restored to him knows that while he was unable to see the shining heavens and the mountains and the stars and the faces of those whom he loved he was not living his true life, so Paul knew that until he was in Christ he had never approached the perfection and glory which God had made possible to the race. It was by no accident that union with Christ exalted and transfigured the whole spiritual nature of man, and raised him to diviner levels of life. Man was made for this; "before the foundation of the world" God had determined that "in Christ" man should find God and God find him.

And now that Paul was conscious that he had come into the line of God's eternal purpose his hopes were immeasurable, and they were hopes which had their root and justification in his actual experience. Already Divine forces were at work in him, and he was certain that while he remained in Christ these forces would continue to work; he was confident that at last they would give him a complete victory over all sin. By his union with Christ he was consecrated to God as a temple is consecrated, or a priest, or a sacrifice; and he could not doubt that the consecration would be made effective by the cleansing of his whole life from the impurity which must trouble and dishonour the righteous God who loveth righteous-

LECT. II.] *ELECTION IN CHRIST.* 35

ness. This then must be the ultimate purpose of God for all who are in Christ. He chose them "*in Him, that they should be holy and without blemish before Him in love.*"

Mr. Matthew Arnold in his "St. Paul and Protestantism" has made a very ingenious and interesting attempt to deprive Protestantism (or, as he commonly calls it, Puritanism,) of the strength it has derived from its appeal to the authority of the great apostle of the Gentiles. But occasionally Mr. Arnold misses his way, and his criticisms touch the very heart of the theology of Paul himself. Discussing the doctrines of Calvinistic Puritanism he says: "the passiveness of man, the activity of God, are the great features of this scheme; there is very little of what man does, very much of what God does."[1] Arminian Methodism, though it puts aside the Calvinistic doctrine of predestination, is, in Mr. Arnold's judgment, open to the same criticism: "the foremost place, which in the Calvinistic scheme belongs to the doctrine of predestination, belongs in the Methodist scheme to the doctrine of justification by faith. . . . Christ, by His satisfaction, gave the Father the right and the power (*nudum jus Patri acquirebat*, said the Arminians) to follow His mercy, and to make with man the covenant of free justification by faith, whereby, if a man has a sure trust and confidence

---

Page 79.

that his sins are forgiven him in virtue of the satisfaction made to God for them by the death of Christ, he is held clear of sin by God and admitted to salvation. This doctrine, like the Calvinistic doctrine of predestination, involves a whole history of God's proceedings, and gives, also, first and almost sole place to what God does, with disregard to what man does."[1]

But very much the same may be said of Paul's own doctrine. If in Calvinistic Puritanism "there is very little of what man does and very much of what God does," and if this is its reproach, the same reproach attaches to the Pauline epistles. If Arminian Methodism is at fault because it gives "first and almost sole place to what God does, with disregard to what man does," Paul is equally at fault.

Mr. Arnold's real controversy is neither with Calvinistic Puritanism nor with Arminian Methodism, but with religion itself. He is a moralist. To him conduct is three-fourths of human life; and religion is "ethics heightened, enkindled, lit up by feeling," "morality touched by emotion." He thinks that "the paramount virtue of religion is that it has *lighted up* morality; that it has supplied the emotion and inspiration needful for carrying the sage along the narrow way perfectly, for carrying the ordinary man along it at all." He remains faithful to the old Astronomy: to him the world of human conduct

---

[1] "St. Paul and Protestantism," pages 84, 85.

is the centre of all the spheres, and around it revolve as useful and subordinate orbs the august objects of religious faith; the sun shines to ripen the harvests which grow in earthly fields; the stars move through the infinite depths of heaven to guide the course of the sailor, perhaps to touch the fancy of the poet. Religion declines to accept this theory of the universe; to religion, God is the centre of all things and God is greater than all things.

To the moralist the supreme object of human life is to be temperate, truthful, just, fearless, industrious, kindly. If reverence for God and the hope of immortality can give fresh sanctions to moral duties and fresh strength to discharge them, the aid of religious faith is gratefully accepted; but faith discharges a secondary and ministerial function. To the man who has seen the glory of God and heard His august voice, life has larger and loftier aims. God fills earth and heaven, time and eternity. His first duty is to God, and that duty includes all others. Life derives its chief interest from God, and finds in Him its true and complete meaning. The intrinsic and natural obligations of temperance, truthfulness, justice, courage, industry, kindness, remain and are indefinitely strengthened; the ideal of all these virtues is heightened and ennobled; but instead of occupying the whole territory of duty, they are only a single province of a wider realm over which the will of God is absolute and supreme.

With this immense enlargement of the area of

duty, with a Divine ideal of righteousness to be fulfilled, with immortal perfection and blessedness to be lost or won, man becomes conscious of his need of a spiritual force beyond his own. He invokes Divine inspiration and receives it. Henceforth he measures, not his own strength, but God's, against all the tasks to which he is called. What he himself does seems nothing; what God does in him, through him, and for him, seems everything.

Mr. Arnold is clear-minded enough to see the contrast between his own way of thinking of human life and conduct and Paul's way. He says that "the voluntary, rational, and human world, of righteousness, moral choice, effort, filled a large place in [Paul's] spirit. But the necessary mystical and Divine world of influence, sympathy, emotion, filled an even larger."[1] That is Mr. Arnold's way of saying that to Paul God was infinitely great. The same thing is true of all prophets and of all men that have exerted great and enduring influence on the religious thought and life of mankind.

And we may measure the real force and depth of every religious movement by the greatness of its conception of God. In century after century, in nation after nation, great religious impulses, which seemed at first to promise a complete and permanent ethical and religious reformation, have soon spent their strength, because their conception of God was defective in

---

[1] Ibid., page 120.

some of its most necessary elements. It is not enough that men know that God is great to punish and great to reward. It is not enough that they recognise in His will an awful authority which it is criminal and disastrous to resist. God should be great to the imagination, filling it with splendour; great to the intellect, commanding its most reverent homage and raising it to its loftiest activity; great to the heart, inspiring it with passionate affection, with perfect trust, with deep gratitude, with glorious hope, and with the awe which will restrain from sin; great to the conscience as the personal revelation of the eternal law of righteousness; infinitely great to all that is noblest in man; great as the Creator of all things; great as the Sustainer of all things; great because of His eternal justice; great because of His infinite love; great as the fountain of all moral and spiritual perfection in His creatures; great as the fountain of all their blessedness. The greater our conception of God, the greater will be our own life. When Christendom comes to know and worship a God in whom all the elements of greatness are found, the evil days of darkness, of superstition, of sorrow, and of sin will for ever pass away, the prayers of saints will be answered, and the fair visions of prophets will be fulfilled.

III.

REGENERATION AND SONSHIP IN CHRIST.

"Having foreordained us unto adoption as sons through Jesus Christ unto Himself, according to the good pleasure of His will, to the praise of the glory of His grace, which He freely bestowed on us in the Beloved."
EPH. i. 5, 6.

THESE words must not be considered alone. They are a link in a golden chain, and we shall not see their full meaning unless we recall the sentences which precede them. "God hath blessed us with every spiritual blessing in the heavenly places in Christ." Why? Because "He chose us in Him before the foundation of the world, that we should be holy and without blemish before Him in love." And this again was because He had "*foreordained us unto adoption as sons through Jesus Christ unto Himself.*"

We may reverse the order of the apostle's thought, and may begin with what he seems to describe as the original and eternal fountain of that great movement of the Divine love and power which will be consummated in our eternal blessedness and glory. Christ is the eternal Son of God; and it was the first, the primæval purpose of the Divine grace that His life and sonship should be shared by all mankind;

that through Christ all men should rise to a loftier rank than that which belonged to them by their creation, should be "partakers of the Divine nature" and share the Divine righteousness and joy. Or rather, the race was actually created in Christ; and it was created that the whole race should in Christ inherit the life and glory of God. The Divine purpose has been thwarted and obstructed and partially defeated by human sin. But it is being fulfilled in all who are "in Christ." They are therefore described as chosen in Him before the foundation of the world, that they should be holy and without blemish before Him in love. If we consent to receive Christ as the Lord and Giver of life we fall into the line of God's eternal purpose, we are God's elect in Him. And that the end for which we are elected may be achieved, "God has blessed us with every spiritual blessing in the heavenly places in Christ."

We have now to consider that original and central Divine purpose which explains and includes all that the infinite love of God has done for our race already, all that the infinite love of God will do for us through the endless ages beyond death; God "*foreordained us unto adoption as sons through Jesus Christ unto Himself.*"

"*Through Jesus Christ.*" Our Lord is always represented as being, in the highest sense and in a unique sense, the Son of God. And without venturing into the lofty, and perhaps perilous, inquiries suggested by the Athanasian Creed, without discussing whether before the incarnation Christ could have been rightly spoken of as the Son or whether His truer name was that which is given Him by John—the Word of God—I may express the conviction that the relation which, when He was in this world, our Lord sustained to the Father represented and revealed an eternal fact, and that the sonship of the earthly Christ has its foundation and root in relations eternally existing in the Godhead. Much more than this the Athanasian Creed could hardly have been intended to affirm.

But passing on to what we know of our Lord as He lived among men, nothing so perfectly represents the impression which His character, spirit, and history produce upon us as the title which describes Him as the Son of God. Other men had been God's servants; He too, as Paul says in the Epistle to the Galatians, was "born under the law"; but to speak of Him as a servant does not tell half the truth. He is a servant and something more. There is an ease, a freedom, a grace about His doing of the will of God, which can belong only to a son. There is nothing constrained in His moral and spiritual perfection; it is not the result of art and painstaking. He was born to it, as we say; He does the will of God as a child does the will of its father, naturally, as a matter of course, almost without thought.

About the Father's love for Him He has never any doubt; and there is no sign that His perfect faith is the result of discipline, or that it had ever been less secure and tranquil than it was in the maturity of His strength. There is nothing to suggest that He had *discovered* God's love for Him. He always knew it; it awakened no surprise. It gave Him peace and strength and blessedness, but produced no passion of rapture. It was His from the first, as the air and the sunlight were His.

The character of His communion with the Father confirms this impression. There is no irreverent familiarity, but there is no trace of fear or even of wonder. It is plain that He lived in the very light of God, saw God as no saint had ever seen Him ; but He is not subdued and overawed by the vision. Prophets had fallen to the ground when the Divine glory was revealed to them ; but Christ stands calm and erect. A subject may lose self possession in the presence of his prince, but not a son.

And when He speaks of the glory which is to come to Him after His death and resurrection, He is still a Son anticipating the honour to which the Father has always destined Him, and which indeed had always been His. I know of nothing more wonderful than the blending of the human and the Divine, the submission of voluntary service with the freedom of natural and essential sonship, in His last great prayer: " I glorified Thee on the earth, having accomplished the work which Thou hast given Me to do. And now, O Father, glorify Thou Me with Thine own self, with the glory which I had with Thee before the foundation of the world." [1]

Christ was God's Son, the first of the human race that ever knew God as a Father. But Paul means us to understand that if we are "in Christ," we too according to God's eternal purpose have become God's sons. The sonship of Christ, as far as this is possible in the nature of things, (or I should rather say, as far as this can be made possible by the power and love of God,) has become ours. The eternal relationship between Christ and the Father cannot belong to us; but all who are one with Christ share the blessedness, the security, and the honour of that relationship; and the life of Christ, which has its eternal fountains in the life of God, is theirs.

For this adoption of which Paul speaks is something more than a mere legal and formal act, conveying certain high prerogatives. We are "called the sons of God" because we are really made His sons by a new and supernatural birth. Regeneration is sometimes described as though it were merely a change in a man's principles of conduct, in his character, his tastes, his habits. The description is theologically false, and practically most pernicious and misleading. If regeneration were nothing more than this, we should have to speak of a man as being more or less regenerate according to the extent of his moral reformation; but this would be

---

[1] John xvii. 4, 5.

contrary to the idiom of New Testament thought. That a great change in the moral region of a man's nature will certainly follow regeneration is true; this change however is not regeneration itself, but the effect of regeneration, and the moral change which regeneration produces varies in many ways in different men. In some the change is immediate, decisive, and apparently complete. In others it is extremely gradual, and may for a long time be hardly discernible. In some regenerate men grave sins remain for a time unforsaken, perhaps unrecognised. Look at these Ephesian Christians. The apostle has to tell them that they must put away falsehood and speak the truth; that they must give up thieving, and foul talk, and covetousness, and gross sensual sin.

He addresses them as "saints." He describes them as having been chosen in Christ before the foundation of the world, and foreordained by God unto adoption as sons unto Himself; and yet he knows that they are in danger of committing these base and flagrant offences. It was hard for them to escape from the vices of heathenism. They were regenerate; but as yet, in some of them, the moral effects of regeneration were very incomplete, the change which regeneration was ultimately certain to produce in their moral life had only begun, and it was checked and hindered by a thousand hostile influences.

The simplest and most obvious account of regeneration is the truest. When a man is regenerated he receives a new life and receives it from God. In itself, regeneration is not a change in his old life but the beginning of a new life which is conferred by the immediate and supernatural act of the Holy Spirit. The man is really "born again." A higher nature comes to him than that which he inherited from his human parents; he is "begotten of God," "born of the Spirit."

There is no doubt a very true sense in which all men may be called God's children. Paul acknowledged the truth of the line of the heathen poet, "We are also His offspring." But the sonship of the race is rudimentary. There is in most men some faint consciousness that, by the law of their nature, their true home is in God's presence, and that perfect strength and blessedness are to be found only in His love. In their trouble and fear they appeal to God as children appeal to a father for pity, for counsel, for safety, for help. Natural instincts which are rarely completely suppressed bear witness to the grandeur of the destiny for which we were created. The capacity for receiving the Divine life is native to us; that we should receive it is an essential part of the Divine idea of human nature. But the actual realization of our sonship is possible only through Christ. Even apart from sin it was possible only through Him. If the Divine life is to be ours, and with the Divine life Divine sonship, we must be one with Christ. And those to whom the gospel comes are made one with Christ in response to their faith in Him. "As many as received Him to them gave

He the right to become children of God, even to them that believe on His name."[1] "Ye are all sons of God, through faith, in Christ Jesus." "Behold," says John, "what manner of love the Father hath bestowed upon us that we should be called children of God·"; and this is not a distinction conferred upon all mankind, for he adds: "for this cause the world knoweth us not, because it knew Him not."[2] "*The adoption of sons*" comes to us through Christ.

Indeed Paul did not believe that even the saints of the old Jewish times were sons of God in the sense in which we are His sons. They had great hopes, but the hopes were not fulfilled. They differed nothing from bondservants. They were under the law. "But when the fulness of the time came God sent forth His Son . . . [to] redeem them which were under the law, that we might receive the adoption of sons."[3] And however hard and technical this way of putting it may seem, it represents a real spiritual fact of transcendent importance, which we may verify for ourselves. Look through the Psalms. They record a very noble and beautiful development of the spiritual life. But no psalmist addresses God as a Father. He is the Creator of all things; the heavens declare His glory, and the firmament showeth His handiwork. He is a Shepherd, who leads us in paths of righteousness for His name's sake. He is a King: He is the Sun, the Shield, the Refuge, the Dwelling-

---

[1] 1 John i. 12. [2] 1 John iii. 1. [3] Gal. iii. 4, 5.

place of His people, their Rock of Defence; but their Father never. Here and there in the Old Testament Scriptures, six or seven times at most in a literature extending over more than twelve centuries, God is spoken of as a father, but the name does not carry with it the nearness of kinship and the tenderness of affection, which are conveyed by the description used in the New Testament, and there is nothing in the spiritual life of the ancient saints which responds to the title. Great as they were, the "spirit of adoption" was not theirs. They "died in faith, not having received the promises, but having seen them and greeted them from afar, and having confessed that they were strangers and pilgrims on earth." Not merely during their earthly life, but after they had passed to their rest, they waited and hoped for the coming of Christ: "God having provided some better thing concerning us, that apart from us they should not be made perfect." Not until the Son of God became man could men, either in this world or in worlds unseen, become the sons of God. The incarnation raised human nature to a loftier level, lifted it nearer to God, fulfilled in a new and nobler manner the Divine idea of humanity. We stand on heights which the ancient saints never reached. John the Baptist was greater than the greatest of the prophets; but the least in the kingdom of heaven is greater than he. God "*foreordained us unto adoption as sons through Jesus Christ unto Himself.*"

And these great and surprising blessings are conferred upon us, not because of any personal merit of ours, but "*according to the good pleasure of [God's] will.*" We had no claim upon Him for gifts like these. Nor in conferring them did He act under the constraint of any law of His own nature which imposed upon Him either a necessity or an obligation to raise us to the dignity of Divine sonship. Everything is to be ascribed to God's infinite love, to His free, unforced, spontaneous kindliness. What He has done for us is "*to the praise of the glory of His grace.*"

Even now Paul has not said enough to convey his conception of the absence of all claim on our part to the blessings which are ours in Christ. He is so eager to make it clear that the whole reason of the honour and blessedness which God has made our inheritance is to be found in God's own love, that he accumulates phrase upon phrase to emphasise and to glorify the spontaneity of the Divine goodness. God "foreordained us unto adoption as sons through Jesus Christ"; this seems sufficient to show that our sonship is not won by our personal effort and righteousness; but to Paul it is not sufficient;—"according to the good pleasure of His will"; it seems impossible to say more than this, but even this is not enough;—"to the praise of the glory of His grace"; nor is the apostle satisfied even now, and he adds, "*which He freely bestowed on us in the Beloved.*" With the infinite suggestiveness of that last word Paul seems to have been content. Christ dwells for ever in the infinite love of God, and as we are in Christ the love of God for Christ is in a wonderful manner ours.

All that constituted the strength and nobleness of Calvinism lies in this account of human salvation. To saintly men who held the Calvinistic creed, which to us seems so hard, so severe, so intolerable, it was radiant with the glow and glory of that passionate joy in the Divine love which Paul expresses in the early part of this epistle. When they contended for the Calvinistic theory of the Divine decrees, they only meant that all things come to us from God, that our redemption from sin and our eternal glory are the effect of His free and spontaneous love. When they said revolting and incredible things concerning the depravity of human nature, and maintained that all the actions of unregenerate men are sinful, that the very virtues of the unregenerate, their justice, their truthfulness, their generosity, their compassion for suffering, are but splendid vices, they meant that we were made to illustrate a Divine righteousness, and that apart from union with God this righteousness is impossible. When they declared that "man by his fall into a state of sin hath wholly lost all ability of will to any spiritual good accompanying salvation," this was nothing more than an attempt to say that all the springs of human goodness are in God. When they insisted that Christ's "obedience and satisfaction" are imputed to us by God, and that by this imputation we are justified, this was only an artificial and unfortunate way of saying that we owe all things to the infinite grace of God, and that God's grace is ours through our union with Christ. Their most extravagant and daring and appalling statements concerning the Divine predestination of the lost to dishonour, wrath, and everlasting death were but the endeavour of devout men, who were filled with immeasurable wonder and thankfulness by their own salvation, to translate into a theological system their profound conviction that they had no stronger claim on the mercy of God than any of those who had been condemned to eternal destruction, and that their salvation was to be ascribed, and ascribed without reserve, to the unsearchable riches of God's grace.

To us it has become apparent that the theory in which they defined the relations between God and the human race involved the gravest slanders both on the Divine justice and on the Divine love. But we should not forget that to men of the loftiest genius, and the noblest and most heroic piety, this theory has appeared to contain the only satisfactory account of the mystery and glory of the moral universe. To them God was infinitely great and glorious, and the theology of Augustine and Calvin asserted His greatness and His glory. We have learned that man, who was created to bear the image of God and to share the sonship of Christ, has also an august dignity, that man's will as well as God's will has authority and force. It is not easy in any scheme of human thought to find room for man when any adequate place has been given to the supremacy of God; but place must be found for both. Of the two extremes—the suppression of man which was the offence of Calvinism, and the suppression of God which was the offence against which Calvinism so fiercely protested—the fault and error of Calvinism was the nobler and grander. The history of the Augustinian and Calvinistic theology in its best times is a fresh and striking illustration of the eternal law, " he that loseth his life shall save it "; for the most heroic forms of human courage, strength, and righteousness have been found in men who in their theology seemed to deny the possibility of human virtue and made the will of God the only real force in the moral universe.

IV.

THE FORGIVENESS OF SINS.

"*In whom we have our redemption through His blood, the forgiveness of our trespasses according to the riches of His grace.*"

—EPH. i. 7.

THE earlier verses of this chapter contain Paul's conception of the Divine ideal of human nature. The region in which his thought is moving lies far remote from that to which we have been so powerfully attracted by recent scientific speculations. Modern science believes that it has discovered traces of the long and dark and difficult path by which human nature has made good its ascent from the lowest levels of life to its present dignity and power. The apostle is interested in inquiries of a loftier order. He is not occupied with the processes by which the Divine ideal of human nature has moved towards its partial fulfilment, but with the Divine ideal itself.

Whether the nature of man, as we know it, came into existence six thousand years ago as the immediate creation of the Divine hand, or whether it is the result of a Divine thought which has gradually accomplished itself through ages of conflict and suffering, the Divine ideal of human life remains the same. It was the Divine purpose "before the foundation of the world" that men should share the life and sonship of the eternal Son of God. It was for this that human nature received its wonderful capacities,—whether these capacities were conferred by a single and isolated creative act, or whether they were the achievement of protracted ages of development. As this was the Divine ideal of the destiny of the race, it was a fundamental law of human nature that its sanctity and righteousness were to be secured by union with Christ: God "chose us in Him before the foundation of the world that we should be holy and without blame before Him in love"; and therefore whatever wisdom, power, happiness, and glory were possible to the race were possible only through Christ: "in Christ" "God blessed us with every spiritual blessing in the heavenly places." We may say that according to the Divine thought the human race was to be a great spiritual organism having Christ for the root of its life and blessedness. Abiding in Christ the race was to abide in God; and only by abiding in Christ could the race achieve the perfection and glory for which it was created.

But the Divine purpose did not suppress human freedom. It could be fulfilled only by the free concurrence of the race with the Divine righteousness and love; and the whole order of the development of the Divine thought has been disturbed by sin. In

His infinite goodness God has delivered us from the immense catastrophe which came upon us through our revolt against His authority. In the text we learn how this deliverance is effected. We were created that "in Christ," not apart from Him, we should achieve the perfection of power and righteousness and should become sons of God; and when we had sinned the fundamental law of our nature was not reversed. "*In Christ*," not apart from Him, "*we have our redemption through His blood, the forgiveness of our trespasses according to the riches of His grace.*"

In these words Paul tells us nothing more than our Lord Himself had told His disciples during His earthly ministry. He said that "the Son of Man came not to be ministered unto, but to minister, and give His life a ransom for many."[1] And when He gave the cup to the twelve at the last supper He said, "Drink ye all of it, for this is My blood of the covenant which is shed for many unto the remission of sins."[2] The apostolic doctrine of the atonement rests on Christ's own teaching.

To understand this doctrine it is necessary to form a clear conception of what is meant by the forgiveness of sins; and those who have had the opportunity of discovering the very loose way in which large numbers of people think about the simplest religious truths will not be surprised if I begin by reminding you that forgiveness is not a change in our minds

---

[1] Matt. xx. 28. [2] Matt. xxvi. 28.

towards God but a change in God's mind towards us. Take an illustration. A son has been guilty of flagrant misconduct towards his father; has insulted him, slandered his character, robbed him, and almost ruined him. The son discovers his guilt and is greatly distressed. He does all he can to atone for his wickedness. He has become a better man, and there is a great change in his mind and conduct towards his father. But it is possible for all the change to be on one side. He may be unable to remove or even to lessen his father's indignation against him. His father may continue for years bitter, relentless, unforgiving. I do not mean to suggest that God will be hard with us when we repent; but if we are to have any clear and true thoughts about this subject we must see distinctly that it is one thing for us to repent of sin and to become better, and quite another thing for God to forgive us.

Nor must the Divine forgiveness be confounded with peace of conscience. I have known many people who were restless and unhappy, dissatisfied with themselves, and unable to find any rest of heart in the Divine mercy. And the reason why the Divine mercy gave them no peace or courage or hope or joy was very plain. They were not troubled by the Divine hostility to their sin, and therefore the assurance that God was willing to forgive them afforded them no relief. It was not God's thoughts about them that occasioned their distress, but their own thoughts about themselves. They did not want to obtain the Divine forgiveness, but to recover their own self respect, which had been wounded by the discovery of their moral imperfections. But it is clearly one thing for God to be at peace with us, and quite a different thing for us to be at peace with ourselves.

There is another possible error. We must not suppose that as soon as God forgives us we escape at once from the painful and just consequences of our sins. The sins may be forgiven, and yet many of the penalties which they have brought upon us may remain. There is a certain alliance between the laws of nature and the laws of righteousness, and there is a similar alliance between the natural laws of society and the laws of righteousness. If a man is guilty of habitual drunkenness he suffers for it. His physical strength will sooner or later be enfeebled; his blood will become foul; his constitution will be undermined; disease will fasten upon him; his intellect will lose something of its clearness and vigour; and his moral force will be lessened. When a man repents of his drunkenness and becomes sober, when he receives God's forgiveness for his drunkenness, he does not escape at once from the natural consequences of his past excesses. The consequences remain for a long time; they disappear very gradually, if they disappear at all. No Divine act arrests the operation of the natural laws which punish the penitent for his former drunkenness.

There are vices, such as flagrant lying, gross treachery, deliberate dishonesty, which involve a man in heavy social penalties. He does not escape these penalties when he repents of the vices and receives the Divine pardon. He is maimed for life. His chances are lost. He will recover with difficulty the confidence of even kindly and generous men. Positions of public trust and honour will be closed against him. He will be excluded from many kinds of usefulness. These penalties will come upon him and will remain upon him by the action of Divine laws which are implicated in the very structure of social life; and no Divine act will lift the penitent beyond their reach and give him back all that he has lost by his wrong-doing. Many of the terrible consequences of sin are untouched by the Divine forgiveness.

What is it then for God to Forgive sins?

Forgiveness among ourselves implies that there has been just resentment against the person whom we forgive, resentment provoked by his wrong doing. When we forgive him the resentment ceases. The resentment may not have quenched our affection. Indeed, the strength of our love often increases the strength of our resentment. An offence which, if committed by a stranger, would be regarded with indifference, creates, if committed by a child, a brother, or a friend, intense moral pain and deep moral indignation.

But to attribute anger and resentment to God is to oppose the whole current of the religious thought of our time. We think of Him as an immense and kindly Power, and a Power can feel neither moral resentment nor moral approbation. It works unconsciously, and according to fixed laws. If it blesses it blesses without delight; if it punishes it punishes without anger. But just in the proportion in which God is regarded as a Power rather than a Person, He loses those attributes of infinite majesty which filled the saints of other ages with reverence and awe. For a Person, however weak and however obscure, is more august than any mere Power however great, however just, however benignant; there are no terms of comparison between them. By excluding from our conception of God the idea of personality, we degrade Him to a rank inferior to ourselves. If God is not a living person I am greater than He.

Or if the idea of God's personality is not altogether suppressed, we are in danger of thinking that His life is passionless. He may have a certain tranquil satisfaction in our happiness and righteousness, but we falsely imagine that we dishonour His greatness if we suppose that He is provoked to moral resentment and indignation by our sin. We think of Him as a summer ocean of kindliness, never agitated by storms.

This was not the conception of Jewish saints; this is not the conception which has formed the faith and righteousness of the Christian church. For myself I worship the God who was revealed in Christ;

having seen Him I believe that I have seen the Father. He wept over the city of Jerusalem; in those tears I see the revelation of the infinite sorrow of the Divine love thwarted and defeated by human sin. On a sabbath day in a synagogue there were men watching Christ to see whether He would heal a man whose hand was withered; if He did they would have a fresh proof that He was a sabbath breaker and this was the charge which they were bringing against Him to destroy His authority as a prophet sent from God. He "looked round about on them with anger, being grieved at the hardening of their heart";[1] in that anger, in that grief, I see the revelation of the Divine anger and the Divine grief when men's hearts are so hardened that while they are hot in their zeal for the mere external forms and institutions of religion they are blind to the noblest manifestations of the Divine righteousness and goodness, and care more for the most mechanical of their religious traditions than for the living triumphs of God's love over the sins and miseries of mankind. And when towards the close of His earthly ministry the indignation of Christ burned with a white heat and He fiercely denounced the Pharisees and all the ecclesiastical authorities of the people, I see in the fires of His wrath a revelation of the wrath of God against men who make great professions of sanctity and religious zeal, but to whom temple and priest

---

[1] Mark iii. 5.

altar and sacrifice, Divine laws and Divine promises, the religious hopes and fears and sorrows of the race, are but the instruments of ambition and covetousness, and who, rather than lose their own wealth, reputation, authority, and ease, will silence the voice of Divine truth, resist religious reformation, slander and crush the prophets of God.

I do not degrade God when I believe that He listens with pity to the cry of the oppressed; I do not degrade Him when I believe that He rises in anger to break in pieces the oppressor. I do not degrade God when I believe that He watches with keen sympathy and delight the heroic struggles of good men to be true and just; I do not degrade Him when I believe that He looks with scorn upon conscious falsehood and dishonesty. I do not degrade God when I believe that He loves men the more because of their righteousness; I do not degrade Him when I believe that He regards not only with disapproval but with resentment those who sin.

When He forgives men His resentment ceases.

The cessation of Divine resentment has effects which do not follow the cessation of just human resentment against wrong doing. A man may forgive a trusted friend who, by a systematic course of fraud extending over many years, has stripped him of his wealth and dragged him down to miserable poverty; but the forgiveness cannot cancel the guilt of the treachery and the fraud. A wife on her deathbed may forgive her husband's persistent neglect, cruelty, and unfaithfulness. The wrongs of years may be forgotten; the tender memories of their early love and happiness may fill her heart; all her resentment may be swept away by the returning tide of the affection she felt for him in the fair morning of life, before the clouds gathered and her miseries began. But the guilt of his villainy is not lessened by her forgiveness. He cannot silence his conscience by pleading that his wife has pardoned him. The brutal offences of those shameful years are still his, though the woman he wronged assured him that she forgave him everything and loved him still. The very generosity of her forgiveness, if his moral nature has not become wholly insensible, will bring his guilt home to him afresh, and increase the anguish of his self reproach. The sins are his; her pardon has not broken the terrible chain which binds them to him.

And there are some considerations which might make us suppose that it is impossible in the nature of things to escape from the guilt of past wrong doing. The sins once committed remain a part of our moral history for ever. What is done cannot be undone; and the continuity of our moral life cannot be dissolved. Conscience, which is the representative of the Divine authority, the witness to the Divine law, holds us responsible for all our sins and refuses to release us from their guilt. You may commit a sin to-morrow; it will be your sin, if you are still alive, thirty, forty, fifty years hence,—yours when you are seventy, though you committed it when you were five-and-twenty. You cannot escape from it. The malignant lie, the act of cruelty, the deliberate dishonesty will cling to you, year after year, and you will not by any moral effort be able to throw it off. When all the people that you injured are dead, the crime will still be yours. You may suffer agonies of humiliation and self reproach on account of it, but it will still be yours. You may endure heavy penalties of another kind for it : public scorn, the loss of social position, the ruin of your fortunes, the breaking up of your home, the alienation and desertion of your own flesh and blood : but it will still be yours. You may sometimes forget it, but it will not cease to be yours because for a time you cease to think of it. Suddenly, in the dead of night, or when you are prostrate with sickness, or when death is drawing near, conscience will spring up in her wrath, armed with an iron lash, and will scourge you for the offence as fiercely as on the morning after it was committed. Conscience has no authority to pardon sin, to cancel your responsibility for it, to treat you as though you were not guilty of it.

But when God forgives us He actually remits our sin. Our responsibility for it ceases. The guilt of it is no longer ours. That He should be able to give us this release is infinitely more wonderful than that He should be able to kindle the fires of the sun and to control, through age after age, the courses of the stars.

He can forgive sin because He is God. Sin is a violation of the eternal law of righteousness, and the eternal law of righteousness is neither above God nor below God. It is not below Him so as to leave Him free to suppress and disregard at His will the eternal contrast between Right and Wrong, to make virtue shameful and vice honourable, to brand and punish truth, justice, and generosity as sins, to command and to reward falsehood, injustice, selfishness, as righteousness. To attribute to Him such a power as this would render it impossible to attribute to Him any moral perfection, and would make Him the tyrant of the universe, not the God. But on the other hand the eternal law of righteousness is not above Him. If it were He would be under authority as we are; He would not be supreme, but would be simply the mightiest and most illustrious Minister of a more august power, its Representative, its Defender, but still its Servant.

The eternal law of righteousness is one with the eternal life and will of God. To quote words which I have used elsewhere: "The supremacy of the law is absolute and irreversible. But when God is truly known, conscience, without revoking or qualifying the acknowledgment of this supremacy, confesses that the authority which it had recognised in an ideal law is the awful and glorious prerogative of a living Person." [1]

---

[1] "The Atonement: the Congregational Union Lecture for 1875." Page 372.

Our supreme duty is to love, trust, and obey God. This includes all other duties; and in every moral offence of which we are guilty the supreme obligation is violated.

The identity between God and the eternal law of righteousness is His characteristic and incommunicable prerogative. This,—not His everlasting existence, not His immense power, not His immeasurable knowledge; this,—not the infinite resources revealed in the vastness, variety, and grandeur of the visible universe which He created, and which through countless ages has rested on His strong and solitary support; this,—not the mysterious energy which originated all forms of conscious life, from its lowest gradations which doubtfully emerge from the dull and blind inertness of matter, to the spiritual strength and splendour of the celestial princes who have their home in His own eternal glory; this identity between the eternal law of righteousness and the life and will of God—constitutes His title to universal obedience and homage, to the love and the worship of earth and heaven.

It is this which gives authority to His forgiveness of sin. When His resentment against us ceases the eternal law of righteousness ceases to be hostile to us. When He pardons our transgressions the eternal law of righteousness no longer holds us responsible for them. The shadow which they had projected across our life, and which lengthened with our lengthening years, passes away. We look back upon the sins which God has forgiven and we condemn them still, but the condemnation does not fall upon ourselves; for God, who is the living law of righteousness, condemns us no longer.

The peace and the blessedness of this release from guilt are wonderful. The soul is conscious of a Divine freedom. It can approach God with happy trust and with perfect courage, for the past is no longer a source of terror, and the future is bright with immortal hope. It has lost a heavy burden which was too great for its strength, and it has a fresh and surprising alertness and joy in all duty. The bitter reproaches of conscience are silenced; for conscience is the minister and representative of God, and when God forgives conscience ceases to condemn.

To those who have known the power of the Divine forgiveness to cancel the guilt of sin, the act is as clearly supernatural as any of the miracles recorded in the Gospels, and it is more wonderful, for it reveals the ascendancy of the Divine will in a region of life far nobler than that in which the physical miracles of the Gospels were wrought.

"*In Christ*" "*we have our redemption through His blood, the forgiveness of our trespasses according to the riches of His grace.*" The relation between the death of Christ and the forgiveness of sins I must reserve for another lecture. Meanwhile I venture to ask those of you who have felt that the infinite mercy of God might forgive us apart from any sacrifice for sins, to consider how much the Divine forgiveness means, that it is the forgiveness of One whose life and will are inseparable from the eternal law of righteousness, and that His forgiveness carries with it an actual extinction of the guilt of the sins which are forgiven.

It is possible that an inadequate conception of the nature and effect of the Divine forgiveness may be at the root of many difficulties concerning the atonement.

NOTE.—Forgiveness may be defined :

(1) In *personal* terms—as a cessation of the anger or moral resentment of God against sin.

(2) In *ethical* terms—as a release from the guilt of sin, which oppresses the conscience.

(3) In *legal* terms—as a remission of the punishment of sin, which is eternal death.

V.

THE FORGIVENESS OF SINS AND THE DEATH OF CHRIST.

"In whom we have our redemption through His blood, the forgiveness of our trespasses according to the riches of His grace." EPH. i. 7.

WE have already considered what Paul means by "the forgiveness of our trespasses"; we have now to inquire what he meant by saying that we have forgiveness in Christ and through the "blood" or death of Christ.

That our Lord Jesus Christ declared that men were to receive redemption or the remission of sins through Himself, and especially through His death, appears from several passages in the Gospels; and the great place which His last sufferings occupied in His thought from the very commencement of His ministry, the frequency with which He spoke of them, the wonderful results which He said were to follow them, the agitation and dismay which He felt as they approached, and His anxiety to pass through them and beyond them, show that to Christ His death was not a mere martyrdom but an awful and glorious crisis in His own history and in the history of the human race.

The apostles Peter, Paul, and John, though each had his own characteristic conception of the work of Christ and the Christian salvation, are agreed in declaring that the ground of our forgiveness is in Christ, and they are also agreed in attributing a mysterious importance and efficacy to His death.

"We thus judge that One died for all, therefore all died." "Him who knew no sin He made to be sin on our behalf; that we might become the righteousness of God in Him." "He was delivered up for our trespasses." "He died for our sins according to the Scriptures." "He gave Himself for our sins." "He suffered for sins once, the Righteous for the unrighteous, that He might bring us to God." "His own Self bare our sins in His body upon the tree." "Herein is love, not that we loved God, but that He loved us and sent His Son to be the Propitiation for our sins." "He is the Propitiation for our sins; and not for ours only, but also for the whole world." "The blood of Jesus His Son cleanseth us from all sin." "God appointed us not unto wrath but unto the obtaining of salvation through our Lord Jesus Christ who died for us." "God commendeth His own love towards us, in that while we were yet sinners, Christ died for us; much more then being now justified by His blood, shall we be saved from the wrath of God through Him." "Being justified freely by His grace through the redemption that is in Christ Jesus: whom God set forth to be a Propitiation, through faith, by His blood, to show His righteousness, because of the passing over of the sins done aforetime, in the forbearance of God; for the showing, I say, of His righteousness at this present season; that He might Himself be just and the Justifier of him that hath faith in Jesus."[1]

But no collection of isolated passages gives an adequate impression of the strength of the proof that both our Lord Jesus Christ and His apostles taught that in Him "*we have our redemption through His blood, the forgiveness of our trespasses according to the riches of [God's] grace.*" This truth is wrought into the very substance of the Christian gospel as that gospel appears in the pages of the New Testament. We may not be able to understand quite clearly why the ground of our forgiveness is in Christ; we may be still less able to discover any special and direct relation between the death of Christ and the act of the Divine mercy in forgiving us; but that the ground of our forgiveness is in Christ, not in ourselves, and that His death has a unique relation to the remission of sins, are facts which lie at the very foundation of the faith and hope and life of the Christian church. Theories of the atonement have varied from age to age; some of them have been very technical and artificial, they were equally remote from the sad realities of the moral life of man

---

[1] 2 Cor. v. 14; 2 Cor. v. 21; Rom. iv. 25; 1 Cor. xv. 3; Gal. i. 4; 1 Pet. iii. 18; 1 Pet. ii. 20; 1 John iv. 10; 1 John ii. 2; 1 John i. 7; 1 Thess. v. 9; Rom. v. 8, 9; Rom. iii. 24-26.

and from the eternal perfections of the moral life of God; some of them were grotesque; some of them morally offensive as well as intellectually incredible; but through all changes of theological thought men have found in Christ, and especially in the death of Christ, the reason and ground of the Divine forgiveness. Theories of the atonement have exercised and baffled the speculation of a long succession of theologians, but the atonement itself has continued to give consolation and courage to all penitent hearts, transforming their despair into hope, their misery into peace, and their terror into perfect joy in the righteousness and love of God.

Perhaps the great mystery is inaccessible to human thought. This is the position maintained by Coleridge in a well known passage in the "Aids to Reflection." What he describes as "the mysterious act, the operative cause" of redemption, is in Coleridge's judgment "transcendent"; "it can be characterized only by the consequences"; and he contends that the apostle Paul describes the redemptive act of Christ, not as it is in itself but by its results in the actual salvation of men. It has an effect corresponding to the effect of paying a ransom for a slave, and is therefore described as the payment of a ransom. It has an effect corresponding to the effect of removing the resentment and anger of a person who has been wronged, and is therefore described as a reconciliation or atonement. It has an effect corresponding to the effect of ancient sacrifices which expiated the offences that excluded from the temple, and it is therefore described as an expiation. These observations are profoundly true, and had the metaphorical character of the terms under which the death of Christ is described in the New Testament been recognised, and the proper limits and functions of metaphorical description been understood,[1] theologians would have been saved from some of the most intolerable theories of this great mystery. To put Coleridge's meaning into simpler language, an illustration which is of excellent use for explaining the effects of the atonement is of no use for explaining the nature of the atonement.

We may perhaps be unable to construct anything that can deserve to be called a theory of the atonement. All our attempts at explanation may at best be only provisional. But I am not inclined to admit that the whole subject is as far beyond the reach of human thought as Coleridge maintained. Something may be known, though there will always remain an infinite mystery to inspire us with reverence and awe.

The two truths which Paul affirms in the text are, in a sense, equally mysterious; but the first may be more accessible than the second. He says, first, that we have forgiveness of our trespasses "*in Christ*," and, secondly, that we have the forgiveness of our trespasses in Christ "*through His blood.*"

---

[1] See note at the end of this lecture.

We are assisted to approach the first truth by
what he has said in the earlier verses of this chapter.
The eternal springs of the diviner life of the human
race are in Christ. Whatever strength and wisdom
and blessedness and glory are possible to us are
possible through Him and through our union with
Him. Christ's eternal righteousness, His eternal
relationship to the Father, the Father's delight in
Him, are the origin of all the greatness for which the
human race was created. It was from Christ, according to the Divine idea of the race, that we were to
receive all things. Every spiritual blessing was conferred upon the race in Him. The race was chosen
"in Him before the foundation of the world," to be
"holy and without blemish before [God] in love."
His sonship was to be the root of ours.

The responsibility,—shall I venture to call it?—the
immense, the glorious responsibility, of our righteousness, rested on Him. In His strength the whole race
was to find strength to do the will of God. His love
for the Father was to sustain our love; His trust in
the Father was to be the life of our trust; His joy
in the Father the perpetual inspiration of our joy.
We were to reveal, in inferior forms, Christ's eternal
perfection,—to *reveal* it, I say; for our perfection
was to illustrate the infinite resources of the moral
life of Christ Himself, and was to be His rather than
our own. The Divine idea of the human race carried
with it the prerogatives of sonship; for if we were
to repeat and illustrate, under whatever limitations,

the characteristic glory and blessedness of the eternal Son of God, it was necessary that we too should be "sons of God" and not merely His servants. In our original creation, it was God's purpose that Christ should be the vine and we the branches. His life was to be ours, and was to be manifested in our righteousness.

This was the Divine idea of the race. It is an idle, and yet an infinitely attractive, dream to speculate on what the history of the race and of every individual of the race would have been if the Divine idea had been freely and loyally accepted by us, and if through generation after generation the idea had revealed more and more fully the infinite wealth of its grace and glory. But we ceased to abide in Christ. We revolted against God. We incurred the Divine resentment. We have come under the condemnation of the eternal law of righteousness.

Now unless the Divine idea of human nature is to be surrendered, the reason and ground of our forgiveness and restoration to God must be in Christ, not in ourselves. Had we continued steadfast in our fidelity we should have lived a life of faith in the Son of God, finding in Him, not in ourselves, the root and ideal perfection of our righteousness, the reason and ground of our sonship and our blessedness ; and through our union with Christ we were to reach the greatness to which the infinite love of God had destined us. Even apart from sin, our whole relation to God was to be determined, not by our own isolated and personal worth, but by the transcendent glory of Christ. It is in harmony with this law that now we have sinned we should have forgiveness in Him. The first of the two truths which the apostle states in this verse,—that in Christ "we have our redemption, the forgiveness of our trespasses according to the riches of [God's] grace,"—is involved in the Christian conception of human nature.

But what special relation can be discovered between the death of Christ and the remission of sins? It is this question that haunts and perplexes many devout minds; and it is this question that, according to Coleridge, admits of no answer. To discover the relation between two terms, both terms must be known; and if the redemptive act of Christ lies wholly beyond the reach of human thought we can never know the relation between that act and the blessings which result from it.

But let us return to that law of human nature which we have already considered. In Christ we have found the ideal righteousness of the race. Shall we be surprised if we also find in Christ the ideal submission of the race to the justice of the Divine resentment against sin? That God should forgive sin apart from a real and effective submission to the expression of His just condemnation of sin is inconceivable; and, holding fast to the great truth that Christ's glorious perfection is the reason and ground of our very existence and of our relation to the universe and to

God, it appears to be in harmony with the fundamental conception of the relations between the human race and Christ that His submission to the pain and loss which came upon the race as the result of sin should be the reason and ground of the Divine forgiveness. According to the Divine idea of the human race Christ's moral relations to the Father are the highest, the perfect expression of ours. But as the result of our sin it is indispensable, if we are to be forgiven, that in us there should be the relation of perfect submission to the righteousness of God in condemning and punishing sin. This relationship has no place, can have no place, in the eternal relations between the Son and the Father. Unless by a supreme act of humiliation, self sacrifice, and love, Christ descends from His glory and stands by our side; unless the dark and awful shadow of our sin falls upon Him; unless He freely consents to have brought home to His very heart the guilt of the race; unless He submits to some experience of the woe and loss by which the guilt of the race is punished: His moral relations to the Father will not be the perfect expression of the relations which must exist between us and God if we are to receive the pardon of sin. Christ's righteousness is the ideal form of our righteousness; Christ's sonship is the ideal form of our sonship; and since our sin has made it necessary that there should be in us a moral submission to the righteousness of the Divine hostility to sin, it seems inevitable that in

Christ this submission should appear in ideal and transcendent perfection. Else we cease to be related to God through Him. But this is an incomplete statement of the truth ; and while stated incompletely it has an appearance of unreality.

The eternal relations between Christ and the Father are the ideal and perfect form of the relations between ourselves and God ; but this is true because the life of Christ is ours, and Christ is the root of our perfection, because He is the vine and we are the branches, because there is no righteousness in us which is not first in Him. In the light of this truth I think that some of the obscurity and mystery of the atonement will be relieved.

For, as I have said already, it seems morally impossible that our sin should be forgiven without a frank, unreserved, and reverential submission on our part to the justice of the Divine condemnation of sin, and to the justice of the Divine menaces against sin. Whatever else may be necessary before the Divine forgiveness can be granted, this seems indispensable. To regard with moral antagonism the Divine resentment against sin, to meet it in a spirit of revolt, to ignore it, are grave offences. For those who have sinned to refuse a real moral submission to the justice of the pain and loss with which God has menaced sin renders reconciliation with God and the pardon of sin impossible. This submission however is a form of righteousness altogether foreign to the eternal righteousness of the Son of God. Nothing analogous to it could have a place in His eternal life with the Father. But there is no righteousness in us which is not first in Him; and if we are to make a true submission to the resentment of God against sin, and to the justice of the penalties in which this resentment is expressed, it seems necessary that He should pass through a moral experience like that which He passed through in the garden and on the cross, and by His own spontaneous submission render our submission possible. His eternal righteousness makes it possible for us to be righteous, for we were created to live in His life; His voluntary endurance of agony, spiritual desertion, and death made it possible for us to consent from our very heart to the justice of God's condemnation of our sin. In another sense than that in which the words are used by the writer of the Epistle to the Hebrews, "He was made perfect through suffering," His submission carries ours with it.

This truth is of such critical importance that I venture to state it in another form. Christ described Himself as the "Way" to the Father, and said "No one cometh unto the Father but by Me."[1] It is a very inadequate and artificial interpretation of these words to allege that Christ has done something or endured something which constitutes a ground on which God can permit us to have access to Himself notwithstanding our sin. Nor is it enough to say that

---

[1] John xiv. 6.

Christ's teaching inspires us with penitence for sin, with true and just thoughts concerning God's condemnation of sin, and with a firm trust in the Divine mercy. It is not something which Christ has done or suffered, it is not something which Christ has taught, that is the "Way" to God; Christ Himself is the "Way." The higher Christian consciousness of nineteen centuries has discovered that Christ is the "Way" to the Father, because in our access to God we are one with Christ; His love for the Father and His trust and joy in the Father become ours. In our approach to God we have fellowship with Christ. Every right and pure and noble and happy affection that floods our spiritual life has its fountains in the life of Christ Himself, and our religious consciousness is a lower form of His own. And since for us as sinful men there can be no right approach to God without a moral submission to the righteousness of the penalties which had been drawn upon us by sin, Christ could not be for us the "Way" to the Father unless Christ's submission had anticipated ours. It is in the power of Christ's own endurance of death, and in fellowship with that endurance, that we submit to the righteousness of God's condemnation of our sin.

The death of Christ has another effect which constitutes it the reason and ground of our forgiveness.

Something more is necessary, if we are to be forgiven, than a real submission to the justice of the Divine resentment against sin. It is not morally conceivable that God should forgive our past sin except there were some security for our future righteousness. He may forgive us before we have been able to break the force of evil custom and to expel evil passions; and indeed it is the glory of the Christian gospel that it assures us at the very beginning of the great and arduous attempt to achieve a perfect righteousness that all the unrighteousness of which we have been guilty is for Christ's sake freely pardoned. The pardon is specially connected with the death of Christ. But I find it difficult to believe that the death of Christ could be a sufficient reason for the forgiveness of sins unless it were a force which destroyed sin.

In the sixth chapter of the Epistle to the Romans Paul develops at considerable length a truth which appears in several other parts of the New Testament; and which attributes to the death of Christ this destructive power. The relations between Christ and those who are in Him are so intimate that His death is their death and His resurrection their resurrection. They were crucified with Him, buried with Him, and they rose again with Him. The truth has been verified in the spiritual consciousness of devout men. The death of Christ is the death of sin. I cannot illustrate this truth at any length, but it is too intimately connected with the great fact that in Christ "*we have our redemption through His blood, the forgiveness of our trespasses according to the riches of His grace,*" to be omitted.

The principal positions which I have maintained are these :

1st. That it is in harmony with the fundamental law of human nature that the reason and ground of our forgiveness should be in Christ ; for the reason and ground of our creation, of our righteousness, and of our blessedness as the sons of God, are in Him.

2nd. That our forgiveness is specifically connected with the death of Christ for three reasons :

(1.) The relations of Christ to the Father are the transcendent expression and original root of our relations to the Father. We are related to the Father through Him. And since the relation of moral submission on our part to the righteousness of God's resentment against sin was an indispensable condition of the forgiveness of sin, it became necessary that Christ Himself should assume this relation of moral submission to the righteousness of God's resentment against sin, that His submission might be the transcendent expression of ours.

(2.) There is no righteousness in us which is not first in Christ. And since our submission to the righteousness of God's resentment against sin was an indispensable condition of our forgiveness, Christ's submission became necessary to render ours possible. His submission carries ours with it.

(3.) His death is the death of sin in all who are one with Him.

There is another aspect of the mystery which is not wholly concealed from us, an aspect which for several centuries has occupied the chief thought of those who have endeavoured to construct a theory of the atonement.

It has been felt that the honour and authority of the eternal law of righteousness would be impaired if the penalties of sin were remitted by a sovereign act of the Divine mercy. For these penalties are not arbitrary. It is just that those who have sinned should suffer. As it belongs to us to obey the law of righteousness, it belongs to God as the Supreme Moral Ruler to inflict the punishment which is due to disobedience. If, after the precepts of the law have been broken, its penalties are arbitrarily cancelled, the law sustains a double injury. It seems insufficient that those who have sinned should repent and sin no more. On what grounds can the punishment which they have already deserved be justly remitted? It seems insufficient that they should make the most complete moral submission to the justice of the punishment with which disobedience is menaced. How can the acknowledgment that punishment is deserved constitute an adequate ground for remitting it?

I have said that it belongs to God as the Supreme Moral Ruler to inflict the punishment which is justly due to our revolt against the eternal law of righteousness and against Himself, to whom that law requires us to yield perfect obedience. The infliction of the punishment is an expression of His condemnation of sin and of His moral resentment against those who are guilty of sin. The life and will of God are so completely one with the eternal law of righteousness that we are unable to conceive that this condemnation and resentment can be suppressed. If it were, there would seem to be a conflict between the eternal law of righteousness and the life and will of God.

The death of Christ contains the solution of these difficulties. For,—

(1.) Christ, the eternal Son of God and the root of our righteousness, having become man, endured death in order to render possible our moral consent to the justice of the Divine resentment against sin, and to the justice of the penalties in which that resentment might have been revealed. Had God withdrawn from us His light and life, and destroyed us by revealing His moral resentment against our sin, this would have been an awful manifestation of the moral energy of His righteousness and of His abhorrence of moral evil. Its moral value would have been infinitely heightened by the intensity of His love for us. But God in the greatness of His love shrank from depriving us of that blessed and glorious destiny for which we were created; and in order to secure our moral submission to the righteousness of His resentment, a moral submission which was the necessary condition of our forgiveness, He surrendered His own eternal Son to spiritual desertion and to death. In this surrender, made for such a purpose, there was a sublimer moral manifestation of the

Divine thought concerning sin than there would have been in condemning the race to eternal death.

(2.) The Lord Jesus Christ is Himself the Moral Ruler of the human race. The moral supremacy of God is manifested and exerted through Him. Through His lips the awful sentence is to be pronounced which will condemn the lost to irrevocable ruin: "Depart from Me, ye cursed, into the eternal fire which is prepared for the devil and his angels."[1] It will be "at the revelation of the Lord Jesus from heaven with the angels of His power in flaming fire" that Divine "vengeance" will come upon them that "know not God" and "obey not the gospel of our Lord Jesus," and then they will "suffer punishment, even eternal destruction from the face of the Lord and from the glory of His might." It was His function to punish sin and so to reveal His judgment of it. But instead of inflicting suffering He has elected to endure it, that those who repent of sin may receive forgiveness and may inherit eternal glory. It was greater to endure suffering than to inflict it.

To sum up in a sentence the principal positions I have maintained in this argument: the death of Christ was an act of submission on behalf of mankind to the justice of the penalties of violating the eternal law of righteousness, an act in which our own submission not only received a transcendent expres-

---

[1] Matt. xxv. 41.

sion but was really and vitally included; it was an act which secured the destruction of sin in all who through faith are restored to union with Christ; it was an act in which there was a revelation of the righteousness of God which must otherwise have been revealed in the infliction of the penalty of sin on the human race. And therefore in Christ "*we have our redemption, the forgiveness of our trespasses according to the riches of* [*God's*] *grace.*"

There is one deep and serious moral objection to the doctrine of the atonement which it may be well for me to notice before closing. It is an objection created by a form of theological rhetoric once very common though it has now disappeared. There was a time when it was not unusual for preachers to speak of the Lord Jesus Christ as enduring the wrath of God which we had deserved; and the same representation of the sufferings and death of Christ was given in treatises from which rhetoric should have been rigorously excluded. Those who suppose that this conception is an integral part of the theory of the atonement naturally recoil from the whole theory with strong moral revulsion. The conception introduces an intolerable fiction into a region where our whole moral nature urgently demands the most august moral realities. It assumes that God fictitiously imputed to Christ sins of which He was innocent, and that on the ground of this fictitious imputation God was filled with wrath against Him. That any serious theologian ever believed either of these revolting propositions is incredible. They had a place in a theological theory, they lent themselves still more frequently to the uses of popular rhetoric, but that they were ever steadily confronted and accepted as real facts I cannot conceive.

Against Christ there could be no resentment in the breast of the Father. In the moment of Christ's most awful agony the Father's moral approval of Him was most intense. "Therefore doth the Father love Me because I lay down My life, that I may take it again."[1] But it was possible for the Father to withhold from Christ the manifestation of His presence and of His love. For God's life is a free, personal life. He reveals Himself and His thought voluntarily. The loss of the sense of His presence is not always an indication that we have incurred His displeasure. It has been the common belief of men who have thought profoundly on the spiritual life that what they have described as "the loss of interior consolation" may be a part of the discipline of a saintly nature, and that the terrible desolation which it inflicts is not necessarily the punishment of exceptional sin, but may be the necessary condition of the development of exceptional righteousness. God may withdraw the manifestation of His presence from a saint, though if the saint had never been a sinner, or if he did not belong to a race of sinners, this severity of discipline would surely be unnecessary.

---

[1] John x. 17.

Christ had never sinned, but He had come into the world to make the sorrow, and as far as He could the very sin of the world His own; and so the supreme woe came upon Him which forced from His heart the cry of agony, "My God, My God, why hast Thou forsaken Me?" It was an awful moment. Darkness—darkness that might be felt—enfolded Him. All vision of God was lost, lost for Him whose life had been a life in the Divine light and love. In that fearful gloom He too had now to walk by faith, not by sight. But His faith in God, and in God's infinite righteousness, did not falter. He submitted with unshaken trust and with undiminished love. His cry of agony is a cry of faith and of filial affection: "My God, My God, why hast Thou forsaken Me?"

It seems almost certain that His terrible moral suffering was the immediate cause of His death. What death really is we do not yet know. What, apart from the Christian redemption, it would have been, we shall never know. To us, however, it must be infinitely more than it can be to inferior races, and it is surrounded in the Scriptures with awful mystery and dread. The breaking up of that physical nature in which our natural life is rooted would have been, but for Christ, an immense and fatal catastrophe. To Christ, the prospect of it seems to have been appalling, and it was made more appalling by the spiritual agonies which He knew would precede and which probably occasioned it. The mystery which surrounds the cross is impenetrable. But we may

venture to say that the laying down of His life was
the supreme achievement of His self sacrifice, His
great and unique act of submission on behalf of the
race to the justice òf the evils which the race had
deserved by sin. And if this is true, then, although
no theory of the relations between His death and the
forgiveness of sin may afford us intellectual satisfaction, and though there are times and moods in the
life of most of us when the greatness and sacredness
of the mystery seem to forbid as irreverent and
profane all attempts to speculate on the manner in
which His death accomplished its great redemptive
purposes, we may still receive with awe and wonder,
with faith and hope and immeasurable joy, the blessed
assurance that He "suffered for sins once, the
Righteous for the unrighteous, that He might bring
us to God," and that "we have our redemption
through His blood, the forgiveness of our trespasses
according to the riches of [God's] grace."

NOTE to Page 72.—"*Analogies* are used in aid of *conviction* ;
metaphors as means of *illustration*. The language is analogous,
wherever a thing, power, or principle in a higher dignity is expressed by the same thing, power, or principle in a lower but
more known form. Such, for instance, is the language of
John iii. 6, 'that which is born of the flesh is flesh ; that which
is born of the Spirit is spirit.' The latter half of the verse
contains the fact *asserted*; the former half the *analogous* fact,
by which it is rendered intelligible. If any man choose to call
this *metaphorical* or figurative, I ask him whether with Hobbes
and Bolingbroke he applies the same rule to the moral attributes
of the Deity? Whether he regards the Divine justice, for

instance, as a *metaphorical* term, a mere figure of speech? If he disclaims this, then I answer, neither do I regard the words *born again*, or *spiritual life*, as figures or metaphors. I have only to add that these analogies are the material, or (to speak chemically) the *base*, of symbols and symbolical expressions; the nature of which as always *taut*egorical (*i.e.* expressing the same subject but with a difference) in contradistinction from metaphors and similitudes, that are always *all*egorical (*i.e.* expressing a different subject but with a resemblance), will be found explained at large in the 'Statesman's Manual,' p. 35-38.

"Of *metaphorical* language, on the other hand, let the following be taken as instance and illustration. I am speaking, we will suppose, of an act which in its own nature and as a producing and efficient *cause* is transcendent, but which produces sundry *effects*, each of which is the same in kind with an effect produced by a cause well known and of ordinary occurrence. Now when I characterize or designate this transcendent act, in exclusive reference to these its *effects*, by a succession of names borrowed from their ordinary causes, (not for the purpose of rendering the act itself or the manner of the agency conceivable, but in order to show the nature and magnitude of the benefits received from it, and thus to excite the due admiration, gratitude, and love in the receivers,) in this case I should be rightly described as speaking *metaphorically*; and in this case to confound *the similarity*, in respect of the effects relatively to the recipients, with *an identity* in respect of the causes or modes of causation relatively to the transcendent act or the Divine Agent is a confusion of metaphor with analogy, and of figurative with literal, and has been and continues to be a fruitful source of superstition or enthusiasm in believers, and of objections and prejudices to infidels and sceptics." — *Coleridge's "Aids to Reflection" (2nd Edition), pp.* 196-198.

VI.

THE FINAL RESTORATION OF ALL THINGS.

"[*The riches of His grace*] *which He made to abound toward us in all wisdom and prudence, having made known unto us the mystery of His will, according to His good pleasure which He purposed in Him, unto a dispensation of the fulness of the times, to sum up all things in Christ, the things in the heavens, and the things upon the earth.*"
—EPH. I. 8–10.

WRITING to the Corinthians Paul entreats them to "receive not the grace of God in vain."[1] Gifts of God which are conferred at the impulse of an infinite mercy and goodness, and through the humiliation and sufferings and death of the Lord Jesus Christ, should fill our hearts with wonder and with gratitude. They are so precious in themselves, they were secured for us at so great a cost, they are the expressions of so glorious a love, that to regard them with indifference is a shameful crime. Nor is it safe to leave any of the gifts of God's grace unappropriated. Those for which we care nothing may be as necessary for our salvation as those for which we care most. We should receive them all with reverence and joy.

---

[1] 2 Cor. vi. 1.

Among these gifts Paul enumerates "*all wisdom and prudence.*" By "*wisdom*" I suppose he means a large knowledge of God, and of the ways of God, and of the will of God; by "*prudence*" the power to perceive how this knowledge affects the guidance of life. A few verses later on he tells the Ephesian Christians that he is constantly giving thanks for them, and that he prays that God will give them "a spirit of wisdom and revelation in the knowledge of Him," that having the eyes of their heart enlightened they may know the greatness of their redemption and of their destiny. It will be convenient to leave the general consideration of the Divine gifts of "wisdom" and "prudence" till we reach that prayer.

In the verses which are now to occupy us the apostle says that God has made "*the riches of His grace*" "*to abound toward us,*" by revealing to us His intention concerning the ultimate destiny of the whole creation. That intention was once an unrevealed "*mystery*"; it was not known to the prophets, psalmists, and saints of earlier ages. It is made known to us now "*according to His good pleasure which He purposed in Him*"[1]; we have not forced the Divine secret; no necessity has compelled God to reveal it; nor has it been revealed as the result of any unforeseen developments in the history of man

---

[1] This is one of the few passages in which I think that the Revisionists have made a change for the worse. Surely Paul meant "which He purposed in *Himself.*"

and the universe. From the beginning of all things it was in the Divine thought that the sorrow and sin of innumerable ages should be brought to a close in what Paul describes as "*a dispensation of the fulness of the times,*" and that in this final movement of the Divine love and power the righteousness and blessedness of heaven and earth should be consummated and made eternally secure. It was God's eternal purpose to "*sum up all things in Christ*"; and to further the accomplishment of His purpose He has at last made it known.

These words bring us face to face with a subject of transcendent interest. There are several passages in the New Testament, and this is one of them, which make it clear that the Divine mercy is ultimately to achieve a complete triumph over misery and moral evil; and these passages, if they stood alone, might give us the impression that all who in any age, in any land, in any world, have erred and strayed from God are to be brought back by the Good Shepherd to the flock and to the fold. This fair vision of universal restoration has from time to time fascinated the imagination and touched the heart of many devout men; and in our days it has become an article of faith with large numbers of Christian people, who find in it the only solution of the difficulties of the universe.

But this epistle, like the other documents contained in the New Testament, was not written for persons who were uninstructed in the Christian faith. The church existed before the Scriptures. The contents of the Christian revelation were made known by living speech, before they were recorded in writing. In an epistle therefore very much is taken for granted. It is not to be interpreted like an act of parliament any more than a speech or a sermon. When I am preaching to a congregation like this I do not feel it necessary to qualify and guard everything I say, in order to prevent it from being misunderstood. I say one thing at a time, and trust to your own knowledge of the broad substance of the Christian faith to supplement the partial statements of a single sermon. If I am preaching on the human aspects of our Lord's earthly history I do not think it necessary to interpolate a declaration of my faith in His Divinity. If I am insisting that only by patient endurance in well doing can you make sure of glory, honour, and immortality, I do not feel obliged to remind you that we owe everything, righteousness in this life and eternal blessedness in the next, to the free grace of God and to the redemption achieved for us by Christ. So when an apostle was writing a letter to a church he wrote freely. He did not write as if the persons who were to read his letter were without knowledge or without sense, or as if they were captious and were likely to force his words to conclusions, which they knew were contrary to some of the principal truths which were received by all Christians.

If anything is certain and clear about the teaching of Christ and of His apostles it is that they warned men not to reject the Divine mercy and so to incur irrevocable exile from God's presence and joy. They assumed that some would be guilty of this supreme crime and would be doomed to this supreme woe. The wheat will be gathered into the garners of God, and the chaff will be burnt up with unquenchable fire. Some men will inherit eternal life; some men will be punished with the second death. Christ Himself, who came to save the world, will say to some: "Depart from Me, ye cursed, into the eternal fire."

This appalling element of Christian teaching was certain to make a vivid impression on the minds of all who received the Christian faith. From the eternal destruction which menaced the impenitent they themselves had been delivered by the infinite mercy of Christ. The greatness of that deliverance was never likely to be long absent from their thoughts. When therefore Paul spoke of God's purpose "*to sum up all things in Christ, the things in the heavens and the things upon the earth,*" they could not misapprehend his meaning. It would be understood that while those who had incurred irrevocable exclusion from the life of God were to receive the just punishment of their sin and to perish, the rest of the moral universe was to be organized into a perfect unity for eternal ages of righteousness and glory.

It is not necessary for us to suppose that this sublime conception of the consummation of all things in Christ was revealed to the apostle by a supernatural voice or in a supernatural vision. I think we can see the path by which he may have been led from the lofty levels of his own spiritual consciousness to those still loftier summits from which he saw afar off the final destiny of the universe. The path was illuminated for him by the Spirit of wisdom and revelation; but it was not a path in the air; as he ascended from height to height he was sure of his ground; in a very true and deep sense every successive discovery had its verification in his own life and in his most certain and assured knowledge of Christ.

Shall we try how far the path is firm for our own feet? Our spiritual consciousness, though less rich and deep than the apostle's, ought to be similar to his; and our knowledge of Christ, though less vivid and less complete than his, ought to include the great outlines of those truths and facts which constituted the substance of his thought. Let us begin at the beginning. Every Christian man that has reached any maturity of Christian development is conscious that the springs of his life are in Christ. Even those of us who have only recently passed into the kingdom of God have some elementary knowledge of this great truth; and as the years go on we have a clearer and still clearer understanding of what Paul meant when he said: "I live; and yet no longer I, but Christ liveth in me."[1] It is in the strength of Christ that we do God's will; our faith in God has

---

[1] Gal. ii. 20.

its root in Christ's own faith in the Father; it is the
peace of Christ which gives us peace; and the joy
of Christ is ours. For each one of us the parable of
the Vine is verified in our own experience; what we
believed at first on Christ's authority we come to
know for ourselves.

But we are not alone in this experience. What is
true of ourselves is true of other Christian people.
Christ's strength is theirs as well as ours; Christ's
faith in the Father is theirs as well as ours; the peace
and the joy of Christ are theirs as well as ours; He
lives in them as well as in us; they too are branches
of the great Vine. We can see in their temper, spirit,
and character, the indications of their union with
Christ. In the saints of other ages and of other
churches, in men who were disciplined by a civilization altogether unlike that by which we have been
disciplined, whose creed was different from ours, who
received with reverence and faith superstitions which
we regard with abhorrence, we discover a wonderful
kinship to what is most living in our own life. There
is a familiar accent in their speech; their secret is
known to us; the sorrows and the joys, the defeated
and the accomplished hopes, the struggles, the reverses,
the triumphs, the surprises, the paradoxes of their
inner life, are akin to experiences of our own. We
catch their meaning at a word. If with natural
reserve they mean to tell us only half their story, we
can supply the rest. The channels in which their
lives flowed were very different from the channels in

which our own lives are flowing, but the streams came from the same eternal Fountain. By whatever external, accidental, temporary differences they are divided from us, they and we are one " in Christ."

Further, we are conscious that our relation to Christ is not provisional and transient. Apart from Him we can do nothing in this world; apart from Him we are sure that we should be able to do nothing in the world to come. To whatever transcendent wisdom, strength, righteousness and blessedness we may rise in the endless ages beyond death, all our perfection will be the manifestation of the infinite resources of the life of Christ. For ourselves, for other Christian people, we can hope for nothing greater or diviner, through all eternity, than complete union with Him. This will be the fulfilment of the glorious purpose of the Divine love.

Thus far the path has been neither uncertain nor difficult to travel. At no point has it been necessary to invent mere speculative theories of the universe, or of the nature and destiny of the human race. We have relied on the most elementary truths contained in the teaching of Christ, truths which are verified and developed in the consciousness of ordinary Christian persons. The church will be organized into a perfect and immortal unity, and will find its perfect and immortal blessedness in Christ; and so the great words of Christ will be accomplished: "The glory which Thou hast given Me I have given unto them, that they may be one even as we are one; I in them,

H

and Thou in Me, that they may be perfected into one. . . . I will that where I am they also may be with Me, that they may behold My glory which Thou hast given Me, for Thou lovedest Me before the foundation of the world."

By an adventurous and sublime movement of thought Paul passes on to the conclusion that what will be true of the church will be true of the whole universe. When through the illumination of the Spirit the church saw in Christ the power and righteousness and glory of God, it also learnt that Christ was the Creator of heaven and earth, that "all things were made by Him, and without Him was not anything made that was made";[1] and that He was also the eternal Word, in whom the mind and will and heart of God were revealed to all God's moral creatures.

How was the relationship between Christ and the universe to be conceived? Had He made it as a mechanic makes a machine? Did He stand apart from it and watch it work? When it was out of His hands had He nothing more to do with it?

This is not the relationship between Christ and ourselves. His incarnation showed that there is a certain kinship between Him and the human race; and our consciousness affirms that He is not only our Creator, but the perpetual source and support of our life and the ideal of our perfection. The relationship

---

[1] John i. 3.

of Christ to mankind was conceived by the apostle
as extending, though doubtless with infinitely varied
modifications, to the whole universe; and in the
Epistle to the Colossians Christ is described as "the
image of the invisible God, the firstborn of all
creation: for in Him were all things created, in the
heavens and upon the earth, things visible and things
invisible, whether thrones, or dominions, or principalities, or powers; all things have been created
through Him and unto Him: and He is before all
things, and in Him all things consist."[1] This remarkable passage, to quote words I have used elsewhere,
"contains Paul's theory of the relations between
Christ and the universe. (1) Christ 'the firstborn'
was, if I may venture to say it, the eternal prophecy
of creation. In Him the perfection and glory dwelt
from eternity, which in the creation have been
manifested in time. What the creation in its ideal
perfection was to be to the Father had, from eternity,
found a transcendent expression in Christ. (2)
When at last the universe was created Christ was the
very ground and root of its existence; it was the
revelation of His thought; its life was 'in Him.'
(3) Nor was the creative act the immediate act of the
Father; the Divine power, if we may use words
which only remotely suggest the truth, travelled
through Christ; all things were created 'through
Him.' (4) Nor, again, was the universe created for

---

[1] Col. i. 15, 16.

itself; its final cause and its consummate perfection are to be found in Christ; all things were created for Him or 'unto Him.' (5) And apart from Him the universe, as a universe, could not continue in existence; it would fall into disorder and sink back into chaos; for 'in Him all things consist.'"[1]

The universe was created to reach its perfection in Christ, and the eternal thought of God has been moving through countless ages of imperfection, development, pain, and conflict, towards this great end. Crossed, resisted, defied, apparently thwarted, by moral evil, the Divine purpose has remained steadfast, has never been surrendered. Its energy has been wonderfully revealed in the incarnation and death of the Lord Jesus Christ. Its final triumph is secure. God will "*sum up all things in Christ, the things in the heavens and the things upon the earth.*" In Him the discords of the universe will be resolved into an eternal harmony; its conflicts will end in golden ages of untroubled peace; it will find God, and in finding God will find eternal unity and blessedness.

Paul's conception of the ultimate organization of the universe itself, as well as of its relations to Christ, has a profound interest. He believed that heaven

---

[1] "The Atonement: the Congregational Union Lecture for 1875." Page 407. The relation of Christ to the universe, and especially to the human race, is developed at some length, pages 403-420.

and earth, thrones, dominions, principalities, and powers are to be included in one perfect and eternal unity. There is to be something more than an immense and majestic confederation of the just and good of all ages and all worlds. The loftiest ranks of God's moral creatures and the most obscure are to share a common life, and are to be one in Christ.

The final perfection and glory of creation are to be the fulfilment of a law which is at present revealed in forms that perplex our understanding, and sometimes almost break down our confidence in the righteousness and love of God. For nearly all the moral mysteries of the world originate in that community of interest and life which extends from generation to generation, and which involves us not only in each other's sorrows but in each other's sins.

I am conscious of personal freedom. When I am tempted to sin, it lies with myself to yield or to resist. Earth and hell confederate could not force me to do wrong. The guilt of my wrong doing is mine, and altogether mine. And yet I do not stand alone. The blood of a hundred generations is in my veins, and the sins and virtues of my remotest ancestors have affected the substance and structure of my brain, the movements of my pulse, the strength of my physical passions, the keenness of all my physical sensibilities. I suppose that it may have been harder for me to live a righteous life last week, because an ancestor of mine in the time of King John was guilty of habitual gluttony, and because another in the time of Henry VIII. was brutally violent in his temper, and because another took the side of the Crown in the time of the Commonwealth and was drunk for a month to show his joy at the return of Charles II., and because another was covetous and miserly in the reign of George III. As the result of the character and habits of our forefathers, some of us are easily kindled to furious anger, some of us are cold and selfish, some of us have to fight with sluggishness, some with grosser and darker passions.

Nor is it only in our physical nature, which so largely determines the development of our moral life, that we are involved in the ill doing or well doing of people whose names we never heard. Our social condition and our moral environment have been created for us by the wisdom and folly, the virtue and the vice, of past generations. Children are born paupers; children are born criminals. Hereditary paupers and hereditary criminals form distinct races, separate from the rest of the community, having their own physical peculiarities which are transmitted from generation to generation, their own traditions, their own social habits, their own unwritten laws. For those who belong to these races by birth it is hard to emerge and to live a better life. Their desperate condition has been aggravated by the neglect and indolence of society. If during the last hundred years there had been the same vigorous zeal for education that exists now, if there had been a more discriminating and less reckless administration of the public provision for the poor, if our criminal laws had been wiser and more righteous, if the relations between the different classes of society had been adjusted more equitably, hereditary pauperism and hereditary crime would by this time have been almost extinguished.

The unfortunate persons who belong to these degraded classes are not alone in their suffering. The evils which rest most heavily on them extend to all ranks of the state. Pauperism and crime impose upon industrious and virtuous people burdens which severely task their strength, and immense and unknown losses which are a perpetual drain upon their wealth. The moral injuries which are inflicted on the community are still more serious. That free and generous spirit of mutual confidence which is necessary not only to the strength and peace of society but to the development of the nobler and more gracious forms of individual character, is destroyed. The natural pity of compassionate hearts for poverty and suffering is chilled and repressed. The most kindly men are afraid to relieve the worst wretchedness, lest they should be encouraging and perpetuating indolence and vice. There is mutual distrust; there is a general sense of social insecurity.

Other moral evils, still more flagrant, are the result of the presence in the nation of large numbers of hereditary paupers and hereditary criminals. The vigorous independence of many who have sprung from an industrious parentage is lessened, and sometimes destroyed, by the institutions and agencies which are created to relieve hereditary misery; and the good morals of many, who in kindlier circumstances would have been honest and exemplary citizens, are contaminated by the vice and the lawlessness which surround them.

But these are only the more conspicuous illustrations of a universal law. The individual life cannot be isolated from the life of the race; we are one with all mankind. We stand together, we fall together. The law which the French call the *solidarité* of the human race, and to which theology has given a gloomy expression in the doctrine of original sin, lies at the root of most of the moral difficulties which through generation after generation have driven men into scepticism and despair.

It may of course be replied that to this great partnership of life and interest which includes all nations and all ages, and from which no tribe however isolated, no individual however resolved to live a separate and lonely life, can altogether escape, the human race owes nearly all its knowledge, its power, its security, its material treasures, and its moral progress. But it is not my immediate purpose to vindicate the law which binds us together; I want to illustrate its constancy and its universality.

The law is not abrogated in the great movement of the Divine love and power for the redemption of mankind. We are not saved one by one. The ancient revelation of God's mercy came to the world through prophets who had received a Divine illumination not granted to the commonalty of mankind, and in whose words men recognised a message from heaven. The supreme revelation of the eternal love and righteousness in Christ was made known to the nations beyond the boundaries of Palestine by the preaching of apostles, and it has been preserved for later centuries in the records of evangelists. In the extension of the knowledge of the history and teaching and laws of Christ from city to city, from land to land, from every generation to the generation that has followed it, God has relied upon the ministry of human intelligence, devoutness, and zeal. He relies upon that ministry still. We learn to trust Him from what other men tell us of His pity, His grace, and His power; we learn to obey Him from what other men tell us of His awful yet benignant authority. The actual righteousness of other men is a perpetual commentary on the true meaning of His precepts; their courage, their peace, and their joy are a perpetual illustration of the true meaning of His promises. He listens to us when we pray alone; but we receive a larger and more gracious blessing when we pray with others. We can worship Him in solitude; but in the common worship of the church we rise to a loftier joy in His glory, and His majesty inspires us with a deeper awe. Every Christian man is a sacrament and a means of grace to his brethren. We are individually the dwelling place of the Holy

Spirit, yet we are living stones in a mightier temple, and are built upon the foundation of apostles and prophets. We are all God's children, and therefore the relations and charities of brotherhood unite us to all our brethren. We are members of the body of Christ, and "whether one member suffereth, all the members suffer with it; or one member is honoured, all the members rejoice with it."[1]

And this same law, the law which is the origin of the darkest mysteries of human life, the law which is asserted in the Divine method of human redemption, is to be illustrated in the blessedness and glory of the universe, when the universe is finally restored to God. Heaven and earth are to be restored to each other as well as to Him. The knowledge of God and the sanctity which have come to *us* in this world of conflict and sin are to flow into the great stream of pure angelic life; and the joy, the strength, the wisdom, and the security, alike of angels and of men, will be indefinitely augmented. As yet, we and they are like countries so remote or so estranged from each other that there has been no exchange of material or intellectual treasures. What the poverty of England would be if we had been always isolated from the rest of the human race we can hardly tell. It is by the free intercourse of trade, and the still freer intercourse of literature, that nations become rich and wise. Sunnier skies and more luxuriant

---

[1] 1 Cor. xii. 26.

soils give us more than half our material wealth, and we send in exchange the products of our mines and the works of our industry and skill. From sages who speculated on the universe and human life in the very morning of civilization, from poets whose genius was developed in the ancient commonwealths of Greece, our intellectual energy has received its most vigorous inspiration; and our religious faith is refreshed by streams which had their springs in the life of ancient Jewish saints and prophets, and of Christian apostles who lived eighteen centuries ago.

What we hope for in the endless future is a still more complete participation in whatever knowledge and love of God, whatever righteousness, whatever joy may exist in any province of the created-universe. Race is no longer to be isolated from race, or world from world. A power, a wisdom, a holiness, a rapture, of which a solitary soul, a solitary world would be incapable, are to be ours through the gathering together of all things in Christ.

We, for our part, shall contribute to the fulness of the universal life. To the principalities of heaven we shall be able to speak of God's infinite mercy to a race which had revolted against His throne; of the kinship between the eternal Son of God and ourselves; of the mystery of His death and the power of His resurrection; of the consolation which came to us in sorrows which the happy angels never knew; of the tenderness of the Divine pity which was shown to us in pain and weariness and disappointment; of the strength of the Divine support which made inconstancy resolute in well doing, and changed weakness and fear into victorious heroism. And they will tell *us* of the ancient days when no sin had cast its shadow on the universe, and of all that they have learnt in the millenniums of blessedness and purity during which they have seen the face of God. The sanctity which is the fruit of penitence will have its own pathetic loveliness for righteous races that have never sinned; and we shall be thrilled with a new rapture by the vision of a perfect glory which has never suffered even temporary eclipse. Their joy in their own security will be heightened by their generous delight in our rescue from sin and eternal death; and our gratitude for our deliverance will deepen in intensity as we discover that our honour and blessedness are not inferior to theirs who have never broken the eternal law of righteousness. Our final glory will consist, not in the restoration of the solitary soul to solitary communion with God, but in the fellowship of all the blessed with the blessedness of the universe as well as with the blessedness of God.

VII.

THE HOLY SPIRIT THE SEAL OF GOD'S HERITAGE AND THE EARNEST OF OUR INHERITANCE.

"*In Him, I say, in whom also we were made a heritage, having been foreordained according to the purpose of Him who worketh all things after the counsel of His will; to the end that we should be unto the praise of His glory, we who had before hoped in Christ: in whom ye also, having heard the word of the truth, the gospel of your salvation,—in whom, having also believed, ye were sealed with the Holy Spirit of promise, which is an earnest of our inheritance, unto the redemption of God's own possession, unto the praise of His glory.*" EPH. i. 11-15.

PAUL has just said that it is the Divine purpose to "sum up all things in Christ, the things in the heavens and the things upon the earth." This is the destiny of the universe. Unmeasured ages of imperfection, conflict, sin, and suffering lie behind us; and it may be that there are unmeasured ages of imperfection, conflict, sin, and suffering still to come. But at last the whole creation is to illustrate and fulfil the Divine thought, and is to reach its perfect unity and ideal perfection in Christ.

That coarse conception of the Divine omnipotence which assumes that a Divine purpose is never obstructed or delayed, and that every Divine volition is immediately accomplished, receives no sanction either from the Jewish or the Christian Scriptures. It

receives no sanction from those discoveries of God
which are accessible through the physical universe
and through the moral nature of man. It looks as
though God did nothing at a single stroke, nothing
by an immediate and irresistible exercise of mere
force. It is His will that the summer should be
beautiful with flowers, and that the autumn should
bring the brown corn and the purple grapes; but
flowers and grapes and corn are not commanded to
appear suddenly, out of nothing; the Divine will
accomplishes itself gradually and by processes extremely complex and subtle. The world itself came
to be a fit home for our race as the result of a history
extending over vast and awful tracts of time. God
intended that it should become what it now is; but
His intention was accomplished by the action,
through age after age, of the immense forces which are
under His control. "Fire and hail, snow and vapour
and the stormy wind," have fulfilled His word. He
gave a commission to millions upon millions of living
creatures to build the limestone rocks. Through
untold centuries vast forests grew and perished, to
form the coal measures. Volcanic eruptions, frost
and heat, the slow movements of glaciers, the swift
rush of rivers, have all had their work to do in
bringing the earth which is our home into its present
condition. This seems to be the Divine manner of
working. The Divine purposes are not achieved
suddenly. God "fainteth not, neither is He weary."
Chaos with all its confusions is only gradually being

reduced to order; the great work is not completed yet; it will reach its term only when all things are finally summed up in Christ.

The same law holds in relation to the moral and spiritual universe. We see it illustrated within narrow limits in the individual lives of good men. They only gradually approach the Divine conception of what they ought to be; their perfection is not consummated in an hour; their knowledge of God and of the will of God gradually widens and deepens; their moral and religious strength is very slowly augmented. It is God's will that they should know Him and know their duty, but they have to be taught. It is God's will that they should be righteous, but they have to be disciplined to righteousness. The law is illustrated on a larger scale in the religious history of the race. The great revelation of God in Christ was not made in the earlier ages of the world. There was a long preparation for it. God began with the most elementary moral duties and with the most elementary religious truths. He taught and disciplined the elect race by picture lessons, by a visible temple, a human priesthood, and a whole system of external rites and ceremonies. There were faint prophecies of the future redemption, but at first they were so obscure as to excite only the most vague and undefined hopes of a Divine deliverance from the evils by which human life was oppressed; and when they became clearer and more vivid they were easily misunderstood. One generation of saints after another passed away, and the Divine purpose was still delayed. And even when the Christ came at last and the kingdom of heaven was set up among men, the hopes excited by that transcendent manifestation of God were not at once fulfilled. After eighteen hundred years the final triumph of the Divine righteousness and love seems still remote.

It is true as Paul says in the text that God "worketh all things after the counsel of His own will"; but it is equally true that His thoughts move slowly, or that to us they seem to move slowly, towards their accomplishment. As yet the universe is incomplete. We cannot tell what God means it to be. Nothing in the heavens above or on the earth beneath has reached its maturity. Paul declares, in his Epistle to the Romans, that "the whole creation," meaning the visible physical universe, "groaneth and travaileth in pain together until now." In this epistle and in the Epistle to the Colossians he tells us that the power and blessedness and security of the principalities of heaven are not yet perfect; the happy spirits that surround the eternal throne are to be organized into a higher unity in Christ, and in Him they are to be brought into a new and nearer relationship to God. That the moral and spiritual development of our own race is still going on, that we are still very far from the perfection which seems possible to us, is only too apparent. The centuries are still distant which will witness those fortunate generations in which all the strength and glory of the physical, the intellectual, and the moral life of man will be at last revealed.

And so the question sometimes occurs to us, whether we have not been born too soon. Is it not possible that just as in the past history of the world inferior and transitional forms of life have given place to nobler and more enduring types, so we in our turn may perish, having answered the purposes of our existence by assisting the next generation to approach a little nearer to the ultimate type of human perfection? Only the wheat will be gathered into the garner of God; the chaff will be driven away by winds, or consumed in the eternal fires. Transitional and imperfect forms of life can have no place in that universe of glory, in which the Divine power and wisdom and goodness will be finally revealed. What then is to be our destiny?

The purpose of God has a majestic simplicity. He will "sum up all things in Christ." Whoever, whatever, can be made to express Christ's thought perfectly, and perfectly to fulfil Christ's will; whoever, whatever, can be made one with Christ, endures. Apart from Him all forms of life and all forms of material existence perish. As age after age drifts by, this law distinguishes between the transient and the eternal. It is as true of angels as of men, as true of the material as of the spiritual universe, that whatever branch abides in Him lives and bears fruit, and that whatever branch does not abide in

Him withers, and the withered branches are cast into the eternal fires and burned. But all that are in Christ have in Him the guarantee of immortal perfection and blessedness.

The

> ". . . one far-off Divine event
> To which the whole creation moves"

may be very distant, but we need not despair. Being in Christ, according to Paul, we have been made the "*inheritance*" of God. God lets go whatever He cannot bring into permanent union with Christ; and whatever apparent strength it may have, whatever loveliness, whatever glory, it passes away. But being in Christ, we are God's eternal possession.

For a moment Paul seems to appropriate this great distinction and blessedness to those who belonged to the Jewish race, "*to the end that we should be unto the praise of His glory who had before hoped in Christ*"; but the Ephesian Christians, who were for the most part Gentiles, were also God's inheritance. They had heard "*the word of the truth, the gospel of [their] salvation,*" and "*having believed*" in Christ, "in Him" they "*were sealed with the Holy Spirit of promise.*" By giving them the Holy Spirit God had set His seal on them, and given them the assurance that they were His.

What Paul meant will become clear if we recall the first occasion on which the Holy Spirit was granted to those who had not been incorporated into the Jewish nation. A great Jewish church was founded in Jerusalem on the day of Pentecost, and it included proselytes as well as those who were Jews by birth. Three thousand received Christian baptism in one day; but as yet neither the leaders of the church nor the commonalty of the faithful had any suspicion that the ancient institutions of Judaism were to pass away, or that the obligations of the Mosaic law were relaxed. Those who had received baptism and who confessed that Jesus was the Christ met day after day in the courts of the temple to worship God, and to rejoice that at last the salvation for which their fathers had hoped had come. Large numbers of Jews, loyal to the traditions of Judaism, streamed into the church. When the apostles were brought before the ecclesiastical authorities they were not charged with provoking the people to neglect the temple worship, or to abandon any of the sacred customs of the Jewish race; their only offence was the boldness with which they had maintained that Jesus was the Christ, and that those who believed in Him would rise from the dead. The number of those who believed soon rose from three thousand to five; and it still continued to increase. Large numbers of the priests professed their faith in Christ.

There can be little doubt that this rapid growth of the church was largely owing to the fact that no question had arisen concerning the special prerogatives of the Jewish people. The church at Jerusalem believed in Jesus as the Jewish Messiah, and confidently hoped that He would fulfil what they supposed to be the predictions of ancient prophets, and the visions of ancient psalmists, by conferring on the Jewish race boundless wealth, supreme political power over all nations, and a splendour surpassing all the magnificence of Rome and of the vanished empires of the eastern world. That the Gentiles were to share the greatness of the descendants of Abraham, and share it without submitting to the customs of the Jewish law, did not occur to them. You remember how severe a shock they received when they discovered their mistake.

In the city of Cæsarea, lying on the coast of the Mediterranean, about seventy miles north-west of Jerusalem, there was living a devout Roman, an officer in the Roman army. He had ceased to be an idolater, but he had not become incorporated with the Jewish race by submitting to the rite of circumcision. He had a vision, and an angel told him to send for the apostle Peter. Peter, after seeing a wonderful vision himself, went to the house of Cornelius, preached the gospel to him and to his Gentile friends; and while Peter was speaking "the Holy Ghost fell on all them which heard the word." Why not? Even John the Baptist had said that Jesus was to bear the sin, not of the Jews alone, but of the world; and in the great commission which Christ had given to the apostles, just before He ascended into heaven, He declared that His authority extended over all mankind, and that they were to make disciples, not merely of Jews and Jewish proselytes, but of all nations, to baptize them all into the name of the Father, the Son, and the Holy Ghost, and to teach them the laws of the new kingdom. As yet however the true genius of the new Faith was not understood; and in telling the story of Cornelius Luke adds, " and they of the circumcision were amazed, as many as came with Peter, because that on the Gentiles also was poured out the gift of the Holy Ghost." Peter saw what the next step must be. Till now no heathen man had been baptized; the kinsmen and friends of Cornelius were, like Cornelius himself, uncircumcised, and among them it is very probable that there were some, perhaps many, who till now had not even been worshippers of the true God. But it was clear to Peter that since they had received the Holy Ghost they had a right to Christian baptism, heathen men as they were; and so they were baptized.

When Peter returned to Jerusalem his conduct was challenged. His defence was irresistible; after telling the story of the visions and of his journey to Cæsarea he went on to say: "As I began to speak the Holy Ghost fell on them, even as on us at the beginning. And I remembered the word of the Lord, how that He said, John indeed baptized with water; but ye shall be baptized with the Holy Ghost. *If then God gave unto them the like gift as He did also unto us, when we believed on the Lord Jesus Christ, who was I that I could withstand God?* And when they heard these things they held their peace, and glorified God, saying, Then to the Gentiles also hath God granted repentance unto life."[1] The descent of the Holy Ghost on Cornelius and his friends was a decisive proof that heathen men who believed held the same rank as Jewish believers, that the divinest blessings and honours of the kingdom of God were theirs, that they too belonged to the elect race and were God's heritage. They were "*sealed with the Holy Spirit of promise.*" Jewish Christians discovered that the exclusive privileges of their race had passed away. Gentile Christians themselves received the assurance that all the prerogatives and all the hopes of God's eternal kingdom were theirs.

But it was not merely on exceptional occasions like this that the Spirit of God descended on those who believed in Christ and so made it apparent that in a new and glorious sense they had come to belong to God. It is evident that the gift of the Holy Ghost was assured by the apostles to all that confessed Christ's authority. This gift was represented as a large and necessary part of the Christian salvation. To the crowds assembled on the day of Pentecost Peter said: "Repent ye, and be baptized every one of you in the name of Jesus Christ unto the remission of sins; and ye shall receive the gift of the Holy Ghost." Nor was this supernatural gift limited to the early years of the Christian Faith. Long afterwards Paul found certain disciples at Ephesus, and there appears to have been something in them that sug-

---

[1] Acts xi. 15–18.

gested to the apostle a doubt whether they possessed "the fulness of the blessing of Christ." He asked them if they received the Holy Ghost when they believed. They said they did not so much as hear whether the Holy Ghost was given. In answer to a further inquiry he learnt that they had received John's baptism. Then he explained to them that John was but the forerunner of Christ, and they were baptized into the name of the Lord Jesus. "And when Paul had laid his hands upon them, the Holy Ghost came upon them and they spake with tongues and prophesied."[1] Throughout the apostolic epistles it is implied that the Holy Spirit made His home with men as soon as they believed in Christ and professed their faith in Him.

Writing to the Galatians, Paul says: "Christ redeemed us . . . . that we might receive the promise of the Spirit through faith."[2] Writing to the Corinthians he says: "Know ye not that ye are a temple of God, and that the Spirit of God dwelleth in you?"[3] In his second epistle to the same church he reminds them twice that God has given them "the earnest of the Spirit."[4] He tells the Christians at Rome that "if any man have not the Spirit of Christ, he is none of His";[5] and that "the sons of God" are those who are "led by the Spirit of God";[6] he also reminds them that the

---

[1] Acts xix. 1–7. [2] Gal. iii. 13, 14.
[3] 1 Cor. iii. 16. [4] 2 Cor. i. 22; v. 5.
[5] Rom. viii. 10. [6] Rom. viii. 14.

Spirit himself bore witness with their spirit that they were the children of God.[1] Elsewhere he describes " love, joy, peace, longsuffering, kindness, goodness, faithfulness, meekness," as " the fruit of the Spirit." [2] Christian men are to " abound in hope, in the power of the Holy Ghost." [3] " The love of God hath been shed abroad in our hearts by the Holy Ghost which was given us." [4] We have " access " in the Spirit to the Father. [5] And Peter, writing to the elect who were scattered abroad through the East, gives them heart and courage in persecution by these inspiring words : " If ye are reproached for the name of Christ, blessed are ye ; because the Spirit of glory and the Spirit of God resteth upon you." [6] Paul charges the members of the churches of Galatia to " walk in the Spirit," [7] and promises them that if they do they will master the power of the flesh. He charges the Ephesians to " be filled with the Spirit " [8] and to " keep the unity of the Spirit in the bond of peace." [9] The Thessalonians are warned not to " quench the Spirit." [10]

But to illustrate the great place which the Spirit of God held in the thought and life of the apostolic churches I should have to add quotation to quotation ;

---

[1] Rom. viii. 16.
[2] Gal. v. 22.
[3] Rom. xv. 13.
[4] Rom. v. 5.
[5] Eph. ii. 18.
[6] 1 Pet. iv. 14.
[7] Gal. v. 16.
[8] Eph. v. 18.
[9] Eph. iv. 3.
[10] 1 Thess. v. 20.

and even then I should give an inadequate impression of the truth; for His presence in the church and in individual Christian men is implied where it is not explicitly referred to, and penetrates the whole substance of apostolic thought.

In the early church the access of the Spirit of God to a man was commonly associated with the mysterious gift of tongues, with the power of prophecy, or with other manifestations of a miraculous kind. It seems to be a law of the Divine action that the beginning of a new movement in the religious history of mankind should be signalised by supernatural wonders which bear emphatic testimony to the new forces that are revealing themselves in the spiritual order, and illustrate their nature. These wonders gradually cease, but the loftier powers of which they are only the visible symbols remain. The miraculous manifestations of the Divine Spirit have passed away, but it was the promise of Christ that the Spirit should remain with us for ever.

I have spoken of the great place of the Spirit of God in the thought and life of the apostolic churches; but He holds as great a place in the teaching of Christ. Early in His ministry he began to speak of "the Spirit which they that believed on Him were to receive";[1] and in the last and greatest of the discourses which He delivered to His disciples He insists that it was expedient for them that He Him-

---

[1] John vii. 39.

self should go away, because only after His death and resurrection could the Spirit come to them.[1] Through many centuries the Jewish nation had been waiting for the advent of the Christ; and now that the disciples of our Lord knew that the Christ was actually with them, they were told that they had still to wait for another advent, the advent of the Spirit. It was no vague spiritual influence of which Christ was speaking, but a person. As Jesus Himself had lived with them, the Spirit was to live with them, and was to live with them for ever.[2] Jesus Himself had taught them as much as they were able to learn; the Spirit was to teach them all things, and to bring back what Jesus had said to their remembrance. He was to guide them into all the truth.[3] He was to reveal the glory of Christ.[4] He was to be what Christ had been to them, and more; a wise Teacher, a strong Defender, a sure support. The promises of the coming of the Messiah had been the consolation and strength of Jewish saints in the darkest and most calamitous periods of Jewish history; these promises of the coming of the Spirit were the consolation and strength of the friends of Christ after His ascension into heaven. For ten days the apostles and their Christian brethren continued to pray that the promises might be fulfilled; and then with "a sound as of the rushing of a mighty

---

[1] John xvi. 7.
[2] John xiv. 16, 17.
[3] John xiv. 25.
[4] John xvi. 13.

wind" and with tongues of fire that rested on the heads of all the faithful, the supreme hour came, an hour not less wonderful than that in which Christ was born, not less wonderful than that in which He died for the sin of the world.

That, for the most part, we are so indifferent to the presence of the Spirit of God is infinitely surprising. We repeat in another form the sin of insensibility of which the Jewish people were guilty when our Lord Himself was visibly among them. Their imagination was filled with the ancient revelations of God to their fathers, with the stupendous miracles which broke the power of their Egyptian oppressors, with the manifestation of God in the clouds and lightnings of Mount Sinai, with the inspiration which had rested on a long line of prophets. The past was sacred to them; but they were so completely under its control that they failed to recognise the nobler disclosures of the righteousness and love and power of God to themselves. And is it not the same with us? We look back upon the days when the Son of God was teaching in the temple, and in the cornfields and on the hills of Galilee; we read the story of His gracious miracles; our hearts are touched by the stainless purity of His righteousness and by the tenderness and strength of His love; we watch with pain and awe and gratitude His sufferings on the cross; and we feel in our heart of hearts that those were the days in which heaven and earth met, and in which God was near to man. The presence of the Spirit,—which Christ Himself declared was to be something greater than His own presence, was to bring clearer light and firmer strength, and completer access into the kingdom of God,—does not fill us with wonder, with hope, with exulting thankfulness. If the Spirit, grieved by our indifference, were to rebuke our sin He might speak to us in words not unlike those in which our Lord Himself spoke to the Jews of His own time: Think not that I will accuse you to the Father; there is One that accuseth you, even Christ on whom ye have set your hope. For if ye believed Christ, ye would trust in Me and reverence Me, for He spake of Me.

It is true that in all evangelical churches there is an acknowledgment, more or less serious, more or less fervent, that it is by the power of the Spirit of God that men are convinced of sin and drawn to trust in Christ for eternal salvation. But while the New Testament recognises very distinctly that work of the Spirit which brings a man to Christ it emphasises far more strongly the privilege and blessedness of that presence of the Spirit which is assured to those who already believe. And this presence is something different in kind from the mere influence which He exerts on those who are not yet in Christ. He can, in mysterious ways which we are unable to trace, touch the central springs of thought and passion in men who have no faith. He can so reach their intellect and their conscience as to enable them to recognise the infinite majesty of God and His infinite love. These discoveries may shake their hearts with fear, or inspire them with faith. But in all this the Spirit is acting upon them from without: there are times when He is near to them and makes His power felt; there are times when His action is suspended, and they are left to themselves. But His relation to those that believe is of altogether a different kind. It is not occasional and transitory. Instead of reaching them from without, His light streams forth from the very centre of their own life, and His power comes to them from eternal springs which are opened in the depths of their own spiritual nature. It is necessary to receive the life of Christ that the Holy Spirit may make us His home, and when that life is ours He dwells with us for ever.

Paul has spoken of us in ver. 11 as being God's "*heritage*"; in ver. 14 we are described as anticipating an "*inheritance*" for ourselves. The Jewish race were regarded as God's heritage; and, being God's heritage, they had great distinctions and blessings. It is the same with all Christians; because we belong in a very special sense to God. Our hopes are infinite. The same Spirit, who is described as the seal impressed upon us by God to make us for ever His own, is also described as "*an earnest*" of the inheritance which is to be ours. His presence in us is the beginning of the blessedness and glory to which we are ultimately destined. It is the sure guarantee that this blessedness and glory will be ours. If by His Spirit God dwells in us now, we shall dwell in

God for ever. And His Spirit dwells in us that He may redeem us completely from all sin and infirmity, and raise us to the power and perfection and blessedness of the Divine kingdom. The ultimate object of God in sealing us with His Spirit was "*the redemption of [His] own possession, unto the praise of His glory.*"

And now let me return for a few moments to the truth which has occupied our chief attention in this lecture.

M. Godet says[1] that the "distinction between the preparatory operation of the Spirit *upon* man . . . and His dwelling *in* man seems at present almost effaced from Christian consciousness." That is a strong statement. It constitutes a serious indictment against the modern church; for the effacement of so great a truth as this must be the result of grave infidelity to Christ and profane indifference to the greatest blessings which He has secured for us by His incarnation and death. Perhaps the words of M. Godet might be somewhat more accurate if they were slightly modified. I am not sure that Christian men—I mean Christian men whose spiritual life is deep and intense—fail to recognise the distinction between what M. Godet describes as "the preparatory operation of the Spirit upon man" and what he describes as "His dwelling in man"; but they suppose

---

[1] "Commentary on the Gospel of John," vol. iii., p. 141 (Clark's translation).

that they cannot hope that the Holy Spirit will dwell in them except after a long and faithful Christian life. There must be, so they imagine, severe and successful discipline of their moral life, victory over their inferior passions, loyalty to all the precepts of Christian righteousness, a perfect faith in God and in the eternal kingdom of God, an ardent love for Him, a deep and unbroken delight in communion with Him; and then the Spirit of God will come to them in the fulness of His power and grace. But that is another form of the old heresy which Luther fought in the great days of the Reformation. Christ came to redeem us, not to confer the blessings of His kingdom on us when we have accomplished our own redemption. Read Peter's words on the day of Pentecost: "Repent ye, and be baptized every one of you in the name of Jesus Christ unto the remission of sins; and ye shall receive the gift of the Holy Ghost." Remission of sins and the gift of the Holy Ghost were promised, not to works, but to faith. They were to come—both were to come—from the infinite grace of Christ to all that believed in Him, and they were to come as the immediate response to their faith.

The ancient promises are unrecalled. By earnest prayer we may obtain from Christ the gift of the Spirit, as we trust we have already obtained the remission of sins.

VIII.

THE ILLUMINATION OF THE SPIRIT.

"For this cause I also, having heard of the faith in the Lord Jesus Christ which is among you, and which ye show toward all the saints, cease not to give thanks for you, making mention of you in my prayers; that the God of our Lord Jesus Christ, the Father of glory, may give unto you a spirit of wisdom and revelation in the knowledge of Him."
—EPH. i. 15-17.

PAUL'S thankfulness for what he heard about *the faith* and religious life of the Ephesian Christians is one of the many proofs that his nature was singularly ardent, generous, and sanguine. He knew that there were some, perhaps many, of them who were emerging only very slowly from the vices of their old heathen days, else he would not have thought it necessary to write what he has written in the later pages of this epistle about the most elementary moral duties. But it was his habit to think of all that was fairest in the lives of Christian people. There were grave faults, there were gross sins, in the church at Ephesus; but he had heard enough of the church to be sure that it had not forgotten what he had taught it eight or nine years before. The faith of the church in Christ was still steadfast, and the reality of that faith was still shown in their spirit and conduct to "*all saints*" (ver. 15). Paul means that they recognised the obligations which were created by a common faith. They themselves were loyal to Christ, and they regarded all Christians as comrades and brethren; and therefore he ceased not to "*give thanks*" for them (ver. 16). That is an admirable temper. We are too much disposed to impeach the sincerity and worth of a man's faith if we see in him a single serious fault. In thinking of communities of Christians we are so saddened —sometimes so embittered—by their moral and religious failures that we are unable or indisposed to recognise in them any trace of the Divine hand, any indication of the presence of the Divine life. That was not Paul's way. He had a keen eye for goodness; whatever might be his sorrow on account of the sins of Christian men, and however sternly he rebuked them for their sins, he rejoiced heartily in every manifestation, however faint, of a genuine desire to do the will of God. He watched the beginnings of a nobler life in his converts as we watch the conflict between the dawn and the heavy darkness of the night. In some of them the rising glory was almost concealed by the dense clouds of heathen ignorance, superstition, and vice; but he could see gleams of light trembling through the gloom. Here and there between the broken clouds there was the clear blue of a diviner heaven. He rejoiced and gave thanks that the light of God had risen upon the darkness; not in a moment, but

K

gradually and certainly, the dim, cloudy, troubled dawn would be followed by a bright and glorious day.

He not only gave thanks for the Ephesian Christians: he prayed for them. He prayed that God would give them "*a spirit of wisdom and revelation,*" that they might know God, and that knowing God they might know the infinite greatness of the Christian hope.

Paul has already reminded his readers that they have received the Holy Spirit, and in the preceding lecture I endeavoured to illustrate the great place which the gift of the Spirit held in apostolic preaching and teaching. Men were urged to believe in Christ that they might receive the Spirit, just as they were urged to believe in Christ that they might receive the remission of sins. They were told that if they acknowledged Christ as their Prince and Saviour the Spirit of God would live with them, as Christ Himself had lived with His earthly friends; or rather, would live *in* them, a perpetual Fountain of light, strength, righteousness, and joy. It was one of the chief glories of the Christian gospel that it assured every man that through Christ he might become the temple of the Holy Spirit. And it is evident from the apostolic epistles that Christian people had the clear and certain consciousness that the promise had been made good; they knew that they had become the home of the Spirit of God.

But the manifestations of the presence and power of the Spirit differ in different men; they differ in the same man at different times. Some He inspires with exceptional faith in God, others with an exceptional passion for the salvation of men; some with a great joy in the Divine love, others with a great reverence and awe for the Divine righteousness. In some He creates a deep devoutness; they live and move and have their being in God; they spend a great part of their life in conscious communion with Him; they are under the control of His presence always; by their prayers they secure for themselves and for the church the largest gifts of the Divine love. He disciplines others to a vigorous and incessant activity in the service of God and of mankind. In those whom He makes strong for service the form of the service varies. In some He breaks up the fountains of pity for human suffering; He kindles in others a fervent indignation against injustice and oppression. He makes some men preachers, others theologians, others reformers, others philanthropists, others statesmen.

There are certain common elements in the life and character of all Christians; but these elements are present in different men with a different energy. All Christians have the spirit of prayer, but some Christians are distinguished by the earnestness and faith of their prayers. All rejoice in God, but in some the joy rises to rapture. All have pity for the sorrows of men, but some are so mastered by their sympathy and compassion that they give their whole life to the service of the miserable. All Christians care, and care a great deal, for the restoration of men to God, but to some this seems to be the only work worth doing: art, literature, politics, business, philanthropy, the great studies of the theologian, the perilous tasks of the ecclesiastical reformer, are regarded with indifference.

If the development of our Christian life and character is healthy as well as vigorous, the manifestations of the Spirit in forms of power and service most remote from our own will be watched with a generous delight. "For even as we have many members in one body, and all the members have not the same office; so we, who are many, are one body in Christ, and severally members one of another."[1]

To some individual Christians, to some churches, to some ages of the church, God has given more of the "*spirit of wisdom and revelation*" than to others. From none indeed is supernatural illumination altogether withheld; for wherever there is real faith in Christ, the Spirit of God must have granted some discoveries of Christ's supreme authority, infinite love, and redemptive power: "no man can say Jesus is Lord, but in the Holy Spirit."[2] But how immense is the contrast between what Paul or John knew of God and what is known of Him by a recent convert

---

[1] Rom. xii. 4.   [2] 1 Cor. xii. 3.

to the faith from some heathen and barbarous race! What he knows has come to him from that same Spirit that flooded the minds of the great apostles with Divine light, but to him the light is as yet very faint and obscure, just enough to show him the path by which to find his way home. These Ephesian Christians had already received Divine illumination, or they would not have been Christians at all; but Paul prayed that the Divine Spirit who dwelt in them would make their vision clearer, keener, stronger, that the Divine power and love and greatness might be revealed to them far more fully. And perhaps in these days, in which men are making such rapid discoveries in inferior provinces of thought, discoveries so fascinating and so exciting as to rival in interest, even for Christian men, the manifestation of God in Christ, there is exceptional need for the church to pray that God would grant it "*a spirit of wisdom and revelation*"; if He were to answer that prayer we should no longer be dazzled by the knowledge which relates to "things seen and temporal," it would be outshone by the transcendent glory of "things unseen and eternal."

The apostle's prayer raises the whole group of questions which are connected with the two great words Inspiration and Revelation, and for the sake of clearness it may be well to remind you that these two words represent two very different things. Revelations may come to men who are not inspired; and men may be inspired who are not entrusted with any new revelations of the Divine thought and will. When the Jewish race stood on the plain before the cliffs of Sinai, and heard, as if from the very lips of God, the ten commandments which were to be the foundation of their national life, their national morals, and their national religion, they received a Divine revelation. They all received it. They had been slaves a few weeks before; they had the ignorance and the vices of slaves; they had lived among heathen people, and though they had not quite lost the tradition of the true God, the superstitions of heathenism had infected their very blood. They were not inspired. I suppose that only here and there was a man who had any glimpse of the eternal and the Divine; but the revelation came to them all. And when the crowd of Galileans listened to the sermon on the mount I suppose that there were among those that listened very few that had any true understanding of what Christ meant. They listened to one of the most wonderful revelations of the mind and heart of God ever given to mankind; but they were not inspired.

God reveals Himself in actions as well as in words. His deliverance of the Jewish people from the oppression of the Egyptian monarchy and His government of the Jews when they had reached the land of promise were a protracted revelation. We retain the ancient Jewish histories because they are the record of that revelation. But all the men that witnessed the escape of the Jews from Egypt were not inspired ; nor were all the men inspired that saw David placed on the throne instead of Saul, nor all the men that saw him driven into the wilderness by the revolt of Absalom, nor all the men that saw the kingdom divided into two hostile states, nor all the men that saw heathen armies desolate the sacred soil and sweep off the population into exile. God was revealing Himself in the deliverances and the sufferings of the Jewish race ; but the men in whose very presence that revelation was going on, the revelation which gives its religious value to the ancient Jewish histories, were not necessarily inspired ; nor indeed did most of them discover anything of the real meaning of the wonderful events they were witnessing.

The whole life of Christ was a revelation. His miracles were revelations of the power and pity of God. His gentleness, His anger, His gracious way with penitent sinners, His stern and indignant condemnation of hypocrites, were a prolonged revelation of the very life of God. But all the men that saw Christ's miracles were not inspired, nor all the men who were touched by His goodness, or who trembled while listening to His menaces.

By the Inspiration which was granted to Jewish prophets they saw in the history of their nation—as their uninspired contemporaries did not see—the Divine laws which the history illustrated. They learnt the thoughts of God from God's way of dealing with themselves and their fathers. The history of the nation was a succession of picture lessons which made plain to them the conditions on which God has made national prosperity depend the causes which according to Divine laws bring about national disaster and ruin. They discovered in the history of the nation illustrations of the Divine longsuffering and mercy and truth, and from what they saw of God in His relations to the Jewish people they passed on to wider and loftier conceptions of the Divine kingdom and its ultimate triumph over the sins and miseries of mankind. The voices and the visions which came to them were *revelations*; but these had a very secondary place in prophetic discipline and endowment. The supreme power of the prophet was that "spirit of wisdom" which enabled him to see God and the laws of God in the actual history of the elect race, and to anticipate from the discovery of what God had done in the past what He would do in the future. The same clearness of vision enabled the prophet to see in the rude virtues of some heathen nations the assurance of their strength and greatness, and in the splendid vices of others the certain omen of their destruction.

The inspiration which was granted to apostles enabled them to discover what was already contained in the life, teaching, death, and resurrection of the Lord Jesus Christ. Special revelations were given to them: like the vision which taught Peter that the old distinction between Jew and Gentile had vanished away; like the visions and revelations of which Paul speaks in the Second Epistle to the Corinthians; like the great apocalypse granted to John in Patmos; but the main substance of what they knew about God and the Divine method of human redemption they discovered in the history and teaching of Christ. Their inspiration enabled them to see what that revelation of God really meant. The light which fell upon it from heaven made the revelation clearer and clearer to them as their Christian life went on; and so Paul's knowledge, as shown in this epistle, is far wider and deeper than that which is shown in his earlier epistles to the Thessalonians. The great *revelation* was made in Christ; the *inspiration* of the apostles enabled them to see the truths and laws which the revelation contained.

To take a rough, a very rough and very imperfect illustration, the thought of God concerning the action of great physical forces is revealed in the constitution and history of the material universe; the genius of the scientific discoverer, like the inspiration of the prophet or the apostle, enables him to discover the Divine thought which is implicated and expressed in Divine facts.

And so the "spirit of wisdom" may also be called the "spirit of revelation"; for until the spirit of wisdom is given the revelation is unintelligible. It becomes an actual revelation when it is understood.

To the apostles inspiration was given in an exceptional measure. They were appointed by the Lord Jesus Christ to lay the foundations of the

Christian church. They had authority to teach all nations in His name. Later ages were to learn His mind from their lips. Theirs was a position of unique responsibility, and their qualifications were unique; for in the Divine order the measures of human duty and the measures of strength conferred for the discharge of it are always equal. That the apostles were inspired as other men are not, requires no external proof. The proof that an exceptional illumination was given to them appears in what they saw of God and the thoughts of God. Their writings are bright with a glory which rests on no other books. For eighteen centuries saintly men, themselves taught of the Holy Ghost, have striven—many of them with all the vigour of genius and all the resources of learning, and with the fresh aids to Christian thought which have come from Christian history and the development of the Christian life under new and unexpected conditions,—they have striven, I say, to reach the frontiers of that truth which the apostles knew and of which the apostles wrote, and they have confessed that at point after point their strength failed, and that the apostles had passed into regions which lay beyond them. This is the real ground on which the special inspiration of the apostles has been acknowledged. It is certain that Paul and Peter and John received an exceptional Divine illumination, because what they have written has continued through age after age to give exceptional illumination to the church. Those who have eyes to see need no evidence that the sun is shining except the sunlight; and this is the kind of evidence which sustains the exceptional inspiration of the apostles. That evidence is stronger to-day than it ever was; for after eighteen hundred years of Christian speculation, of Christian learning, of Christian controversy, after eighteen hundred years during which an unbroken succession of saints have been living in communion with God, the writings of the apostles still shine with a unique brightness.

But in kind the inspiration of the apostles was the same as that which Paul prayed might be granted to the Christians at Ephesus, the same as that which we ourselves may hope to receive from God.

Supernatural revelation, as I have said, came to the apostles on special occasions; but these occasions seem to have been rare, and in one case at least a supernatural revelation only enabled an apostle to anticipate a discovery which might have come to him as the result of a deeper knowledge of the mind of God as already revealed in Christ. The vision which Peter saw at Joppa, and which gave him courage to receive Cornelius into the church, conveyed no fresh truth, no truth which was not already contained in the revelation of God in Christ. To us it is wonderful that any man who had known Christ could have failed to see that He had come to seek and to save the lost of all races and of all lands, and to save them just as they were. But, whatever may have been made known to the apostles by special supernatural revelations, the substance of their faith was what the illumination of the Spirit enabled them to discover in Christ.

Apostolic revelations are not granted to us. Inspiration is not granted to us in the same measure in which it was granted to the apostles, for our work is inferior to theirs; but it will be granted, if we seek it, in whatever measure the exigencies of our personal duties and of our work for others require.

The authoritative teaching of the Christian church has never recognised with sufficient clearness and firmness this glorious prerogative of the Christian life. Theologians and ecclesiastical rulers have dreaded the outbreak of fanaticism if all Christian people were encouraged, or permitted, to hope for the immediate illumination of the Holy Spirit. In the Church of Rome His direct guidance has been practically limited to councils, to popes, and to a few eminent saints. In the great Protestant churches, although it has been acknowledged that individual Christians are taught of God, the anxiety to defend the supremacy of the Holy Scriptures as the only authoritative source of religious knowledge has led to the virtual suppression of the truth that the "spirit of wisdom and revelation" may come to the commonalty of the church.

But we should never be afraid to accept the infinite grace of God. In Luther's time men were afraid that the doctrine of justification by faith would corrupt the morals of the church, by relaxing the motives to righteousness. Luther had the courage to believe that error could never be friendly to holiness and that truth could never be the ally of sin. He preached the doctrine which many sagacious theologians regarded with dismay, and it ennobled and invigorated the morals of half Europe. A similar courage in accepting and asserting the inspiration possible to all Christians would not lessen but confirm the authority of prophets and psalmists, evangelists and apostles.

The real danger arises from those mechanical and superstitious conceptions of inspiration which would have long ago disappeared had the great churches frankly received the definite teaching of the New Testament concerning the illumination of the Spirit that is granted in varying measures to all Christians. Excited and enthusiastic men have discovered that the illumination of the Spirit is really promised to all those who believe in Christ; they have supposed that in the case of the apostles and evangelists the illumination of the Spirit suspended the action of all the ordinary faculties of the mind, that the men who received inspiration in its highest forms saw visions, heard voices, and were mastered by irresistible impressions; they have naturally inferred that if they themselves were to receive the teaching of the Holy Spirit He would manifest Himself in the same abnormal ways. They have therefore mistaken the wild fancies of a morbid imagination and the waywardness of incipient insanity for the light and teaching of the Spirit of Truth. They have confounded inspiration, which is assured to all Christian people, with revelations which have been granted only to exceptional men in exceptional times, and which are surrounded by exceptional guarantees of their reality. A great truth which the leaders of the thought and faith of the church refuse to acknowledge will almost certainly be grossly misunderstood by ignorance and fanaticism.

Perhaps the safest description of the gift which is promised to all Christians is that which is contained in the text. It is the "*spirit of wisdom.*" It is not a blind impulse, resulting in a conviction having no intelligible grounds; it is not an impression having nothing to justify it except the obstinacy with which we hold to it. When the Spirit of God illuminates the mind we see the meaning of what Christ said and of what Christ did. We simply find what was in the Christian revelation from the beginning. The discovery is no private and personal distinction. What *we* have seen in Christ, if our vision is clear and true, other Christian men will be able to see in Him for themselves. There is nothing violent, nothing abnormal, in the experience of those who are thus illuminated by the Holy Spirit; they simply obtain the more efficient use of a faculty which is necessary to the integrity of human nature.

If I am asked how we are to distinguish between what is revealed to us by the Spirit of God and what we discover by the energy and penetration of our own thought, I can only reply that the question seems to me to rest on a misconception of the nature of spiritual illumination. The "wisdom" which the Spirit grants us is not a "wisdom" separable from the ordinary activity and discernment of our own minds; it is not something alien to our own higher life; it becomes our own wisdom, just as the vision which Christ miraculously restored to blind men was not something foreign to them but their own. They saw what before they had only handled, and the nobler sense revealed to them what the inferior sense could not make known; they saw for themselves what they had only heard of from others. The reality of the supernatural work was ascertained by the new discoveries it enabled them to make of the world in which they were living. Analogous effects follow the illumination of the Holy Spirit. When the "*spirit of wisdom and revelation*" is granted to us, "*the eyes*" of our heart, to use Paul's phrase in the next verse, are "*enlightened*"—*our own eyes*,—and we see the glory of God.

Apart from this illumination no true knowledge of God is possible to man.

IX.

THE RESURRECTION AND GLORY OF CHRIST IN RELATION TO THE HOPE OF THE CHURCH.

> "*Having the eyes of your heart enlightened, that ye may know what is the hope of His calling, what the riches of the glory of His inheritance in the saints, and what the exceeding greatness of His power to usward who believe, according to that working of the strength of His might which He wrought in Christ, when He raised Him from the dead, and made Him to sit at His right hand in the heavenly places, far above all rule, and authority, and power, and dominion, and every name that is named, not only in this world, but also in that which is to come: and He put all things in subjection under His feet, and gave Him to be head over all things to the church, which is His body, the fulness of Him that filleth all in all. And you did He quicken, when ye were dead through your trespasses and sins, wherein aforetime ye walked according to the course of this world, according to the prince of the power of the air, of the spirit that now worketh in the sons of disobedience; among whom we also all once lived in the lusts of our flesh, doing the desires of the flesh and of the mind, and were by nature children of wrath, even as the rest:—but God, being rich in mercy, for His great love wherewith He loved us, even when we were dead through our trespasses, quickened us together with Christ (by grace have ye been saved), and raised us up with Him, and made us to sit with Him in the heavenly places, in Christ Jesus: that in the ages to come He might show the exceeding riches of His grace in kindness toward us in Christ Jesus.*" EPH. i. 18.—ii. 7.

THERE is something in this passage to discourage the Christian preacher. Paul knew that what he was writing on the great subject that was kindling his whole nature to a passion of enthusiasm and rapture would convey no real knowledge to the Ephesian

Christians unless the same Spirit that rested on him rested on them. And therefore, at the outset of that wonderful movement of thought which we are now to consider he prayed that God would give them "a spirit of wisdom and revelation" that they might have a true knowledge of God. And if they were to know the greatness of the Christian hope, the future glory of the saints, the exceeding greatness of the Divine power which was already revealing itself in the Christian church, the eyes of their heart must be Divinely enlightened. His own teaching would be of no avail; they must be taught of God.

It remains true that things eternal and Divine—and these are the things about which every preacher has to speak—can never be seen and known except under the illumination of the Spirit of God. There is a "light which lighteth every man," and which is sufficient to enable every man to apprehend the elementary facts and rudimentary principles of God's relations to mankind; but as soon as we attempt to pass to the higher provinces of Christian truth, the light which is common to the race fails us and we need a larger inspiration. We ourselves must be inspired if we are to follow the teaching of inspired apostles.

There is something, I say, discouraging in this. On most other subjects, if a speaker has a clear understanding of the truths which he is trying to illustrate, and if he has any faculty of exposition, he can be tolerably sure of being able to make his meaning plain to every intelligent listener. A Christian preacher can have no such confidence.

But if there is something discouraging in this, there is also something animating in it. It was not the Divine purpose that the glories that were revealed to apostles should be unknown to the commonalty of the faithful; and since these glories cannot be known except by the inspiration of the Holy Spirit, this inspiration will be given to all Christian men that devoutly seek it.

Every man that believes in Christ receives not merely the remission of sins, but the very life and light of God. The life may be almost suppressed, the light almost quenched, through moral and religious carelessness, through neglect of the ethical and spiritual laws of Christ, through infirmity of faith; but while we retain our union with Christ the life and the light remain. When the Christian preacher is conscious that his vision of truth is wanting in clearness and brightness, and that he is unable to express plainly and vividly even that which is plain and vivid to himself, he may remember that those to whom he is speaking have a diviner Teacher. He is speaking to inspired men. The spiritual truths of which he can give only an inadequate and fragmentary account are directly revealed to those who listen to him, by the illumination of the Divine Spirit.

In attempting to make our own the truths contained in the passage which is now before us, I think it will be well to begin with Paul's representation of our Lord's resurrection and ascension to the Divine glory.

I.

The descent of the Son of God from His eternal majesty to the infirmities and sorrows and temptations of this mortal condition is so transcendent a revelation both of the love of God and the possible greatness and blessedness of man that we need not be surprised that to many profound Christian thinkers the incarnation has seemed to constitute the whole of the Christian gospel. When we pass from the incarnation itself to the atonement for the sin of the world, which our Lord achieved by His death, wonder is added to wonder, glory to glory, and it seems impossible that any further revelation can approach the infinite interest attaching to the birth and the death of Christ. But even the atonement did not end the succession of wonders which began with the incarnation.

I will not dwell at length on the importance of the Resurrection of Christ in relation to the revival of the faith of Christ's original disciples, the founders of the Christian church. But I must remind you that if Christ had not visibly emerged from the darkness and mystery into which He passed when He died, if His body had remained in Joseph's sepulchre, if He had not reappeared to His apostles and His other earthly friends, it looks as if their faith would have been destroyed.

"We *hoped* that it was He which should redeem Israel"; these words of the two disciples to whom our Lord appeared on the road to Emmaus seem to express the condition of mind of all the disciples of our Lord during the gloomy interval between His death and His resurrection. Their faith was gone. Their Master—so it appeared—had been crushed by His enemies. No vague and doubtful visions created by an excited imagination, visions seen by solitary persons in solitary places, could have restored their confidence. The great Teacher whom they had received as the Messiah had been crucified. His crucifixion seemed to contradict all ancient prophecies. It was in violent contradiction to all their own expectations and hopes. Apart from His visible return to them, His return to them in circumstances which would exclude all doubt that He had triumphed over death, it is hardly conceivable that they could have recovered their own faith in Him; it is quite inconceivable that they could have had the courage to attempt to persuade other men that He was the Christ. To His original disciples the shock of the crucifixion was so appalling that, apart from His resurrection, they could hardly have recovered the legitimate impression of His earthly ministry.

But the resurrection of our Lord and His visible reappearance are of immeasurable importance to ourselves. Apart indeed from His resurrection we might still have seen adequate reason for believing that in Jesus of Nazareth the Eternal Life was manifested in a human character and in a human history. I have admitted that the crucifixion was so severe a shock to the faith of our Lord's earthly friends that had they not seen Him again their faith in Him as the Messiah would never have revived; and it is hard, no doubt, to conceive what our own religious faith and life would have been if our Lord's history had closed with His death and burial. But, for myself, I think that if He had not predicted His resurrection from the dead, and if we had had no knowledge of His resurrection, the story of His earthly ministry would have exerted, if not the same authority over me, yet the same kind of authority that it exerts now. My conscience would have done homage to Him as the eternal law of righteousness speaking through human lips and visibly illustrated in a human life. The sermon on the mount would still have been to me the proclamation of the laws of a Divine kingdom, and of that kingdom I should still have regarded Christ as the Divine Founder. His unique declarations that He was the Way to the Father; that He was the Truth, the eternal truth as contrasted with all the shadows of reality which surround us in this visible and transient universe; that He was the Life, and that only in union with Him can the perfect and eternal life possible to human nature be achieved,—would still, I think, have commanded my unfaltering confidence. I should still have found rest of heart and immortal hope in His assurance that His blood was shed for the remission of sins.

But it seems to me that if, after His death, He had never reclaimed and transfigured His physical nature, I should have felt that in His earthly life there had been only a transient alliance between the Divine and the human, that He had *manifested* Himself in a human form and a human history but had not actually become man; and that He had now withdrawn Himself from all human limitations into the eternal glories of the infinite life of God, and was in no sense a man any longer.

He would still have been my Prince, but He would not have retained that nature which made Him accessible to temptation and which sometimes made it hard even for Him to keep the Divine law. He would still have been my Saviour; but He would not have retained those human sympathies which do so much to attract and confirm my faith in His pity and His love. I should have had to appeal to a Divine mercy and a Divine power which had been revealed in the human Christ, but the human Christ would have been lost for ever. The loss would have been immense, and, as it seems to me, without any compensations. The resurrection of Christ is the assurance that this loss has not been inflicted upon us: the human Christ is still ours.

But how is it that Paul speaks with such a passion of emphasis of "*the working of the strength of* [God's] *might which He wrought in Christ when He raised Him from the dead*"? The apostle seems struggling with an idea too large for expression.

The Divine power manifested in the resurrection of Christ appears to him so immense that he accumulates epithet on epithet to describe it. What is the explanation of the extraordinary strength of the apostle's language?

Our Lord Himself raised the dead. He raised the daughter of Jairus and the son of a widow at Nain. He raised His friend Lazarus of Bethany after he had been dead four days. These miraculous acts were no doubt very wonderful; but the writers of the four Gospels record them without any expression of astonishment, and there is not even a passing reference to any one of them in any of the epistles. Why should the resurrection of our Lord Himself have been described by Paul with this vehemence and intensity of language? Why should he have spoken of it as if it were the great triumph of the power of God?

The answer to these questions is to be found in the unique character of our Lord's resurrection. When the daughter of Jairus was brought back to life, she returned to the same life that she had lived before she died; she was a child again in her father's house. We know nothing of her later history; but if she lived many years she passed through all the common experiences of the race; she ate and drank and slept; she grew up to womanhood; she may have married; she had the ordinary cares and sorrows and joys of womanhood; illness came to her as it came to others, and at last she died a second time and was buried. It was the same with the young man at Nain. He went home with his mother, continued to work at his trade, took once more the place in the common ranks of men which for a few hours had been vacant, lived and died like other men. It was the same with Lazarus. He came from his sepulchre to the quiet house in Bethany from which his dead body had been carried, and lived with his sisters as he had lived before. There is no reason to believe that his intellectual powers had received any sudden enlargement, or that his moral life had risen to any extraordinary heights of grandeur, or that in any other respect he had become a very different man from what he was before. He took up the broken threads of life just where he had left them, and was the same man that he had always been, except that the days of death and the hour in which at the command of Christ he returned to the common paths of men must always have been recalled by him with a certain wonder and awe.

But the resurrection of Christ was not a return to the life which death had interrupted. It was the beginning of a new life under altogether new conditions. The Resurrection was followed by the Ascension. God "*raised Him from the dead, and made Him to sit at His right hand in the heavenly places, far above all rule and authority and power and dominion, and every name that is named not only in this world, but also in that which is to come ; and He put all things in subjection under His feet.*"

I have the impression that many Christian people impoverish these great words. During His earthly life our Lord was in a position of absolute dependence on the Father.[1] Between His earthly humiliation and the glory which He had with the Father before the world was, the distance was immeasurable. He took "the form of a servant," a slave; and I think that many Christian people have never caught any glimpse of the transcendent change which has now passed upon Him. They know indeed that His sufferings are over, and that He has perfect blessedness in the perfect love of God. They suppose that His present home is a world of great visible splendour, that His form is radiant with glory, and that He is decorated with titles of supreme dignity. But as during His earthly history He was one of ourselves, although His person was Divine, so they imagine that in heaven He is only one of the glorified; the first in rank, the centre of universal love and honour and worship; but nothing more. As He travelled with men along the common levels of human life when He was here; so they imagine He will travel with us along the loftier levels of that glorious life

---

[1] I do not mean to imply that "subordination," or in a very true sense "dependence," may not be predicated of the present relation of Christ to the Father. "Subordination" must, I think, be predicated of the Eternal Word even before the incarnation. But in Christ's earthly history His dependence on God was like our own. It is this which I think has ceased.

which we hope for on the other side of death, one of ourselves, although endowed with a nobler righteousness, with a larger wisdom, and a diviner joy. His access to God must be nearer and more intimate than ours, in heaven, as it was on earth. He must have a clearer and fuller vision of God's thought. But He will share with us through eternity the blessedness of contemplating the glory of God and the perpetual manifestations of God's infinite love and righteousness.

But this is not Paul's conception of Christ. Paul attributes to Him a real and effective sovereignty over all worlds, seen and unseen. He is not merely surrounded with the pomp and circumstance of supreme authority. He does not merely watch, with a perfect sympathy of joy, the infinite activities of the Divine life and the tremendous manifestations of the Divine power, as a son might watch the successive triumphs of his father's heroism and his father's genius. He Himself is Lord of all. He controls and governs all the immense forces of the material universe; He controls and governs the more immense and awful forces of the moral and spiritual universe. He, the Christ whom men knew on earth, He—and not another—He who was born at Bethlehem, who was a child in the home of Joseph and Mary at Nazareth, who grew in wisdom and stature, who was tempted, who delivered the sermon on the mount, whose arms enfolded little children, who was betrayed by Judas, who was charged with treason against Cæsar and with blasphemy against God, who was scourged, who was crucified,—He, and not another, is Lord of all. This is the explanation of the emphasis with which Paul speaks of the great power of God that was manifested in the exaltation of Christ. When He was on earth He sat by the well and slept in the ship because He was weary; now His strength must never be spent. Although He was filled with the Divine Spirit His knowledge was limited by human conditions, not only in His childhood but in His maturer years; now His knowledge must cover every province of the universe of God. The incarnation was wonderful: that it should have been possible for the Eternal Word who "was in the beginning with God," and who "was God," "by whom all things were made," to descend from the eternal splendours of Divine supremacy and to become man, is an infinite mystery. But that, having become man and retaining His humanity, it should have been possible for Him to reascend to those heights of authority and glory is also an infinite mystery.

This, I repeat, is the explanation of the emphasis and energy with which Paul dwells on the greatness of the Divine power as illustrated in the resurrection, ascension, and glorification of Christ. During His earthly life He was unequal to the great tasks of supreme authority, just as He was unequal during His childhood to the tasks of His public ministry. By the natural growth of His intellectual and moral nature in youth and manhood, by the discipline of labour and sorrow, by fellowship with God, by the inspiration and power of the Holy Spirit, He gradually reached that mature wisdom, strength, and righteousness which were necessary for His public activity. But He still had "the form of a servant," and His powers were powers for service, not for sovereignty; for service indeed of unique moral grandeur, but still for service. With His resurrection and ascension into heaven there came an extension, an expansion, an exaltation of the powers of Christ's human nature which corresponded with His transition from humiliation to the glory of the Father. "*The working of the strength of* [God's] *might*" rendered Him capable of a knowledge so immense, enriched Him with a wisdom so Divine, inspired Him with a force so wonderful, that Christ, the very Christ that was born at Bethlehem and was crucified on Calvary, became the real and effective Ruler of heaven and earth.

Do you say that the human nature of Christ cannot have been invested with this transcendent greatness, and cannot sustain these transcendent activities, —that the human Christ may share the honour and blessedness of the Eternal Word, but that these immense powers must be attributed solely and exclusively to the Divine Person who assumed humanity for the purposes of human redemption?

I admit that they must be attributed to a Divine Person; but the Person of Christ was Divine during

His earthly life, as truly Divine then as it is now. In Christ the eternal Son of God became man; and He has not ceased to be man. In Christ, a Divine Person once made human nature the organ of a life of perfect obedience; in Christ, a Divine Person now makes human nature the organ of supreme and universal sovereignty. In Christ, the eternal Son of God accepted all the limitations of human life, "taking the form of a servant, being made in the likeness of men; and being found in fashion as a man He humbled Himself, becoming obedient unto death, yea the death of the cross"; and in Christ the Eternal Word is now enthroned "above all rule and authority and power and dominion," and God has "put all things under His feet." Paul asserts this truth in another epistle. After describing, in words which I have already quoted, the voluntary humiliation of Christ, he goes on to say: "Wherefore also God highly exalted Him and gave Him a name which is above every name; that in the name,"—not of the Eternal Word or Son of God,—but "in the name of *Jesus* every knee should bow, of things in heaven and things on earth, and things under the earth, and that every tongue should confess that *Jesus Christ* is Lord, to the glory of God the Father."[1]

The words of Christ Himself are decisive. Just before His ascension He said to His apostles, "All authority hath been given unto Me in heaven and

---

[1] Phil. ii. 9-11.

on earth." It was not an otiose and oriental sovereignty which He claimed, a sovereignty of luxurious splendour and ease, separated from all the real and substantial attributes of power. He spoke as one who was about to rule as well as reign, and who knew that He would have the power to do it.

And even before His death He had described the forms in which His great power was to be exerted. He had said that the hour is coming in which all that are in the tombs are to hear the voice of the *Son of man* and to come forth;[1] that the *Son of man* will come in His glory, and all the holy angels with Him, and before Him shall be gathered all the nations; that He will divide the just from the unjust, will condemn the lost to their irrevocable ruin, and welcome the saved to their eternal blessedness.[2] He, "the Son of man," is to raise the dead and to judge the world. He is not merely to witness the manifestation of the great power of God in the resurrection; the resurrection is to be His own work. He is not merely to concur in the decisions of the perfect knowledge and infinite righteousness of the Father; He Himself is to judge the human race. These great claims are definitely made for Himself as "the Son of man," and they are the complete assurance of the truth that these amazing acts of wisdom and of power are to be the acts of the very Christ that lived among men. It is therefore legitimate to conclude

---

[1] John v. 25-28.   [2] Matt. xxv. 31 *seq.*

that all the other wonderful prerogatives and works which He claims are prerogatives which illustrate the dignity and the power, not merely of the Eternal Word, but of the Christ in whom the Eternal Word became man. He is the Way to the Father. He gives eternal life. He is the permanent root of the higher life of man, and apart from Him we can do nothing. It is by Him that all saints are kept from evil in this world. He returned to the Father that He might prepare a place for them in the world to come.

The transcendent development of the powers of Christ which Paul in this passage attributes to "*that working of the strength of* [God's] *might which He wrought in Christ when He raised Him from the dead and set Him at His own right hand in the heavenly places*" was anticipated by our Lord before His death; it was necessary to the great works which He said He was to perform, and to the unique relations which He said He was to sustain to the spiritual life of the race.

Paul's closing words are "dark with excess of light." The Christ who is thus exalted "*far above all rule and authority and power and dominion*" is not to be separated from those whose nature He shares and whom He has redeemed from sin and from eternal death. The supremacy of Christ is to be asserted in His union with His saints. God gave Him to the church "*to be head over all things.*" He is supreme in the church as well as in the rest of the universe; and the church is "*His body*" in which all the wealth and the energy of His life are revealed, the perfect organ of His will, the very home of His glory. And yet it is not in the church alone that the power and glory of Christ are manifested. He gives to the whole creation its substantial being; apart from Him it would be a phantom universe; He is the centre and support of universal law; the spring of universal life; the author of all beauty and of all joy and blessedness: He "*filleth all in all.*"

II.

And now Paul reminds the Ephesian Christians that "the exceeding greatness of God's power" which raised Christ from the dead had been revealed in other forms. "YOU *did He quicken when ye were dead through your trespasses and sins.*" Human nature has no enduring life apart from God. Separated from Him "who only hath immortality" our nature not only sinks into degradation, it is destined to "eternal destruction." Death has begun in every man who by his "*trespasses and sins*" has separated himself from the eternal fountains of life that are in God. The noblest elements of his nature are dead already, and unless he is raised from the dead the death will extend until he is completely and irrevocably destroyed.

There was a time, Paul says, when the Ephesians were "*dead,*" and he gives a terrible description of their moral condition in those evil days. They lived according to the customs and traditions of *this* world; not having the Divine life they could not live under the control and inspiration of the laws and glories of the Divine kingdom. They were confederate in their moral temper and disposition with the great leader of revolt against the authority and righteousness of God. This evil power is described according to a rabbinical tradition as having his home in "*the air*," beneath the happy seats of the saints and of the angels who have kept their first estate, and yet above the sphere of human life. The rabbinical conception, when stripped of the wild conceits and fancies which were associated with it, is an intelligible one; the awful representative of sin has powers immeasurably above our own, and yet he can have no place among the principalities and thrones of heaven; he was therefore supposed to reign in a sphere intermediate between heaven and earth: he was "*the prince of the power of the air.*"

Morally, he is described by Paul as the prince "*of the spirit that now worketh in the sons of disobedience.*" The contrast between those who were in Christ and those who were not was vividly present to the mind of the apostle. The kingdom of God had been established on earth, and the Ephesian Christians had passed into it; but the old kingdom of evil to which they had once belonged was still standing, and the spirit of revolt was still working in those who had not escaped from it.

And it was not only those who had been rescued by Christ from heathenism that had once lived among the sons of disobedience. Paul says, "*we all*" lived among them; we Jews as well as you Gentiles; we all "*lived in the lusts of our flesh, doing the desires of the flesh and the mind*," governed, not by invisible and eternal laws, not by the just and righteous will of God, but by our own impulses and passions; and we were all "*by nature children of wrath even as the rest.*"

This phrase is sometimes quoted as though it were intended to affirm the dreadful doctrine that by our mere birth we incur the Divine anger and that apart from any voluntary wrong-doing we are under the Divine curse. This appalling theory receives no sanction from either the Old Testament or the New. It is taught in the Westminster Confession, which declares that by their sin Adam and Eve "became dead in sin and wholly defiled in all the faculties and parts of soul and body"; that as they were "the root of all mankind, the guilt of this sin was imputed and the same death in sin and corrupted nature conveyed to all their posterity, descending from them by ordinary generation"; and that "every sin, both original and actual, being a transgression of the righteous law of God . . . doth in its own nature bring guilt upon the sinner, whereby he is bound over to the wrath of God and curse of the law, and so made subject to death, with all miseries, spiritual, temporal, and eternal"; and these words of Paul's are quoted in support of the dogma. It is taught in the Articles of the Church of England, which declare that "original sin . . . is the fault and corruption of every man that naturally is engendered of the offspring of Adam . .. . whereby man is very far gone from original righteousness, and is of his own nature inclined to evil, so that the flesh lusteth against the spirit; and therefore in every person born into this world it deserveth God's wrath and damnation."

This is not the doctrine either of Christ or of Paul. In Paul's language nature is opposed to grace as the natural is opposed to the supernatural. Those who are in a state of nature are living their own life without the inspiration of the Holy Spirit. "The light which lighteth every man," and which, if they had followed it, would have brought them to God, they have gradually darkened until nearly every ray is extinguished. They have broken the law written on the heart, and instead of rising into that union with God for which they were created, and in which they would have achieved the perfection of their life, they have by their own acts separated themselves from Him and so have become "*children of wrath.*" This terrible destiny is, I repeat, according to Paul not their inheritance by birth, but their inheritance by choice. They are "*dead through their trespasses and sins.*"

From this condition of nature all Christians have emerged. "*God being rich in mercy, for His great love wherewith He loved us, even when we were dead through our trespasses, quickened us together with Christ and raised us up with Him and made us to sit with Him in the heavenly places, in Christ Jesus.*"

The union between Christ and those who through faith and the power of the Holy Spirit are one with Him is so intimate and complete that in His resurrection, in the measureless enlargement and glorification of all the capacities and powers of His human nature, and in His enthronement at the right hand of God, they rise to new and diviner levels of life. The joy and the glory of their Lord are theirs.

The great words of Christ, "Abide in Me and I in you," "I am the Vine, ye are the branches, he that abideth in Me, and I in him, the same beareth much fruit," extend beyond the limits of this mortal life; as they are the assurance of the possibility in this world of a righteousness transcending our own strength, they are the assurance of the certainty in the world to come of a glory transcending all imagination and hope.

> "Lord, in Thy people Thou dost dwell,
>   Thy people dwell in Thee;
> O blessedness unspeakable !
>   O wondrous unity !
>
> One with Thee all Thy life they know,
>   And all Thou hast possess;
> In Thee they underwent all woe,
>   And wrought all righteousness.
>
> They rose upon Thy rising day,
>   With Thee to heaven did soar;
> Thou livest evermore, and they
>   Shall live for evermore.

> When Thou Thy kingdom shalt obtain
> And put Thy glory on,
> Thine endless reign shall be their reign,
> The King and they are one."[1]

Now we can see why it was that when Paul prayed that the illumination of the Holy Spirit might be granted to the Ephesian Christians, that they might know what is "the hope" which belongs to those that are called of God, he went on to speak of the resurrection and glory of Christ. "*The exceeding greatness of* [God's] *power to usward who believe*" has been already illustrated in "*the working of the strength of His might which He wrought in Christ when He raised Him from the dead and set Him at His own right hand in the heavenly places.*" God will confer on us a greatness and a blessedness corresponding to the greatness and blessedness which He has conferred on Christ. No promises of "glory, honour, and immortality" can adequately represent the wonderful future of those who are to dwell for ever in God; but in the ascent of Christ from His earthly humiliation to supreme sovereignty, in the corresponding development of the intellectual and moral energies of His human nature, we see how immense is that augmentation of power and of joy to which we are destined.

We are not merely to escape from the sorrows, the sins, and the temptations of our present condition; nor are we merely to carry with us to some fairer and

---

[1] "Golden Chain of Praise," by T. H. Gill.

happier world our present capacities of knowledge, of righteousness, and of bliss; our whole nature is to be expanded and enlarged by the great power of God.

III.

There is another aspect under which Paul presents the eternal greatness and blessedness of those who are in Christ. He describes them as God's "*inheritance*" (chap. i. 18). The form of thought was suggested by the unique relations of the Jewish race to God. In the very earliest pages of their sacred books the Jews were taught that the God who had revealed Himself to their fathers was not a mere local and national divinity, but the Creator of the heavens and the earth, and yet the Jewish people were in a special sense His own. This was the ground on which prophets and psalmists appealed to God for protection in times of national calamity, and for mercy in times when the nation was guilty of flagrant sin. Moses told the people that, when God menaced them with destruction because of their offences, he prayed to the Lord and said: "O Lord God, destroy not Thy people and Thine inheritance which Thou hast redeemed through Thy greatness, which Thou hast brought forth out of Egypt with a mighty hand." In his great song he said, "The Lord's portion is His people, Jacob is the lot of His inheritance." Solomon in his prayer at the dedication of the temple urged the same plea in entreating God to show mercy to the people even when through their sins they were suffering captivity: "Give them compassion before them that carried them captive, that they may have compassion on them; for they be Thy people and Thine inheritance, which Thou broughtest forth out of Egypt, from the midst of the furnace of iron." When foreign armies had invaded the country and laid it desolate, a psalmist represented God Himself as enduring loss and dishonour: "O God, the heathen are come into Thine inheritance; Thy holy temple have they defiled; they have laid Jerusalem on heaps."

The actual history of the Jewish race was a history of shame as well as of glory; the Divine ideal of their national life was defeated by their perversity and sin. And yet for a long succession of centuries they enjoyed unique prerogatives. The laws which lay at the foundation of their civil and ecclesiastical institutions were Divine. They were delivered from great national disasters by special interpositions of the Divine hand. Divinely inspired prophets were their ethical and religious teachers. Their temple, their priesthood, their ritual, the exceptional laws which regulated their personal life, were a Divinely ordered discipline of faith and righteousness. And at last it was among them that the Eternal Word became flesh and laid the foundation of the kingdom of God among men.

Those who are "in Christ" are God's eternal "*inheritance*"; all the resources of His wisdom and power will contribute to the perfection of their righteousness, their wisdom, and their joy; and He will defend them from all peril as He defends the foundations of His own eternal throne. We are His, "*that in the ages to come He* [may] *show the exceeding riches of His grace in His kindness toward us in Christ Jesus*"; and only the measures of His infinite power and infinite love can determine "*the riches of the glory of His inheritance in the saints.*"

The Christian gospel is a great appeal to the hopes of mankind. The revelation of the love of God in the incarnation of the Lord Jesus Christ and His death for the sin of the race, and the wonderful blessings with which the Christian life is enriched even in this world, are but the assurance of other manifestations of the Divine grace in the golden ages of the endless future. We have only told half the story of the Divine love when we have spoken of the descent of the Son of God from His greatness and majesty to the sorrows and conflicts of this earthly life ; and that half of the story is incredible until we make it clear that He came in order to lift up the race to the heights of God. The true home of man is in eternal light and eternal blessedness ;—

> "And our life
> Is not so sweet here or so free from strife,
> Or glorious deeds so common, that if we
> Should think a certain path at last to see
> To such a place, men then should think us wise
> To turn away therefrom and shut our eyes."

Perhaps if our own imagination were radiant with

the splendours of an endless life in God, if to our own faith those splendours were never wholly concealed by the dense clouds of earthly care and sorrow, and if sometimes they broke through the clouds in triumphant floods of glory, if the gospel on the lips of the church were thrilled with the passion of the exulting hope of reigning with Christ on His throne as well as touched with the pathos of the sad memories of His cross, many a weary and troubled heart that now listens to the gospel with languid interest would be filled with a sudden rapture of wonder and joy, and, having discovered the infinite possibilities of a life in Christ, would surrender itself trustfully to His authority and love.

NOTE.—After the larger half of this volume had been written I met with the following passage in Canon Westcott's "Gospel of the Resurrection," a book which with the companion volume, "The Revelation of the Risen Lord," I earnestly recommend to my readers:—

"The Epistle to the Ephesians and the writings of St. John contain, in a Divine commentary on the Resurrection, of which Christian history is the gradual and partial fulfilment, the complete solution of the greatest problems to which the thoughts of men are now being turned, the solidarity of humanity and the relation of our World to the whole Kosmos." (*Notice to the Second Edition.*)

X.

SALVATION BY GRACE.

"*For by grace have ye been saved through faith; and that not of yourselves: it is the gift of God: not of works, that no man should glory.*"   EPH. ii. 8.

TO a superficial criticism it may appear that this epistle could not have come from the hand of the apostle Paul. In the epistles to the Romans and to the Galatians, which by universal consent were written by him, there are certain characteristic words, characteristic phrases, characteristic forms of thought, which in the epistle to the Ephesians never appear. The very symbol of the Pauline theology is the great doctrine of justification by faith; but in this epistle the doctrine of justification by faith is not once asserted. The word "justification" does not occur; the specific idea for which the word stands does not occur. The intellectual form under which the Christian redemption is conceived is different from that which is found in the earlier expositions of the Pauline gospel.

With growing years there was a growth in Paul's apprehension of the contents of the Christian revelation. The illumination of the Divine Spirit which rested on him from the first shone more and more unto the perfect day. The intellectual forms in which he conceived and expressed the truth which came to him were determined partly by his personal genius, by his intellectual culture and environment, by his moral and spiritual history, his conflicts, failures, and triumphs, partly by the varying aspects of that great controversy which he had to maintain with error and sin. When he wrote the epistles to the Galatians and the Romans he was in the agony of his struggle with those Christian teachers who were endeavouring to perpetuate in the Christian church some of the imperfect and transitory elements of Judaism. The conflict did not really relate to the mere external ceremonies of the ancient religion, but to its ethical and spiritual methods. The Jewish people had been trained to conceive of the relations between God and man as based on law. There were certain commandments to be kept, as the condition of securing or retaining the prerogatives and hopes which were the inheritance of the elect race. It was hardly possible indeed for a devout and thoughtful Jew to imagine that the great inheritance had been earned by Jewish virtue or sanctity; for there was no proportion between the faith of Abraham, Isaac, and Jacob, and the glory which God had conferred on them and on their descendants. The inheritance, as Paul says in writing to the Galatians, was not the reward of obedience to the law, it was the free promise of God to Abraham, who trusted in the Divine righteousness and truth.[1] But if a Jew was not to forfeit his great position he had to obey carefully a whole system of positive precepts.

And so the idea of law was one of the great formative principles of Jewish religious life. The Divine claims on the Jew were incessant, and they met him everywhere. Not to satisfy them was to incur guilt and penalty. How to escape the condemnation of the law, how to stand right with it, or in other words, how to be justified, was the constant object of Jewish anxiety and effort.

And the conception of our relations to God which was represented and enforced by Jewish institutions was, as far as it went, a true conception. There is an eternal law of righteousness, which is one with the just and perfect will of God. This law we are under infinite obligations to obey. If we obey it, we are right at once with God and with the law; if we violate it, we are under condemnation. The authority of this majestic law is asserted by conscience: while we are obedient conscience is at peace with us; as soon as we are disobedient conscience condemns us. When therefore the Jewish teachers insisted on the authority of law, on the terrible results of breaking the law, on the necessity of justification, they had the conscience of men on their side, and they were in harmony with one part of the eternal truth

---

[1] Gal. iii. 18.

of man's relations to God. Any system of religious thought which finds no place for this severe conception is fatally deficient, is essentially false, and can never train men to a perfect life. The relations between man and God may be conceived and stated, not adequately, not completely, but in part, in terms of law.

And in controverting the heresies of Judaizing teachers, whose strength was largely derived from this element of truth in their teaching, Paul meets them on their own ground, the ground familiar to him. He too had been disciplined by Judaism. The idea of law had become a part of the fibre of his thought; it had been the centre and root of his whole religious life and action. He had been passionately anxious to be right with the law, to avoid everything which it prohibited, to do everything which it required. To be condemned or to be justified, these were the supreme issues of life. And "as touching the righteousness which is in the law" he had been "found blameless."

But an hour came when the law was revealed to him in a new and august, but most awful, form, requiring a virtue quite beyond his strength, condemning thoughts, dispositions, habits, which he could not renounce. That was a terrible discovery. But he did not, in his despair, deny the authority of the law which demanded an impossible righteousness; he confessed that it was "holy, just, and good." Nor did he try to persuade himself that his relations to

God could not be properly represented in terms of law; this would have been antinomianism. His mind still revolved round the old question which this legal relation to God suggests, How can a man be justified? and he found the answer to it in Christ. We are to be justified by faith in Him.

That was a conception of the Christian redemption expressed, to use the phrase I have used so often, in terms of law. It is a forensic conception; and that forensic conception rests on a profound and eternal fact. In the forgiveness of those who believe on the Lord Jesus, and their release from the just and awful penalties of their sin, the principles of the eternal law of righteousness are not suppressed but are asserted in the highest and most august form. Those who believe in Christ are not merely forgiven, —Forgiveness is the act of an authority which is above law; they are justified,—Justification is the act of an authority which expresses and administers law. And in his epistles to the Romans and Galatians Paul illustrates and maintains the truth that we are not merely forgiven for Christ's sake but justified by faith in Him.

He meets the Judaizing teachers where they stand, gives a real satisfaction to those demands of the conscience and the moral nature which they were endeavouring to satisfy by recalling the external and symbolic institutions which had vanished away. And when men's hearts are shaken with fears created by the requirements of law, and when their whole conception of their relations to God is based upon the idea of His moral authority, the very substance of the gospel is the assurance that according to the principles of the spiritual order created by Christ we are justified, not by works, but by faith. At such a time and to such men the doctrine of justification by faith is the truest, completest account of the contents of the gospel of Christ.

But to Paul the doctrine of justification by faith was not a final statement of Christian truth. It was not a formula which could be used mechanically for constructing schemes of Christian doctrine and which made it unnecessary for him to recur to the actual relations between God and the human race. The theological method that draws out a long series of conclusions from definitions was not Paul's method. This method, with whatever logical skill and rigour it may be handled, will result in the creation of a theology which will have two great demerits. Beginning with a mere intellectual definition, every deduction from it will have a technical and formal character; and every fresh deduction will be more technical and more formal than that from which it was drawn, till at last the remoter conclusions will be wholly destitute of reality and life. The system will be false as well as formal. For the method assumes that the definition is not only true but adequate; and this assumption is always erroneous. No definition contains a complete account of the relations between God and man.

The apostle would have been flung to the lions or crucified rather than surrender his testimony to the doctrine of justification by faith. It was the energy with which he maintained this doctrine and the vehemence with which he assaulted whatever teaching compromised or corrupted it, that made many Christian Jews regard him with distrust and even with hostility. It was this which made the synagogue in nearly every city that he visited, both in Asia Minor and in Europe, the centre of a fierce hostility against him which often broke out into violence. But the thought of Paul retained its freedom. He was not imprisoned within the walls of any formula. He was continually recurring to those Divine facts which no formula can completely represent. His doctrine of justification by faith was not a mere fetish. He could write a whole epistle, an epistle dealing with the central glories of the Christian revelation, and say nothing about justification by faith from the beginning to the end of it.

Paul, I repeat, was not imprisoned within the walls of a formula, but was continually recurring to facts. It is true that our relations to God may be defined in terms of law. He has sovereign authority, and we are under the most stringent obligations to obedience. He is the Moral Ruler of the universe, and we are His subjects. His will is inseparable from the eternal law of righteousness to which the conscience does homage and whose claim it enforces. Any account of the relations between God and ourselves which does not include this conception is not only defective but fatally defective, is absolutely and ruinously erroneous. But this conception does not exhaust the Divine relations to the human race. There are other relations between God and man which cannot be expressed in terms of law; and it is with these relations that Paul is dealing in this epistle. He says nothing about Justification because he is not moving in that region of law in which he vindicated the Christian redemption against the Judaizers; the Fact which his account of Justification by faith represented in one form is represented here in another. His mind and heart are filled with the Divine grace.

To some of us that beautiful word has been soiled by unclean hands, tainted by contact with corrupt and pernicious forms of religious thought. Grace has been too often represented in forms which dishonoured the righteousness of God, and were unfriendly to the righteousness of man. In our modern religious language it occurs less frequently than in the language of our fathers. But the word is too precious to be surrendered. Among the Greeks it stood for all that is most winning in personal loveliness, for the nameless fascination of a beauty which is not cold and remote but irresistibly attractive and charming. It was also used for that warm, free-handed, and spontaneous generosity which is kind where there is no claim or merit, and kind without hope of return; a disposition lovely in itself, and winning the admiration and affection of all who witness it. This beautiful word, with all its beautiful associations, has been exalted and transfigured in its Christian uses.

Grace transcends love. Love may be nothing more than the fulfilment of the law. We love God, who deserves our love. We are required to love our neighbour, and we cannot refuse to love him without guilt. But grace is love which passes beyond all claims to love. It is love which, after fulfilling the obligations imposed by law, has an unexhausted wealth of kindness.

Grace transcends mercy. Mercy forgives sin, and rescues the sinner from eternal darkness and death. But grace floods with affection the sinner who has deserved anger and resentment, trusts penitent treachery with a confidence which could not have been merited by ages of incorruptible fidelity, confers on a race which had been in revolt honours which no loyalty could have purchased, on the sinful joy beyond the deserts of saintliness.

The eternal righteousness of God is that which constitutes His dignity and majesty, makes Him venerable and august; but His grace adds to His dignity an infinite loveliness, to His majesty an ineffable charm, blends with the awe and devout fear with which we worship Him a happy confidence, and with our veneration a passionate affection.

Our salvation,—this is the central thought of the Epistle to the Ephesians,—is the achievement of God's grace. God's free, spontaneous love for us, resolved that we who sprang from the dust, and might have passed away and perished like the falling leaves after a frail and brief existence, should share through a glorious immortality the sonship of the Lord Jesus Christ. God chose us in Him before the foundation of the world, that we should be holy and without blame before Him in love ; He blessed us with every spiritual blessing in the heavenly places in Christ. This was the wonderful idea of human greatness and destiny which was formed by the grace of God. According to the Divine purpose, which it lies with us to accept or reject, the very righteousness of the Son of God is to be ours, His access to the Father, the eternal peace and blessedness of His own eternal life. The race declined from the lofty path designed for it by the Divine goodness. But as by the grace of God Christ was to be the root of our righteousness and blessedness, as the ground and reason of our ethical and spiritual greatness were in Him, so in Christ God has revealed the root, the ground, the reason of our redemption. We have our redemption through His blood, the forgiveness of our trespasses according to the riches of God's grace. There is nothing abnormal in the forgiveness of our sin being the result of Christ's death; all our possible righteousness was to be the fruit of the perfection and energy of His eternal life.

The original idea of the Divine grace, according to which we were to find all things in Christ and Christ was to be the root of a perfection and glory surpassing all hope and all thought, was tragically asserted in the death of Christ for human salvation. Our fortunes—shall I say it?—were identified with the fortunes of Christ; in the Divine thought and purpose we were inseparable from Him. Had we been true and loyal to the Divine idea, the energy of Christ's righteousness would have drawn us upwards to height after height of goodness and joy, until we ascended from this earthly life to the larger powers and loftier services and richer delights of other and diviner worlds; and still, through one golden age of intellectual and ethical and spiritual growth after another, we should have continued to rise towards Christ's transcendent and infinite perfection. But we sinned; and as the union between Christ and us could not be broken without the final and irrevocable defeat of the Divine purpose, as separation from Christ meant for us eternal death, Christ was drawn down from the serene heavens to the shame and sorrow of the confused and troubled life of our race, to pain, to temptation, to anguish, to the cross and to the grave, and so the mystery of His atonement for our sin was consummated. In His sufferings and death, through the infinite grace of God, we find forgiveness, as in the power of His righteousness and as in His great glory we find the possibilities of all perfection.

Our union with Him is not dissolved. Through His death we receive forgiveness, through His death we die to the sin which brought the death upon Him; and in His resurrection and ascension we see the visible manifestation of that eternal life which we have already received, and which will some day be manifested in us as it has been manifested in Him.

It is at the close of this sublime movement of thought that the apostle asserts and re-asserts, with an accent of triumph, that we have been saved by grace. And if we have been saved by grace, then it must be through faith and not by works; for grace and faith are correlative. If human salvation has its origin in the infinite grace of God, if by that grace it is carried through to its eternal consummation, then our true position is one of immeasurable trust and immeasurable hope. If on God's side everything is of grace, then on our side there can be nothing of merit. We have only to receive the infinite blessings of the Divine love. We have to surrender ourselves to that stream of eternal benediction which has its fountains in the eternal depths of the Divine nature. We have to make way for the free unfolding in our life and destiny of the Divine idea and purpose.

The apostle is not content with stating the great truth once for all. He states it affirmatively and then negatively: then affirmatively again; and closes with a final negation. "*By grace have ye been saved,*" and to exclude the possibility of missing his meaning, he adds "*not of yourselves.*" This is not enough: "*it is the gift of God*"; nor is this enough; to make it clear that the gift is absolutely free, he adds "*not of works, that no man should glory.*" Even now he is not satisfied; the good works which are possible to us cannot be the ground and condition of salvation; for they are its result: "*We are His workmanship, created in Christ Jesus for good works which God afore prepared that we should walk in them.*" As the branch is created in the vine, we are created in Christ; as the fruits of the branch are predetermined by the laws of that life which it receives from the vine, so our "*good works*," which are the result of our union with Christ, are predetermined by the laws of the life of Christ which is our life and the strength of all our righteousness.

The doctrine of Justification by faith is here, but is included in truths of a wider range and a loftier order. We have passed from the region of law to the region of the free personal relations between God and those who were created to share the life and glory of His Son. But in this region too our position is one of dependence and of faith.

When the discovery of God's infinite grace has once been made, and as long as the vision of it is unclouded, this earthly life is touched with a celestial brightness. God, the infinite and eternal God, does not cease to be great, but His greatness is softened with a tenderness which forbids all fear. He does not cease to be our Moral Ruler, but His authority—though not relaxed—has an infinite charm. Sometimes a change passes upon our imaginative conception of the Divine life. To many of us in our earlier days the life of God was an ocean—an ocean which no line could fathom, an ocean without a shore and without an horizon, without a tide and unvexed by storms. There is something monotonous and oppressive in this sublime immensity; through age after age the infinite waters are never augmented, and they neither ebb nor flow. That conception of God is unfriendly to the vivid realization of His free, personal life. It is a conception which trains us to think of Him as an infinite force, governed by necessary laws, rather than a living Person.

But when we discover the Divine grace, the life of God is no longer an ocean but an infinite stream flowing fresh from eternal fountains, bright with a thousand gleaming lights, with rainbows of beauty about it, and filling the universe with glorious music as it flows. He is a living God. We find in Him a spontaneous personal affection, an affection for individual men, and not merely an infinite love extending over the race as the sky bends over the earth. Grace transcends law, and the energies of the Divine nature are no longer governed by eternal necessities of righteousness, nor even, if that conception is possible, by eternal necessities of love. These necessities exist, but beyond them and above them are free Divine volitions inspired by an infinite affection. This discovery, under forms so fair, of the personality of God exalts our own personal force, and raises us at last to the perfection of personal freedom.

But this is rather what we hope for in those distant regions of blessedness which lie beyond death than what we can achieve while we are still environed by mortal imperfection. It is enough if in some rare and happy hours this wonderful vision is permitted to assure us of the transcendent glory of our position and destiny; enough if when the vision has passed away the remembrance of it adds something to the courage and patience with which we endure our transitory sorrows, something to the joy and vigour with which we do the will of God.

XI.

CHRISTIAN MEN GOD'S WORKMANSHIP.

"For we are His workmanship, created in Christ Jesus for good works, which God afore prepared that we should walk in them."
—EPH. ii. 10.

IN the next chapter of this epistle there is a noble phrase which receives very much of its significance from the fact that Paul wrote it far on towards the close of his life. He speaks of the "unsearchable riches of Christ." I doubt whether the phrase would have occurred to him in the earlier years of his ministry; if it had and we had found it in either of the epistles to the Thessalonians, or in the epistle to the Galatians, it would have meant far less than it means here. For when he wrote to the Ephesians he had been preaching about Christ for very many years, and as the years passed by his knowledge of Christ became broader and deeper; but the phrase shows that he still felt that, after all that he had said, very much remained unsaid, and that after all he had learned very much remained unknown.

"The unsearchable riches of Christ." I trust that many of us understand Paul's mood when he wrote those words. There is a very true sense no doubt in which we may say that the gospel is very simple. We may write in half a dozen lines the supreme fact which is the substance and heart of the whole of the revelation which has come to us through Christ. But year after year the wealth of the revelation is perpetually growing. Twenty or thirty years ago, when we first discovered that we could trust in Christ for eternal salvation, we said, and we had a right to say, that we believed the gospel. To-day if we are asked whether we believe the gospel we are rather inclined to answer, Yes, as much as we know of it; and we are prepared to believe all the rest. The gospel is very simple: "God so loved the world that He gave His only begotten Son that whosoever believeth on Him should not perish but have eternal life." That is the simple gospel; but its simplicity is the simplicity of the ocean or of the boundless heavens. "The knowledge is too wonderful for us; it is high, we cannot attain to it." Not in this world, and I suppose not in the next. Through the bright and blessed ages of our immortal existence we shall still be speaking of "the unsearchable riches of Christ."

In the text we have a part of the gospel which is rarely apprehended by us in the first months or years of our religious history. Some of you can perhaps remember when it came to you as something surprising; fresh as if it had just been spoken by the lips of an angel who had left the throne of God to bring you the news. For a long time you had acknowledged Christ as your Prince and your Saviour, and you knew something of the peace and something of the strength which are the inheritance of all, who believe in Him; but this transcendent fact that you had been "*created in Christ Jesus*" was a startling discovery, as wonderful as anything you learnt when you found Christ or when Christ found you for the first time. It may be that there are some of you Christian people to whom this part of the gospel is still like mountain heights concealed by mists and clouds. God grant that the sunlight may soon be strong enough to scatter all that conceals it, and to reveal it to you in all its majesty. And although, as I have said, this aspect of truth rarely comes to us early in the Christian life, it may be that this is precisely that part of the gospel of Christ which some of you who are conscious that you are not Christians at all may most need to learn. It is not quite clear that the same elements of the gospel that come home to those who have lived a very bad life and have forgotten God altogether will also have supreme power for those who are not far from the kingdom of heaven. Perhaps one reason why some men do not believe the gospel is that they have not often heard that part of it for which their moral and spiritual history has prepared them. Every man should hear in his own tongue the wonderful works of God, and should hear the works which will seem most wonderful to him. It is possible to make void the gospel as well as the law by our tradition.

"*Created in Christ Jesus:*" the words suggest far-reaching speculations which I must not pursue just now, about the Divine ideal of humanity and about how that ideal is suppressed by human folly and sin; they suggest inquiries about the ideal relations of all men to Christ, relations which are only made real and effective by personal faith in Him.

But Paul was thinking of those who by their own free consent were in Christ, of those who, as he says, had been "saved by faith." Of these it was actually true that they were "*God's workmanship created in Christ Jesus.*"

How are we to get at the gospel which these words contain? Let us try.

Most of us I suppose who have any moral earnestness are at times very dissatisfied with ourselves; yes, with *ourselves*. We think it hard that we should be what we are. We complain not only of the conditions of our life, which may have made us worse than there was any need that we should be, but of our native temperament, of tendencies which seem to belong to the very substance of our moral nature. We have ideals of moral excellence which are out of our reach. We see other men who have a goodness that we envy, but which is not possible to ourselves. There is something wrong in the quality of our blood. The fibre of our nature is coarse, and there is nothing to be made of it. There is a wretched fault in the marble which we are trying to shape into nobleness and beauty, and no skill or strength of ours can remove it.

The Calvinistic doctrine of original sin is incredible, but there are times when we discover strange moral facts about ourselves which drive us to a theory almost as gloomy. Do none of you remember being startled, say when you were five-and-thirty or forty, at finding in yourselves faults and imperfections, tendencies to forms of sin, of which you had never seen any sign before? And when they began to appear, did none of you ever say to yourselves: "Why these are the very things which I saw in my father when he was about the same age! Perhaps he mastered them, perhaps he did not. When as a child I noticed them in him they seemed to be altogether foreign to my own nature, but now that I am touching the age at which they appeared in him they are beginning to show in me"? And is it not partly the secret of the special sympathy we have with many of the faults of our children that these faults recall the faults of our own childhood and our own youth? There is something infinitely saddening in this. When we were young we fought with certain sins and killed them, they trouble us no more; but their ghosts seem to rise from their graves in the distant years and to clothe themselves in the flesh and blood of our children. We might be ready to impeach our parents, and to charge on them the faults of temperament which make some forms of virtue and righteousness so hard to us and some forms of sin so easy; but our lips are closed, for our children in their turn may impeach us. This transmission,—I will not say of special tendencies to sin,—but of physical and moral conditions which make us terribly accessible to special temptations to sin, appears even when parents fight a good fight and win a secure victory. When there is no moral resistance to the vice which is akin to us the heritage of evil is enlarged and made more appalling. Drunkenness indulged in through two or three successive generations will so enfeeble the moral capacity for resistance to the vice as almost to extinguish moral responsibility for it. Violence of temper indulged in for two or three generations will approach very nearly to insanity. By a beneficent law it seems as if this awful accumulation of hereditary vice is soon arrested. The race grossly infected with hereditary corruption dies out. Experience verifies the truth of the ancient words that the iniquities of the fathers may be visited on their children to the third and even to the fourth generation, but there the entail ceases, the race perishes; but the entail of manly virtue, of sobriety, of industry, of piety, is not cut off; the mercy descends through thousands of generations of them that love God and keep His commandments.

There is no evading these truths. The facts on which I am insisting form the materials of a large part of the tragedy of our moral life. We are conscious of our moral freedom; we know we can resist, and ought to resist, the temptations to which our constitution exposes us. We are not fated to *fall* under these particular perils, but we *are* fated to struggle against them ; and this is what we resent. Why could we not have had an easier destiny? Why were we condemned to perpetual conflict? Why were our possibilities of goodness limited by conditions over which we had no control and which were never open to our choice? If the forces which are adverse to our perfection were outside us, the case would be changed ; but it is we ourselves who are at fault. The evils we are fighting against were born with us, and they grow with our growth and strengthen with our strength.

And ours is not an exceptional wretchedness. The special infirmities of men vary. One man finds it hard to be just, another to be generous ; one man finds it hard to be quiet and patient under suffering, another to be vigorous in work ; one man has to struggle with vanity, another with pride, another with covetousness, another with the grosser passions of his physical nature ; one man is suspicious by temperament, another envious, another discontented ; one man is so weak that he cannot hate even the worst kinds of wrong doing, the fires of his indignation against evil never burst into flame ; another is so stern that even where there is hearty sorrow for wrong doing he can hardly force himself to forgive it frankly. The fault of our nature assumes a thousand forms, but no one is free from it. I look back to the ancient moralists, to Plato and to Seneca and to Marcus Antoninus, and I find that they are my brethren in calamity. The circumstances of man have changed, but man remains the same.

How are we to escape from the general, the universal doom? We want to remain ourselves, to preserve our personal identity, and yet to live a life which seems impossible unless we can cease to be ourselves. It is a dreadful paradox; but some of us know that this is the exact expression of a dumb discontent which lies at the very heart of our moral being. Is there any solution? Paul tells us what the solution is, Christian men are "*God's workmanship created in Christ Jesus.*"

The Adam of the symbolic story contained in the early chapters of Genesis reveals what God meant man to be. The symbolic story of his fall reveals how man came to be what he is. Adam stands for the race, and represents the failure and defeat of the Divine idea of human nature. But in Christ there is a fresh beginning, and a new race comes from Him. He becomes the actual and not merely the ideal root of the life of those who, to use the apostolical phrase, are "*in Him.*" In many startling forms, the variety of which is the witness to the transcendent greatness of the spiritual fact they represent, Christ is declared to meet the very want of human nature that I have been endeavouring to illustrate. Let me hear your trouble once more; state it how you please; do not be afraid of exaggeration; put it in the strongest form in which your despair can utter itself.

Your whole life, you say, is at fault, through imperfections of temperament and constitution which came to you at your birth. Nothing could help you except you could be born afresh. Granted; "except a man be born anew he cannot see the kingdom of God," and this new birth, not in any feeble metaphorical sense, but in a sense most gloriously real and transcending the metaphor instead of falling below it, is precisely what is possible to you through Christ. As your present life, which has been so miserable a failure, came to you from your parents, and bears in it the deep and ineffaceable impression of what your parents were and of what their ancestors were, a new life may come to you from Christ, the beginning of that life being the new birth.

Put your trouble in another form: you tell me that what you are is the result of the follies and vices of a long line of progenitors, that as you bear in your complexion, your features, and even in curious tricks of manner, their image and superscription, so your moral qualities have come to you as an inheritance; that your ancestors first of all, and then your circumstances and education, have made you what you are, and that you wish to God they had made you something very different. I will not quarrel with this way of putting it. I will not ask for the qualifications of your statement which I might press for; let it be as you have said; you have been manufactured by your birth and circumstances, and are dissatisfied with the result. Then place yourself in God's hands, and you,

O

shall be His "*workmanship created in Christ Jesus to good works.*" Or to put it as St. Paul puts it elsewhere, " if any man be in Christ he is a new creature." I might go on for hours; I do not think you can state your case in any extreme way which has not been anticipated by Christ and His apostles.

You say you cannot help yourself, and that your ways of life are the natural fruit of what you are, that thistles must grow thistles, that you cannot get peaches from a crab tree. Let it be so; but you may be made a branch of the great Vine, and the nobler life that is in Him will show itself in your character in heavy clusters of righteousness and charity. You say that there is no hope for you in this life, death and only death can break up the villainous structure of your nature. If you could die and begin again you might have a chance, but that would be your only chance. I do not object to that way of putting it. "Are ye ignorant that all ye who were baptized into Christ Jesus were baptized into His death? We were buried therefore with Him through baptism unto death; that like as Christ was raised from the dead through the glory of the Father, so we also might walk in newness of life. . . . Our old man was crucified with Him, . . . that so we should no longer be in bondage to sin."[1]

Yes, we were made for this, for something higher

---

[1] Rom. vi. 3-6.

than is within our reach apart from the reception of the life of God. There are vague instincts within us which are at war with the moral limitations which are born with us. It is not merely the men who sink into the foulest sins, the men who have no courage, no vigour, no magnanimity in them, that are conscious of a restless, eager, and sometimes passionate attempt to transcend the measures of human righteousness. Nor is it the base and ignoble alone that find themselves unable to touch the ideal of goodness by which they are haunted. On mountain heights of victorious moral achievement the stars are still beyond our reach, and we have no wings to stretch away to the sky; our feet are still on the earth, however high we may have the vigour and the constancy to climb. Our aspirations,—to use a feeble word which we heard incessantly five-and-twenty years ago, and the disappearance of which from popular literature and speech is perhaps a sign that the generous ambitions of those times have sunk,—our aspirations are after a perfect righteousness and a diviner order; but we cannot fulfil them. They will die out through disappointment; they will be pronounced impossible unless we discover that they come from the fountains of a Divine inspiration, unless we have the faith and patience of the saints of old who waited, with an invincible confidence in the goodness and power of God, until the words of ancient prophecy were fulfilled and more than fulfilled in Christ. The prophets of the earlier centuries prophesied of the grace that was to come to later generations; their prophecies were dark and indistinct, and even to themselves almost unintelligible. They inquired and searched diligently concerning the salvation which they knew was to come, though they could not tell the time or the manner of its coming. And these aspirations of the individual soul are also prophecies; by them the Spirit of Christ is signifying to us the hopes which are our inheritance; they come from the light which lighteth every man. But their fulfilment is not reserved for others; they may be fulfilled to ourselves. All that we have vaguely desired is now offered us in the glorious gospel of the blessed God; in Christ we become "*His workmanship created in Christ Jesus unto good works.*"

But is it all real? Where are the proofs of it? Are Christian men themselves conscious of a redemption as wonderful as the apostle describes? Did I not admit that this truth is rarely grasped by Christian people in the early years of their Christian life? How should this be possible if they are really "*God's workmanship,*" "a new creation," if they are "born again" through the power of the Holy Ghost? Well, there seems to be some sense in a reply which I saw the other day to questions of this kind; children, as far as we know, do not feel how wonderful a thing it is to be born; at the time they do not think much about it; they have no knowledge of what it means and what is to come of it. And this is often true, perhaps generally true, of the second birth. We believe in

Christ, acknowledge Him as Prince and Saviour, trust Him for the Divine life; but we are born the second time, as we were born the first time, without knowing what has happened to us. All life in its beginnings is weak and timid in its movements, and it is a folly to attempt to worry it into a precocious activity. Be patient; the life will show its strength in good time.

All life has to create an organization for itself by appropriating the materials within its reach. The rude popular conception of Adam, that he was dust one moment and the next a vigorous man of thirty, is surrendered now. That is not God's way of creating living things. It is certainly not the order of the spiritual life. There is first the blade, then the ear, then the full corn in the ear. The second birth is followed by years of infancy. The Divine life develops slowly according to the conditions of its environment. It must have time to grow. Often the soil is unkindly. Often the life is starved for want of the means of strength. If the moral powers have been badly disciplined, if the moral habits are very defective, and if the natural temperament is hard, gross, brutal, it will be a long time before the new and Divine force wins supremacy. There will not be an immediate transformation of character. The conscience is only gradually enlightened; but as the light comes it is welcomed, and the will is conscious of being reinforced by a new power; the early struggles with moral evil are rewarded by a clearer and larger knowledge of moral duty, and a Divine energy sustains the endeavours to keep the Divine law. Still the growth in goodness is slow. The robustness of manly strength comes with the vigour of manhood, not in the childhood of the religious life; but still it comes. There is no sudden outburst of the nobler spiritual affections; the passions of manhood are not possible in childhood, and the spiritual affections of a saint belong to the maturity of the saintly life.

But we are God's "*workmanship created anew in Christ Jesus.*" The branch is in the vine, though as yet the leaf has hardly escaped from its sheath and the flower is only timidly opening itself to the sun and air. We are God's "*workmanship.*" The Divine idea is moving towards its crowning perfection. Never let us forget that the life which has come to us is an immortal life. At best we are but seedlings on this side of death. We are not yet planted out under the open heavens and in the soil which is to be our eternal home. Here in this world the life we have received in our new creation has neither time nor space to reveal the infinite wealth of its resources; you must wait for the world to come to see the noble trees of righteousness fling out their mighty branches to the sky, and clothe themselves in the glorious beauty of their immortal foliage.

And yet the history of Christendom contains the proof that even here a new and alien life has begun to show itself among mankind: a life not alien indeed, for it is the true life of our race, but it is unlike what had been in the world before. The saints of every church, divided by national differences, divided by their creeds, divided by fierce ecclesiastical rivalries, are still strangely akin. Voice answers to voice across the centuries which separate them; they tell in different tongues of the same wonderful discovery of a Divine kingdom; they translate every man for himself into his own life the same Divine law. We of obscurer rank and narrower powers read their lives, and we know that we and they are akin; we listen to their words, and are thrilled by the accent of home. Their songs are on our lips; they seem to have been written for us by men who knew the secret we wanted to utter better than we knew it ourselves. Their confessions of sin are a fuller expression of our own sorrow and trouble than we ourselves had ever been able to make. Their life is our life. As men draw to men everywhere rather than to creatures of inferior rank, naturally assuming the brotherhood which springs from their common nature, so we draw to Christian men everywhere. They and we are brethren, whatever their church, whatever their creed. We and they belong to a new race. A new type of character has been created. Christ lives on in those whose life is rooted in Him. It is not His teaching merely, it is not the force of His example merely, that has contributed this new moral element to the history of mankind. It is wonderful with how little Christian knowledge this new type of character is possible. The instincts of the life received from Him count for more than mere intellectual acquaintance with the

Christian creed. Concerning some things there is no need to give teaching to Christian men, as there is no need to teach a primrose how to blossom or a blackbird how to sing. They are "taught of God to love one another," they are "*God's workmanship created in Christ Jesus unto good works.*"

And so as St. Paul says, "we are saved by grace, not of works"; the works, the characteristic works, of the Christian life are the result of our salvation, not its cause. The works are "*prepared for us.*" They are determined by the law of our new life. The fruit of the branch hangs on it because the branch has been grafted into the vine; to ask for the fruit first as the condition of the grafting would be to make the blunder of those who insist on making amendment of life the foundation of faith instead of insisting on faith as the foundation of amendment. Christian righteousness is not what God asks for as the condition of your forgiveness and restoration to Himself: one of the greatest of His gifts to those whom He pardons is the power to live righteously. We come to Him that the tree may be made good, and that so the fruit may be good too. We place ourselves in His hands, that He may create us afresh, that through the power of His Spirit we may have a new life. And we do not assume our true position until we surrender all things, virtues as well as vices, strength as well as weakness, that we may make a fresh beginning, and that the will of God may be perfectly accomplished in us.

XII.

JUDAISM AND CHRISTIANITY.

" *Wherefore remember, that aforetime ye, the Gentiles in the flesh, who are called Uncircumcision by that which is called Circumcision, in the flesh, made by hands; that ye were at that time separate from Christ, alienated from the commonwealth of Israel, and strangers from the covenants of the promise, having no hope and without God in the world. But now in Christ Jesus ye that once were far off are made nigh in the blood of Christ. For He is our peace, who made both one, and brake down the middle wall of partition, having abolished in His flesh the enmity, even the law of commandments contained in ordinances; that He might create in Himself of the twain one new man, so making peace; and might reconcile them both in one body unto God through the cross, having slain the enmity thereby: and He came and preached peace to you that were far off, and peace to them that were nigh: for through Him we both have our access in one Spirit unto the Father. So then ye are no more strangers and sojourners, but ye are fellow-citizens with the saints, and of the household of God, being built upon the foundation of the apostles and prophets, Christ Jesus Himself being the chief cornerstone; in whom each several building, fitly framed together, groweth into a holy temple in the Lord; in whom ye also are builded together for a habitation of God in the Spirit.*" EPH. ii. 11–22.

THE great truth which the apostle asserts in this passage does not kindle in our hearts any enthusiasm of wonder or of gratitude. That we Gentiles should take equal rank with the Jewish people in the kingdom of God, should share with them, in this world and the next, all the blessings of the Christian redemption, does not surprise us. For eighteen hundred years the Divine kingdom has appeared to be ours rather than theirs.

But Paul was a Jew, and though he had become a Christian he retained a vivid sense of the religious supremacy which had been the pride and glory of his race. Through many centuries the Jews had regarded the uncircumcised heathen with contempt. The poorest, the meanest, descendant of Abraham was nearer to God who made the heavens and the earth than the noblest of the Gentiles. For any man who had Jewish blood in his veins and whose imagination and passions had been fired with the glorious memories and still more glorious hopes of the Jewish people, it was impossible to escape altogether from the traditions of his race. In Paul these traditions heightened the rapture with which he declared that the Gentiles were heirs of " the unsearchable riches of Christ." This amazing gospel was always fresh to him; there was a touch of strangeness in it to the last.

In the first half of this chapter he has been reminding the Ephesian Christians that they were raised from the dead with Christ, the Jewish Christ; that the Divine life which has been revealed in Him is theirs; that they share the security, the blessedness, and the glory of His eternal throne; that in the ages to come God will show the exceeding riches of His grace in His kindness towards them in Christ Jesus. And now he seems to feel how surprising it is that he, a Jew, should be writing in this strain to

Gentiles, should be surrendering all the ancient prerogatives of his race, should be conceding to heathen men all the glories of that kingdom which for sixteen centuries had been the hope and strength and consolation of the descendants of Abraham.

Had the claims of the Jewish people been without any foundation? Had there been no real difference between the elect nation and the rest of mankind? This was very remote from Paul's belief. Now that the great thought of God concerning human redemption had been accomplished, the distinction between Jew and Gentile had disappeared; but during the long period of preparation and discipline the whole heathen world was in a position of religious inferiority. To the Jews had been revealed the coming of a wonderful time, when their God would be the actual Ruler not only of the Jewish people themselves but of all mankind. In anticipation of that blessed age Jewish psalmists had called upon the heavens to rejoice and upon the earth to be glad: "Make a joyful noise unto the Lord, all the earth; make a loud noise, and rejoice and sing praise. Sing unto the Lord with the harp; with the harp, and the voice of a psalm. With trumpets and sound of cornet make a joyful noise before the Lord the King. Let the sea roar and the fulness thereof; the world and they that dwell therein. Let the floods clap their hands; let the hills be joyful together before the Lord: for He cometh to judge the earth, with righteousness shall He judge the world, and the people with His truth."

What form this kingdom was to assume neither poet nor prophet defined very closely. The imaginative descriptions of the final reconciliation of heaven and earth are full of splendour, of splendour as dazzling as that of the clouds touched by the rising glory of the dawn; but how these glowing visions were to pass into actual history it was impossible to anticipate. This however was certain: a great Prince was to appear among the descendants of Abraham, and He was to reign on the throne of David. He was to have "dominion from sea to sea and from the river unto the ends of the earth." The wild Bedouin of the desert, whom no conqueror had been able permanently to subdue, were to bow before Him; and remote islands were to send Him tribute. All kings were to do homage to Him, and all nations were to submit to His authority. He was to be a descendant of Abraham; and yet, according to poetic vision, He was to be exempted from the limitations of mortality. Men were to fear Him "as long as the sun and moon endure, throughout all generations." His name was to "endure for ever," was to be "continued as long as the sun," and under His reign there was to be universal righteousness and perpetual peace.

And because the Christ was to appear among the Jewish people and was to be one of themselves, they were formed into a Divine "*commonwealth*," organised under the laws of a Divine polity, a commonwealth separated by God Himself from the rest of the human race. Divine "*covenants*" were made with them in which the great "*promise*" was renewed. They were sustained through all the tragic vicissitudes of their extraordinary history by this great "*hope.*" God Himself had His home among them; their temple was His palace; they received revelations of His will through inspired prophets; their national fortunes were, in a very exceptional sense, under His control.

In all these particulars there was an immense contrast between the Jewish people and all heathen nations. In those great and honourable privileges which were conferred upon the Jews because the Christ was to belong to the Jewish race, the Gentiles had no share; they were "*separate from Christ.*" It is true that in the original revelations made to Abraham it was made clear that the blessings bestowed upon him and his descendants were, in some way, to extend to all mankind; and it is also true that this large and generous conception of the prerogatives of the Jewish people reappeared in the later periods of Jewish history. Since all nations were to be under the rule of the great Prince, all nations were to share the security and peace and prosperity of His benignant reign. It would have been natural therefore, if from the very first the Gentiles had had some organic relation to the Divine polity of the chosen people. And Paul seems to suggest that this would have been the fulfilment of the Divine idea. But the Gentiles were "alienated *from the commonwealth of Israel*," as if, for some reason, the lines between Jew and Gentile had to be drawn deeper and firmer than was originally intended.

According to the merciful purpose of God, the supremacy of the Jews was to be the source of religious benefit to those who were not Jews. The Jews were to be a nation of priests, but other nations were to be worshippers in the Divine temple. Supernatural revelations were made to the Jews, but Jewish prophecy was to make the will of God known to all mankind. The Divine method—this seems to be Paul's thought,—was to maintain some real and intimate relations between the Jewish people and all other races. But, perhaps because of the rapid development of idolatry and the increase of moral corruption among the Gentiles, this could not be carried into effect. The Gentiles were not "aliens" from the commonwealth of Israel, persons who had never any rights of relationship to that commonwealth; they were "*alienated*" from it; the rights they once had they had lost. Nor was this all. The national existence of the Jewish people, their national history, their national institutions, were a visible prophecy and assurance of the ultimate establishment of the kingdom of God among men; by the alienation of the Gentile nations from the commonwealth of Israel they became strangers, foreigners, to "*the covenants of promise*"; they had "*no hope*" of the final triumph of the Divine righteousness and love; for them the final issues of the history of the world were dark, troubled, uncertain; their golden age was in the past and was irrevocably lost, while the golden age of the Jewish people was in the future. Even this does not exhaust the contrast between the moral and religious condition of the pagan races and the moral and religious condition of the Jews. While the Living God was revealing Himself in supernatural ways to the elect nation, in the laws which He gave for the conduct of their national and personal life, in promises and threatenings, in severe national chastisements and in great national deliverances, in prophecies and in miracles, no supernatural revelations of the same kind came to the Gentiles. It looked as if God had forsaken them; they were "*without God in the world.*"

Paul did not indeed believe that their moral condition was as desperate as it seemed to be. Speaking to the Athenians he said: "God made of one every nation of men for to dwell on all the face of the earth, having determined their appointed seasons, and the bounds of their habitation: that they should seek God, if haply they might feel after Him and find Him, though He is not far from each one of us; for in Him we live and move and have our being; as certain also of your own poets have said, For we are also His offspring."[1] In his speech to the people of Lystra Paul blends the two truths, the truth that God had in some sense left heathen races to themselves, and the truth that revelations of His greatness and goodness still remained with them: "We also are men of like

---

[1] Acts xvii. 26–28.

passions with you, and bring you good tidings, that ye should turn from these vain things unto the living God, who made the heaven and the earth and the sea and all that in them is; who in the generations gone by *suffered all the nations to walk in their own ways; and yet He left not Himself without witness* in that He did good, and gave you from heaven rains and fruitful seasons, filling your hearts with food and gladness."[1] Nor was it only in this outward and visible manner that God asserted His authority among the Gentiles. In Paul's epistle to the Romans he recognises that inward ethical revelation which God makes to all mankind; among the heathen there are those who are loyal to the obligations of duty and who "show the work of the law written in their hearts, their conscience bearing witness therewith."

But to Paul the moral confusion and the religious desolation of the Gentiles were appalling. He believed that they were enduring the just penalties of their own sins and the sins of their ancestors. In that terrible description of the heathen contained in the first chapter of the Epistle to the Romans he attributes their vices to the Divine justice manifesting itself in awful wrath. They had forsaken God, and therefore "God gave them up in the lusts of their hearts unto uncleanness," "gave them up unto vile passions," "gave them up unto a reprobate mind." That description is a terrible commentary on what he

---

[1] Acts xiv. 15–17.

meant by the Gentiles being "*without God in the world.*"

Everything was changed by the coming and the death of Christ. "*Now in Christ Jesus ye that once were far off are made nigh in the blood of Christ.*" By the Lord Jesus Christ the whole world had been brought within the range of the grace and redemptive power of God.

"*For He is our peace.*" The question has been raised whether Paul meant that Christ had brought to an end the ancient separation of the pagan world from "the commonwealth of Israel," and had thus established peace between the Jew and the Gentile; or whether, in addition to this, he meant that Christ had brought to an end the deeper and more fatal estrangement between the human race and God.

Paul himself has made his meaning clear. As he had just stated with such tremendous emphasis the contrast which had existed for many centuries between the religious position of the Jew and the religious position of the Gentile, it was only natural that he should declare that this contrast had now disappeared. The external institutions of Judaism, "*the law of commandments contained in ordinances,*" had been the "*middle wall of partition*" between the elect nation and the rest of the world; these institutions had isolated the Jews from all pagan races, and had restrained within the limits of the elect race the great revelation of the righteousness and love of God; and the reason for the existence of these institutions ceased at the coming of Christ. He was the true Temple, the true Priest, the true Sacrifice; and He came to found a spiritual kingdom in which descent from Abraham was to confer no privileges. By bringing to an end the religious supremacy of the Jew, Christ brought to an end the estrangement, the "enmity," between Jew and Gentile. He created in Himself "*of the twain one new man, so making peace.*"

But this was only part of His work. He came that He "*might reconcile them both in one body, unto God through the cross*"; and by that reconciliation He made "*peace*," not only between Jew and Gentile, but between earth and heaven.

And He "*came and preached peace to you*," the Gentiles, "*that were far off, and peace*" to the Jews, "*to them that were nigh.*" The image, as I have said elsewhere,[1] present to the apostle's mind is that of an imperial power sending messengers to provinces with which it had been at war, messengers whose first business was to make known that the war was over. And this reconciliation between God and the human race had been accomplished "*in the blood*" and "*through the cross*" of the Lord Jesus Christ. Through Him, and as the result of this reconciliation, both Jew and Gentile have their "*access in one Spirit unto the Father.*" The restoration of the universe to an eternal unity in Christ has begun; the old division

---

[1] "The Atonement: the Congregational Union Lecture for 1875." Page 257.

between the descendants of Abraham and the heathen world has disappeared; in their religious life, all Christians of all nations, whatever their temporary and external distinctions, are already one in Christ: the Gentiles are "*no more strangers*" in the Divine commonwealth, but "*fellow citizens with the saints,*" no more "*sojourners,*" but "*of the household of God.*" There is now rising a nobler and more majestic temple than that which had been for many centuries the centre of Jewish worship and the home of the visible symbol of the Divine glory; a temple of which Christ Himself is the corner stone, and "*the apostles and prophets*" of the new Faith "*the foundation.*" Into this temple the Gentiles were being built as living stones. "*Each several building,*"—the church at Ephesus, which was largely composed of Gentiles, as well as the church at Jerusalem, which was almost exclusively composed of Jews,—each Christian community, is included in the immense plan, has its relations adjusted to the rest of the great structure, and in Christ being "*fitly framed together groweth into a holy temple in the Lord.*" This process is described as the work of the Divine Spirit. It is by His teaching and by the inspiration of His strength that we are "*builded together for a habitation of God.*"

The relations between the Old Testament and the New, between Judaism and Christianity, are exciting anxious interest. The controversies concerning the authorship and the age of many of the ancient Jewish books, controversies which have occupied a considerable number of distinguished scholars during the last forty or fifty years, have recently been forced on the attention of ordinary Christian people. This passage seems naturally to suggest the consideration of the position which it is our duty to assume in relation to this question.

Paul recognises the Divine origin of the institutions of Judaism. Their Divine origin is assumed throughout the New Testament. From the first page of the Gospel of Matthew to the last page of the Apocalypse of John it is always acknowledged that God, who revealed Himself in Christ, and who through Christ had achieved the redemption of mankind, had through a long succession of centuries revealed Himself to the Jews. This is not only assumed, it is often explicitly asserted.

The reality of this ancient revelation is confirmed by the contents of the sacred books of Judaism. You may regard the early chapters of the book of Genesis as a collection of mythical traditions; you may offer some natural explanation of the miraculous incidents of the Exodus; you may challenge the historical trustworthiness and impartiality of the books of Kings and Chronicles; you may contend that the book of Deuteronomy was written in the time of Josiah, and that the Levitical institutions were not completely organised till the time of the exile; it still remains true that a supernatural and Divine glory rested on the history of the Jewish race. For many centuries Jewish prophets declared that the universe bore witness to the one Supreme God. In the earlier ages they may have been most deeply impressed by the awfulness of His power; but to the devout Jew God was always the Moral Ruler of men, and while in the greatest of heathen empires the heavens were becoming, through one generation after another, darker and darker with incredible superstitions, among the Jews there were brighter and yet brighter discoveries of the Divine righteousness, the Divine pity, and the Divine love. No external evidence is necessary to prove that the psalmists and the prophets were illuminated and inspired by the Spirit of God. Their happy trust in the Divine goodness, their exultation in the Divine righteousness, the agony of their penitence when they had broken the Divine law, the pathos of their appeals to the Divine mercy, are a sufficient proof that they had heard the voice and seen the face of God. Only the vision of the Divine glory could have created the rapture of their joy; only the loss of that vision could have occasioned the bitter anguish with which, out of the depths of a great despair, they cry to the God who had forsaken them. And still, after the lapse of so many centuries, after changes so vast in the intellectual, the moral, and the religious life of mankind, their words soothe our sorrow, quiet our agitation, invigorate faith, and kindle the fires of devout affection. We know that God revealed Himself to them, for through them God reveals Himself to us.

No exceptional genius for religion can be attributed to the Jewish people, in explanation of the contrast between the religious truth contained in their sacred books and the religious knowledge of the rest of mankind. For it is clear from the Jewish histories themselves that down to the time of the exile the nation had a passionate lust for every form of pagan worship, and that neither the traditions of the great events in their national life nor the menaces of the prophets were sufficient to restrain them from gross and licentious idolatry.

The rise, the growth, the enduring strength of the great Jewish hope is another decisive proof that Jewish Patriarchs, Psalmists, and Prophets received light from the very presence of God. Through age after age, when Abraham, Isaac and Jacob were living the life of Bedouin chiefs on the plains of Syria, a thousand years later when through the victories of David and the peaceful reign of Solomon the nation had touched the highest point of its secular glory, five hundred years later still, when the exiles in Babylon had just returned to their own land, prophet after prophet, poet after poet, consoled the sorrows or heightened the joys of their fellow countrymen by the confident assurance that the time would come when from among themselves would arise a righteous Prince, who would be the Leader of a great reformation and the author of a great redemption.

This lofty hope, so both psalmists and prophets declared, was no mere dream of patriotic enthusiasm, but rested on the strong promise of God. And when Christ came He declared that the hope and the promise were now to be fulfilled.

You cannot explain the religious contents of these ancient Jewish books by any theories about the monotheistic tendencies of the Semitic races. The only rational explanation is that which is offered by the repeated declarations of the books themselves, that in some wonderful way "the word of the Lord." came to the prophets of the Jewish people.

But it does not follow from this that Jewish patriarchs, Jewish heroes, Jewish kings, who displayed some great moral and religious qualities, exhibited a faultless morality deserving of our homage and imitation. Nor does it follow that the ethical knowledge even of those who were conspicuous for their religious faith was very much in advance of the ethical knowledge of their race and of their age. Most intelligent Christian people have, I suppose, come to see that it was impossible that the ethics of the sermon on the mount should have been made the law of conduct in the earlier ages of Jewish history; the larger revelation and the nobler morals are indissolubly connected with each other.

It may however still be necessary to insist upon what after all is a very simple and obvious truth, that a loyal faith in the supernatural revelations made to the Jewish race does not require us to believe that every book that the Jewish people counted sacred was assigned by them to its true date and its true author, or that the accuracy of the historical contents of these books is guaranteed by Divine inspiration. We may receive with grateful reverence those discoveries of God which are contained in the Jewish scriptures, we may be completely convinced that to psalmists and prophets there came visions and voices from the upper heavens; and yet we may feel under no obligation to acknowledge that the chronicles which were kept of later Jewish history, and the traditions which were preserved of the fortunes of Abraham and his immediate descendants, are absolutely trustworthy.

I think that the speculations of some recent scholars on several of these questions are extremely precarious, and that some of their most remarkable conclusions are extremely arbitrary. These ancient books appear to me more remarkable the more closely I study them; they appear to me not only to contain a unique history, but to possess ethical and literary qualities which are also unique. I see no reason for believing that the Jewish scholars by whom they were arranged made any grave mistakes either about the dates at which they were written or about their authorship. But I claim freedom for those who think differently. These are not questions which can be peremptorily determined by an appeal to the authority of Christ or of His apostles. They recognise the Divine origin of the institutions of the

LECT. XII.] JUDAISM AND CHRISTIANITY. 217

Jewish nation; but they never invest with the Divine authority the written history either of the institutions or of the nation. They recognise the Divine origin of the religious contents of the ancient Jewish literature; but on the critical questions concerning the literature itself Christ and His apostles have not spoken. These questions must be left to the determination of critics.

I am glad to be able to sustain what I have said on this subject by a quotation from an English author whose clear strong sense gives great authority to his words. And perhaps his opinion will be regarded of still greater value because he wrote before the modern critical attack on the books of the Old Testament had begun. The quotation is from Archdeacon Paley's well known book on the Evidences of Christianity.

Archdeacon Paley says:

"Undoubtedly our Saviour assumes the Divine origin of the Mosaic institution; and independently of His authority I conceive it to be very difficult to assign any other cause for the commencement or existence of that institution, especially for the singular circumstance of the Jews adhering to the unity when every other people slid into polytheism; for their being men in religion, children in everything else; behind other nations in the arts of peace and war, superior to the most improved in their sentiments and doctrines relating to the Deity. Undoubtedly also our Saviour recognises the prophetic character of many of their ancient writers. So far therefore we are bound as Christians to go. But to make Christianity answerable with its life for the circumstantial truth of each passage of the Old Testament, the genuineness of every book, the information, fidelity, and judgment of every writer in it, is to bring, I will not say great, but unnecessary difficulties into the whole system. These books were universally read and received by the Jews in our Saviour's time. He and His apostles, in common with all other Jews, referred to them, alluded to them, used them. Yet, except where He expressly ascribes a Divine authority to particular predictions, I do not know that we can strictly draw any conclusion from the books being so used and applied, beside the proof, which it unquestionably is, of their notoriety and reception at that time. In this view our scriptures afford a valuable testimony to those of the Jews. But the nature of this testimony ought to be understood. It is surely very different from what it is sometimes represented to be, a specific ratification of each particular fact and opinion, and not only of each particular fact but of the motives assigned for every action, together with the judgment of praise or dispraise bestowed upon them. St. James, in his epistle, says: 'Ye have heard of the patience of Job, and have seen the end of the Lord.' Notwithstanding this text, the reality of Job's history and even the existence of such a person has always been deemed a fair subject of inquiry and discussion amongst Christian divines. St. James's authority is considered as good evidence of the existence of the Book of Job at that time, and of its reception by the Jews, and of nothing more. St. Paul in his Second Epistle to Timothy has this similitude : 'Now, as Jannes and Jambres withstood Moses, so do these also resist the truth.' These names are not found in the Old Testament ; and it is uncertain whether St. Paul took them from some apocryphal writing then extant, or from tradition. But no one ever imagined that St. Paul is here asserting the authority of the writing if it was a written account which he quoted, or making himself answerable for the authenticity of the tradition ; much less, that he so involves himself with either of these questions as that the credit of his own history and mission should depend upon the fact whether Jannes and Jambres withstood Moses or not. For what reason a more rigorous interpretation should be put upon other references it is difficult to know. I do not mean that other passages of the Jewish history stand upon no better evidence than the history of Job, or of Jannes and Jambres (I think much otherwise); but I mean that a reference in the New Testament to a passage in the Old does not so fix its authority as to exclude all inquiry into its credibility, or into the separate reasons upon which that credibility is founded, and that it is an unwarrantable as well as unsafe rule to lay down concerning the Jewish history what was never laid down concerning any other, that either every particular of it must be true or the whole false."—(*Paley's "Evidences of Christianity,"* Part III., chap. 3.)

The admirable sagacity of these words might have saved many excellent Christian people from difficulties which have almost destroyed their Christian faith. And if these words were remembered by some whose faith is untroubled they might prevent that passionate and unreasonable hostility to free criticism which menaces Protestant Christendom with divisions perilous both to religious belief and to religious life.

XIII.

THE GRACE GIVEN TO PAUL.

"*For this cause I Paul, the prisoner of Christ Jesus in behalf of you Gentiles,—if so be that ye have heard of the dispensation of that grace of God which was given me to you-ward; how that by revelation was made known unto me the mystery, as I wrote afore in few words, whereby, when ye read, ye can perceive my understanding in the mystery of Christ; which in other generations was not made known unto the sons of men, as it hath now been revealed unto His holy apostles and prophets in the Spirit; to wit, that the Gentiles are fellow-heirs, and fellow-members of the body, and fellow-partakers of the promise in Christ Jesus through the gospel, whereof I was made a minister, according to the gift of that grace of God which was given me according to the working of His power. Unto me, who am less than the least of all saints, was this grace given, to preach unto the Gentiles the unsearchable riches of Christ; and to make all men see what is the dispensation of the mystery which from all ages hath been hid in God who created all things; to the intent that now unto the principalities and the powers in the heavenly places might be made known through the church the manifold wisdom of God, according to the eternal purpose which He purposed in Christ Jesus our Lord: in whom we have boldness and access in confidence through our faith in Him. Wherefore I ask that ye faint not at my tribulations for you, which are your glory.*"
—EPH. iii. 1-13.

HAVING asserted the generous freedom of the Christian redemption which confers upon men of all races citizenship in the commonwealth of the saints, makes them members of the household of God, and builds them into one stately temple consecrated by the Divine presence and glory, Paul was about to address to the Ephesian Christians those practical exhortations which are contained in the fourth, fifth, and sixth chapters of the epistle.

But he adds a pathetic urgency to these exhortations by describing himself as "*Paul the prisoner of Jesus Christ*"—the one whom Christ has put in chains[1]—"*in behalf of you Gentiles*"; and this description sets his imagination on fire, and awakens in his heart a passion of gratitude. "*A prisoner of Christ*"—he can desire no more honourable title; "*on behalf of* [the] *Gentiles*"—he can be appointed to no more honourable service. It will be well, he thinks, for the readers of his epistle to be reminded of the "*grace*" which God had conferred on him in appointing him to preach to heathen nations "*the unsearchable riches of Christ.*" Not that they required to be informed of his special commission, for they knew it already;[2] there was not a Christian church in any part of the world that was ignorant of it.

God had made known to him "*by revelation*" the great truth that "*in Christ*" the Gentiles were "*fellow-heirs and fellow-members of the body and fellow-partakers of the promise*"—of the great promise which through so many centuries had been the consolation and strength of Jewish saints; and "*through the gospel*"

---

[1] Meyer, *in loc*.
[2] In the expression which Paul uses—"if so be that ye have heard"—he does not imply that he thought his hearers might perhaps be ignorant of his vocation to be the apostle of the Gentiles. He assumes that they knew it.

they were to pass into the actual possession of their blessedness (ver. 6). This was the Divine purpose from the beginning; and even Jewish prophets and psalmists had seen that the heathen were to share in the righteousness and peace and prosperity of the kingdom of the Messiah, for this was essential to the universality and grandeur of that kingdom; but the elevation of the heathen to the same height of dignity as the Jew was "*in other generations not made known to the sons of men as it hath now been revealed unto* [God's] *holy apostles in the Spirit*" (ver. 5). It was therefore a "*mystery*,"—a Divine thought which had been long unknown, but which had been at last revealed.

Paul says that the knowledge of this "*mystery*" had come to him by "*revelation.*" At Christ's appearance to him when he was on his way to Damascus he had been told that he was to preach to the heathen. It was to them as well as to his own countrymen that he was to be sent "to open their eyes, that they may turn from darkness to light, and from the power of Satan unto God, that they may receive remission of sins and an inheritance among them that are sanctified by faith in Me."[1]

But I am not sure that these words alone would have made it quite clear to Paul that the religious supremacy of the Jewish race, derived from Divine institutions and Divine revelations, and consecrated

---

[1] Acts xxvi. 17, 18.

by the sorrows and glories of more than two thousand years, was now to pass away. Through the power and grace of Christ the heathen might receive the remission of sins and an inheritance among those that were consecrated to God and made an "elect nation"; they might escape from the power of Satan and so be liberated from a worse bondage than that from which the Jewish people were delivered under the leadership of Moses; they might pass into a kingdom diviner than that ancient commonwealth which had received its laws and its polity from Heaven; and yet they might not take equal rank with those who belonged to the sacred race. The heathen that repented of sin and acknowledged the authority of Christ might be among the commonalty of the saved, and the descendants of Abraham might retain the prerogatives of nobles and princes. Something beyond the general commission to preach the gospel to the Gentiles was necessary before Paul was likely to see that in the new temple of God "the middle wall of partition" had been broken down, and that in Christ Jew and Gentile were now equally near to the inner sanctuary, and that through their faith in Him they had the same "*boldness*" and the same "*confidence*" in their "*access*" to God (ver. 12).

And even if Paul's original commission had been more explicit and decisive, I should have been conscious of dissatisfaction if the great truth that the human race has been made really one in Christ rested exclusively on the authority of this wonderful revelation. I believe in the reality and in the supernatural character of Paul's vision; the glory which shone round about him was the glory of Christ; the voice which he heard was the voice of Christ. But it is not God's way to rest truths of this order on the bare authority of supernatural visions and supernatural voices. And Paul's treatment of the great truth both in this epistle and elsewhere shows that to him it had other evidence than that which it derived from the words which he heard in the great crisis of his personal history.

To Paul the truth had in the very highest sense of the word been "*revealed.*" The illumination of the Spirit had shone upon it and made it clear and certain. It was involved in his whole conception of the Divine method of redemption. It was in Christ— not in Abraham—that God "blessed us with every spiritual blessing in the heavenly places"; it was in Christ—not in Abraham—that God "chose us before the foundation of the world, that we should be holy and without blemish before Him in love." The honour which belonged to the descendants of Abraham was a great honour as long as it lasted, but it had been superseded by a diviner distinction conferred upon all that were in Christ; for in Christ God "foreordained us unto adoption as sons unto Himself, according to the good pleasure of His will, to the praise of the glory of His grace." It was not on the bare authority of a voice or a vision that Paul declared that the Gentile had equal rank with the Jew in the Divine kingdom; the voice or vision might have assured him of the *fact* that the equality existed; but to Paul the equality was *necessary*, it was implicated in what he knew of the relation of Christ to all that were one with Him; and therefore he says in the Epistle to the Colossians (chap. iii. 11) that in Christ "there *cannot* be Greek and Jew, circumcision and uncircumcision, barbarian, Scythian, bondman, freeman; but Christ is all in all."

By what he had written in this epistle "*in few words*" the Ephesian Christians could "*perceive*" his "*understanding in the mystery of Christ.*" He was not merely entrusted with a Divine message, the terms of which he was bound to repeat accurately; he understood the Divine thought and purpose. The "mystery" had been made plain to him. He goes on to say that the "mystery" had been revealed not only to himself, but to God's "*holy apostles and prophets in the Spirit.*" In describing "*the apostles and prophets*" of the new Faith as "*holy*" Paul does not attribute to his apostolic brethren or to himself, —for he too was an apostle,—any personal sanctity; he merely means to say that they are "consecrated" persons; and he has already attributed the same consecration to all the Christians at Ephesus, they are the "saints" as well as "the faithful in Christ Jesus."

The same revelation, the same illumination of "*the Spirit*," had come to the rest of the apostles that had come to Paul himself. The question arises, why to them any such revelation should have been necessary. To Paul who had not been among the personal friends of our Lord while He was on earth, and who during the time that he was with Ananias at Damascus after his conversion could have heard only imperfect and incomplete reports of our Lord's teaching, the illumination of the Spirit might have been necessary in order to enable him to apprehend the "mystery." But why was this illumination necessary to the other apostles? Early in our Lord's ministry they had heard Him say that "many shall come from the east and the west, and shall sit down with Abraham and Isaac and Jacob in the kingdom of heaven."[1] Towards the end of His ministry they had heard Him describe the coming of the Son of man in His glory when "all the nations" shall be gathered before Him and when He will say to the righteous, to the righteous among the heathen: "Come ye blessed of My Father, inherit the kingdom prepared for you from the foundation of the world."[2]

When He was told that certain Greeks who had come to worship at Jerusalem at the feast of the passover wished to see Him He answered: "The hour is come that the Son of man should be glorified . . . Now is the judgment of this world, now shall the prince of this world be cast out. And *I*, if I be

---

[1] Matt. viii. 11.   [2] Matt. xxv. 31–34.

lifted up from the earth, will draw all men unto Myself." [1]

In His conversation with the Samaritan woman which I suppose John heard, and which, if he did not hear it, had come to the knowledge of the apostles through the report of the woman, Christ had distinctly declared that the sanctity of the institutions of Judaism was about to pass away: "The hour cometh when neither in this mountain nor in Jerusalem shall ye worship the Father . . . The hour cometh and now is when the true worshippers shall worship the Father in spirit and truth; for such doth the Father seek to be His worshippers. God is a Spirit; and they that worship Him must worship in spirit and truth." [2] The temple was the centre of the religious and national life of Judaism, the visible symbol and guarantee of the sacredness of the elect race; when the Jewish temple ceased to be sacred, the sacredness of the Jewish race was lost. In the great commission given to the apostles immediately before our Lord's ascension He recognised no distinction between Jew and Gentile, and gave no hint that Jewish believers were to have a higher rank or larger blessings in His kingdom than the rest of mankind. "All authority," He said, "hath been given unto Me in heaven and on earth," the whole human race were His subjects; and therefore they were to "make disciples of all the nations, baptizing them

---

[1] John xii. 32. [2] John iv. 21-24.

into the name of the Father, and of the Son, and of the Holy Ghost; teaching them to observe all things whatsoever I commanded you."[1]

These passages are only illustrations of the largeness and universality of the aims of Christ as illustrated in His own words; and we should have thought that the apostles would have learnt from Him, without any subsequent revelation, that in the new kingdom the old distinctions between the Jews and the rest of mankind were to have no place. But it is clear from the history in the early chapters of the Acts of the Apostles that this was an aspect of our Lord's teaching which even the apostles had not understood; an impressive warning that we ourselves may miss the meaning of the very plainest words of Christ. It was the vision which Peter saw in a trance at Joppa that gave him courage to go to the house of Cornelius at Cæsarea and to preach the gospel to him and to his guests. "Ye yourselves know," said the apostle to the Roman soldier and "his kinsmen and his near friends," "how that it is an unlawful thing for a man that is a Jew to join himself or come unto one of another nation; and yet unto me hath God showed that I should not call any man common or unclean."[2] And then Cornelius told the story of the vision which he himself had seen and which had led him to send for Peter: "Four days ago, until this hour, I was keeping the ninth hour of

---

[1] Matt. xxviii. 20. [2] Acts x. 28.

prayer in my house; and behold, a man stood before me in bright apparel, and saith, Cornelius, thy prayer is heard, and thine alms are had in remembrance in the sight of God."[1] In the presence of the double vision Peter made a great discovery and expressed it in the memorable words: "Of a truth I perceive that God is no respecter of persons; but in every nation he that feareth Him and worketh righteousness is acceptable to Him."[2] But even then the Christian Jews who were with Peter, and who had heard the account of the visions which had come to him and to Cornelius, did not suppose that heathen men who had not received circumcision were henceforth to be equal with themselves in the Divine kingdom. For the narrative in the Acts, after giving a summary of Peter's discourse, goes on to say: "While Peter yet spake these words, the Holy Ghost fell on all them which heard the word. And they of the circumcision which believed were amazed, as many as came with Peter, because that on the Gentiles also was poured out the gift of the Holy Ghost. For they heard them speak with tongues and magnify God."[3] The victory of the new spiritual freedom over the exclusiveness of the ancient faith was not yet secure. When Peter went back to Jerusalem his conduct at Cæsarea was challenged by some of the Jewish Christians. He had to tell the story of

---

[1] Acts x. 30, 31.   [2] Acts x. 34, 35.
[3] Acts x. 44-46.

his vision at Joppa and of the vision of Cornelius and of the descent of the Holy Spirit on Cornelius and his friends; and he closed the story with the decisive question: "If then God gave unto them the like gift as He did also unto us, when we believed on the Lord Jesus Christ, who was I that I could withstand God?"[1] Judaism died hard. For a generation large numbers of Jewish Christians regarded with bitter hostility the release of the Gentile converts from the obligations of the Mosaic law, and cherished for their "uncircumcised" brethren the traditional Jewish scorn. But "the apostles and prophets" were convinced that with the new age the old institutions had passed away. The illumination of the Spirit completed the revelation which had begun in supernatural visions; and when Paul, some years later, met the leaders of the Jewish church at Jerusalem they received him frankly and acknowledged that he had a Divine commission to preach to the heathen his large and generous gospel.

I doubt whether Paul would have chosen to be the apostle of the Gentiles had the choice been left to himself. Never, even to the last, does the moral and religious condition of the Gentile world appear to have caused him as much distress as the moral and spiritual condition of his own race. There is no passage in his epistles which reveals an agony of earnestness for the conversion of the heathen like that

---

[1] Acts xi. 16.

which he felt for the conversion of the Jews, and which breaks out in the pathetic passage in the Epistle to the Romans: "I have great sorrow and unceasing pain in my heart. For I could wish that I myself were anathema from Christ for my brethren's sake, my kinsmen according to the flesh."[1] When he was first called to the apostleship he might naturally have thought that his true work was to preach the gospel to Jews. Was he not one of themselves, a Hebrew of the Hebrews, a Pharisee, blameless in his observance of all their sacred laws? Had he not spent his youth in accumulating Jewish learning? Was he not perfectly familiar with all the intricacies of Jewish speculation? Was not the method of Jewish thought his own? The struggles through which he himself had passed on his way from the old Faith to the new, would they not enable him to enter into the very heart of his countrymen who would have to pass through similar struggles? All the most passionate forces of his nature made him long to bring his own people to Christ. But when it became clear that Christ meant him to preach the gospel to the heathen he frankly accepted the commission. At first it may have seemed to him the less noble task. But as years went on, his imagination as well as his heart became completely filled with the grandeur of his vocation. When, during his imprisonment in Rome, he wrote this epistle his conception of his

---

[1] Rom. ix. 2, 3.

work was loftier than ever. He had caught the spirit of the imperial city. His soul had expanded beyond the traditions of his people. He was haunted by visions of conquests more remote than had ever been achieved by the Roman arms and of an empire more extensive than that which was governed from the palace of the Cæsars. He saw that the kingdom of Christ included all nations, effaced the ancient limits which had divided race from race, imposed upon all mankind the authority of the same righteous laws, granted to all men the same security, the same rights, the same freedom, the same access to God in this world, the same glory in the world to come. And he saw that he had been elected by Christ to take a chief part in founding this universal empire. He had been chosen to pass beyond the frontiers of Judaism and to declare to all nations that the Lord Jesus Christ had not come to confer exceptional prerogatives on a single race, but to restore the whole world to the light and life and blessedness of God. He could conceive of no greater office. He was amazed by the contrast between the grandeur of his commission and his own unworthiness: "*Unto me who am less than the least of all saints is this grace given, that I should preach among the Gentiles the unsearchable riches of Christ.*"

His enthusiasm was still further heightened by the conviction that the regal spirits that dwell in the light of God were watching from their thrones the gradual accomplishment of that Divine purpose which was to be finally fulfilled in the restoration of the human race to unity in Christ. Even to "*the principalities and the powers in heavenly places*" there was a new and wonderful revelation of "the *manifold wisdom* of God," in the extension of the kingdom of God from the Jews to the Gentile world, and in the triumph of the Divine love over the divisions, the sorrows, and the sins of mankind.

In what way this makes known the wisdom of God Paul does not explain. To ourselves with our modern habits of thought it may seem that "*the manifold wisdom of God*" is illustrated in the tribute which the church has received from all ages and from all nations. It was not in Judæa alone that the hand of God was controlling the course of national history during the ages which preceded the coming of Christ. The separation of race from race, by mountains and seas, by differences of language, by differences of civilization, had resulted in the growth of many types of national character. Every distinct type had some unique qualities, some unique form of power, some unique virtue, some unique grace. Had there been a premature breaking down of the divisions which separated nation from nation, the development of the resources of human nature would have been less rich and varied. But at last the hour came for the emerging of a higher and completer form of life in which were to be blended the final results, purified and transfigured, of all the discipline to which the several races of mankind had been subjected. The faith of the Jews, the philosophy of the Greeks, the political virtues of the Romans have all contributed to enlarge and deepen the thought and life of the church. In future generations the mighty streams of India and of China, which still flow apart, will find their way into the common channel. The church is the heir of the genius, the heroism, the virtues, the sufferings of all the ages of human history. But this is a modern conception, and is remote from Paul's method of thought.[1]

His words in this place recall a memorable passage in the Epistle to the Romans. He has been warning the Gentile Christians against exulting over the fall of the Jews; has been maintaining that though, as the result of the crimes of the Jewish people, the glory which had once rested upon them had passed to the Gentiles, the Jews had not been finally forsaken and that at last they would obtain mercy. But it is evident that to the apostle the ways of God were surrounded with darkness and mystery. How it could have happened that when the kingdom of God was established on earth the children of the kingdom should have excluded themselves from it, and that its glories should have become the inheritance of the heathen, he could not understand. The future was as mysterious as the present. For the time was to come when the Jews were to learn from

---

[1] But it appears very conspicuously in Clement and in other great teachers of the Alexandrian church. Clement was in some senses of the word a "modern."

Gentile faith and zeal to acknowledge the sovereignty of the Jewish Christ. He knows that God is ordering the course of the world's affairs wisely, but the Divine ways are beyond his comprehension. He exclaims: "O the depth of the riches both of the wisdom and knowledge of God; how unsearchable are His judgments, and His ways past finding out."[1]

It was now several years since he wrote those words, and perhaps the great problem which he states rather than solves in the earlier epistle was beginning to be clearer to him. But whether or not he himself had found any solution of it he was still confident that in the way in which the Gentiles had come to have so great a place in the Divine kingdom there was a wonderful illustration of "the manifold wisdom of God"; and he believed that what was obscure to himself would be open and plain to "the principalities and the powers in heavenly places."

The enthusiasm with which the apostle speaks of preaching the gospel to the heathen is contagious. His words burn on the page, and our hearts take fire as we read them. What was the secret of this exultation in the gospel and in his commission to make the gospel known to all mankind? The question is a large one, and I shall not attempt a complete answer to it; but considerable light is thrown upon it by the contents of this epistle.

1. Paul had *a vivid intellectual interest in the*

---

[1] Rom. xi. 33, 44.

Christian gospel. To him it was a real revelation of the most wonderful and surprising truths concerning God and the relations of God to the human race. It urged his intellectual powers to their most strenuous activity. It never lost its freshness. It was never exhausted. From the beginning of his apostolic ministry to its close, if we may judge from those of his epistles which have been preserved in the New Testament, the boundaries of that immense kingdom of truth which was revealed to him in Christ and by the illumination of the Spirit of Christ were always advancing. In this epistle he has travelled far beyond the limits which he reached in the Epistle to the Romans.

I believe that in all the great movements of religious reform that have permanently elevated the religious life of Christendom there has been a renewal of intellectual interest in the Christian revelation. Some forgotten aspects of the gospel have been recovered; the theological definitions which had for a generation or two been a sufficient expression of the results at which human speculation had arrived concerning the great facts of revelation have been challenged and discredited, and the mind of the church has been brought into immediate contact with the facts themselves; the methods which had determined the construction of theological systems have become obsolete, and the work of reconstruction has tasked the genius and the learning of the leaders of Christian thought; the central principles of the gospel have received new applications to individual conduct and to the organization of social life; in all these ways a fresh and keen intellectual interest has been excited in Christian truth, and the intellectual interest has deepened moral and spiritual earnestness.

If at the present time the religious life of the church is languid, and if in its enterprises there is little of audacity and of vehemence, a partial explanation is to be found in that decline of intellectual interest in the contents of the Christian Faith which has characterized the last hundred or hundred and fifty years of our history.

There has been, no doubt, a very vigorous interest in critical questions and questions of apologetics; but these questions lie on the extreme edge of the territory of Christian thought; they raise controversies which are very remote from the central and inspiring elements of the Christian gospel. There has also been a great interest in the historical and external aspects of the life of our Lord and the work of His apostles; but the geography of the Holy Land, the crimes of the family of Herod, the functions and powers of the sanhedrim, the opinions and customs of the Essenes, the rivalries of the Pharisees and Sadducees, the laws of Roman municipalities and Roman colonies, though they afford some subsidiary aids to the illustration of the narratives of the New Testament, render us very little service in apprehending the substance of the Christian revelation.

We must renew the intellectual interest of the church in the Christian revelation itself—not in its "evidences" merely, not in the historical circumstances of the age in which Christ appeared, not in the modes of life and thought which prevailed among the people who listened to His teaching and witnessed His miracles—if we are to recover the ardour, the vehemence, and the passion of Paul. The intellect has its rights, as well as the conscience and the heart; and if religious truth does not meet the just demands of the intellect as well as of the moral nature, it will be regarded with languid interest and will at last be either silently abandoned or rejected with open hostility and scorn.

2. The heart and imagination of Paul were filled with *the infinite and eternal blessings which were the inheritance of the human race in Christ.* For human sin there was the Divine forgiveness. For human weakness in its baffled attempts to emancipate itself from the tyranny of evil habits and evil passions there was Divine redemption. For human uncertainty and doubt in the presence of the great problems of life and death there was the illumination of the Spirit and free access to God. For restless discontent at the limitations of human virtue there was the possibility of a transcendent righteousness through union with the life of the Eternal Son of God. Paul believed in "the unsearchable riches of Christ."

We shall never recover his enthusiasm as long as we dwell chiefly on the external and incidental benefits which follow the acceptance of the Christian gospel.

M. Condorcet, in his Life of Voltaire, speaks of the defenders of religious faith as having been reduced by Voltaire to what he describes as "the humiliating necessity" of relying on the argument derived from its political expediency. The phrase was justly chosen. It is a humiliation to which the apologists of Christianity should never have stooped. In stooping to it they surrender their whole case.

To defend our assertion of the awful authority of God by urging that where this authority is recognised the difficulties of human governments are lessened, and a readier obedience is secured for human laws; to apologise for trying to persuade men of the infinite love revealed in the incarnation and the death of the Lord Jesus Christ by pleading that we are giving consolation and patience to the poor, whose miseries and discontent might otherwise be a peril to the institution of property and to the stability of the state; to argue that in speaking to men of judgment to come, and in urging them "by patient endurance in well doing to seek for glory, honour, and immortality," we are strengthening the obligations of those common virtues which contribute to the wealth of nations;—this is treachery to our cause. To urge a similar defence of Christian missions to the heathen is equally ignoble and equally fatal to the intensity and fervour of Christian zeal.

It is true, no doubt, that by the influence of Christian missionaries barbarous races have been civilized, have been trained to habits of industry, have come to live in better houses and to wear better clothing; have even—and this I have sometimes heard alleged as a strong reason for generous contributions to a missionary society—have even become customers for the goods of Manchester, Birmingham, and Bradford. But with what amazement, with what immeasurable contempt, Paul would have listened to arguments like these! If the gospel of Christ is true, these incidental advantages which follow the triumph of the Christian Faith are petty and insignificant when compared with the infinite blessings which Christ has brought within the reach of all mankind.

As a Christian minister at home I decline to have the value of my work estimated by the extent to which it lightens the work of the police and diminishes the cost to the ratepayers and the nation of maintaining workhouses and jails.

As an advocate of Christian missions to the heathen, I decline to have the value of missionary faith and heroism measured by the annual value of the new markets in Africa and the Pacific for English hardware and cotton goods. Give to every cluster of miserable huts in Central Africa and in the islands of the South Pacific the material wealth and splendour of the foremost cities of Europe; transform their savage chiefs into cultivated statesmen; let their people be trained to discuss the philosophy of Plato and to admire the majesty of the genius of Æschylus;

let them become famous for their brilliant discoveries in science; let them create a literature with an original grace, beauty and dignity: and all this would be as nothing compared with what you have done for them, in bringing them home to God, in assuring them of the tenderness and strength of the love of the Father whom they had forgotten, in opening to them the fountains of eternal life and eternal righteousness, in making them the heirs of eternal glory. This was Paul's faith; and this faith was, in part, the source of his invincible energy and his passionate enthusiasm.

XIV.

FILLED UNTO ALL THE FULNESS OF GOD.

" For this cause I bow my knees unto the Father, from whom every family in heaven and on earth is named, that He would grant you, according to the riches of His glory, that ye may be strengthened with power through His Spirit in the inward man ; that Christ may dwell in your hearts through faith ; to the end that ye, being rooted and grounded in love, may be strong to apprehend with all the saints what is the breadth and length and height and depth, and to know the love of Christ which passeth knowledge, that ye may be filled unto all the fulness of God. Now unto Him that is able to do exceeding abundantly above all that we ask or think, according to the power that worketh in us, unto Him be the glory in the church and in Christ Jesus unto all generations for ever and ever. Amen."

—EPH. iii. 14–21.

PAUL'S description of God as "*the Father, from whom every family in heaven and on earth is named*," is unique. Unfortunately the charm and the force of it cannot be represented in an English translation. The Greek word represented by "*family*" is used to denote not only a family, but a clan, a tribe, a nation, a race—any number of men who are thought of as the descendants of one father.[1] We have no analogous word in our own language, and therefore the felicity of Paul's expression cannot be

---

[1] They are a πατριὰ as coming from one πατήρ.

transferred into English. What he means is this:—
You have a name for those who belong to the same
family, the same tribe, the same nation, the same
race, by which you describe them as the descendants
of a common ancestor,—a name which implies that
their unity is not the artificial creation of human law,
but consists in their relationship to a common father;
this name bears witness to the relationship of all the
families and tribes of men, and of all ranks and orders
of angels, to the eternal Fountain of all created life.
God is the true Father of all races in heaven and on
earth; and the unity of a family, a tribe, a nation, in
its common ancestor, has its original and archetype in
the unity of angels and men in Him.[1] This great and
noble conception of the unity of heaven and earth
in God is characteristic of that form of Christian
theology which is illustrated in this epistle and in
the epistle to the Colossians. It appears elsewhere[2];
but in these two epistles, which were written about
the same time, it is developed with extraordinary
boldness and with a vehement and glorious eloquence. As yet, according to Paul's conception, the

---

[1] Angels were, I suppose, conceived of by Paul neither as isolated individuals nor yet as a multitude of individuals characterized by a monotonous uniformity of powers and perfections.
He thought of them as grouped together in ranks, orders, and,
if I may venture to use the word, "nationalities," distinguished
by differences like those which are created among ourselves by
differences of descent. Hence he could by analogy speak of
them as "families" in heaven.

[2] *e.g.* 1 Cor. xv. 24.

Divine idea is unfulfilled. Its orderly development has been troubled, thwarted, and delayed by sin, by sin in this world and in other worlds. But it will be fulfilled at last. In Christ "were all things created, in the heavens and upon the earth, things visible and things invisible, whether thrones or dominions or principalities or powers; all things have been created through Him and unto Him"[1]; and in union with Christ, the eternal Son of God, heaven and earth will be restored to the eternal Father.

There are two great prayers in this epistle. The first is in the first chapter. It seemed to Paul that the gospel was so wonderful that it was impossible for men to see the glory of it unless they were taught of God, and therefore after his lofty account of God's purpose to bring the heavens and the earth into an eternal unity in Christ, he tells the Christians at Ephesus that he was continually praying that God would give them "a spirit of wisdom and revelation in the knowledge of Him," and that the eyes of their heart might be enlightened that they might know the hope to which God had called them, and "the glory of His inheritance in the saints." Spiritual illumination is necessary if we are to know the contents of the Christian gospel; for the gospel reveals invisible and eternal things lying far beyond the frontiers of the common thoughts of men.

The second prayer takes another form. Its central

---

[1] Col. i. 16.

idea is strength. Strength is necessary as well as Light. We cannot *know* the gospel unless its glories are divinely revealed to us; and the spiritual *energy* necessary to receive it and to hold it fast must also come from God.

"*I bow my knees unto the Father from whom every family in heaven and on earth is named that He would grant you, according to the riches of His glory, that ye may be strengthened with power through His Spirit in the inward man.*" By "the inward man" Paul means our central and highest life; and he prays that the life itself—not any particular function of it—may be strengthened. Life is a mystery in its lowest as well as in its loftiest forms, but I suppose that we all attach a more or less definite conception to words which describe life as vigorous or feeble. When we say that a man's physical life is energetic we do not mean to say that any particular organ is strong, that he has great muscular force, can lift heavy weights and walk long distances; we mean to describe something which appears to us to lie within and beneath the physical organisation, and which inspires the whole. When we speak of a man's intellectual life as strong or weak we do not mean that some particular faculty is admirable or the reverse of admirable; a particular faculty may be singularly vigorous, and yet the man may give us the impression of intellectual feebleness; a particular faculty may be very deficient in vigour, and yet he may give us the impression of intellectual strength.

If we say that a man is remarkable for his intellectual energy, we think of him as having in the very centre of his intellectual life a free and inexhaustible fountain of force and activity. It is the same in the spiritual life. There is a certain imperfection in many of us which I do not know how to describe except by saying that, though at times particular spiritual faculties may appear to be vigorous, the central life is weak. There are men whose zeal for the evangelization of the world is often very real and very fervent, but who give us no impression of spiritual strength. There are others who are often inspired with a passion for Christian perfection, but in them too there appears to be no real vigour. There are others who seem spiritually weak, though their vision of spiritual truth is very keen and penetrating. There are others who seem capable of very lofty devotion,—of awe, of vehement religious emotion, of rapture in the Divine love and in the hope of glory, honour, and immortality, and who yet give us the impression that they are wanting in those elements of life which constitute spiritual energy. In every one of these cases, to use language which suggests rather than expresses the truth, the vigour is not derived from the central fountains of life, but from springs that are more or less distant from the centre. The man himself is wanting in force though there are spiritual forces at work in him. Those of us who are conscious that this is our condition should pray to God that we "*may be strength-*

ened with power through His Spirit in the inward man."

It has been questioned whether the next clause in the prayer, "*that Christ may dwell in your hearts through faith,*" is merely explanatory of the first, or whether it describes another and a higher blessing. Did Paul mean that we must be "strengthened through [God's] Spirit in our inward man" *in order* that Christ may dwell in our hearts? Or did he mean that the power of the Divine Spirit is never separated from Christ, is indeed dependent on the life and presence of Christ, and that to have spiritual strength is really the same thing as to have Christ dwelling in us?

The question may be settled, I think, by an appeal to the experience of Christian people. There are times when Christ comes to us and when the heart is animated with the blessed hope that He has come to remain with us for ever. We have already learnt that apart from Him we can do nothing, and now all things are possible to us. The new heavens and the new earth wherein dwelleth righteousness are ours, and we live in the light of God. Evil passions die down, and evil habits seem to fall away from us like the chains of Peter at the touch of the angel. Christ brings with Him a clearer knowledge of God and of duty; a firmer purpose to keep the laws of the kingdom of heaven; a new ardour of affection for all Christian men; a more generous charity for all mankind; a more intense delight in righteousness; a deeper joy in the infinite love of God; a more vivid hope of immortality. We are lifted by His presence above ourselves, and into a fairer world than this. These are the Divine hours of life.

But in our relations to Christ we are not passive. If He is to "abide" in us we must "abide" in Him. He comes at the free impulse of His infinite mercy, but He does not make His home with us unless, if I may venture to use the phrase, we have strength to detain Him. And many of us are conscious that we have no firm hold of Christ. He comes to us with blessings which surpass all our hope and all our thought, but we let Him go. How it is we can hardly tell, but in a few days or weeks all our blessedness is over.

The apostle suggests the explanation. Christ can "*dwell*" in our hearts only "*through faith*"; and faith, though in its beginning the cry of helpless weakness and the birth of despair, is in its maturer forms the expression of the noblest strength. It is the result of the concurrent action of all the higher forces of the spiritual life in their most intense energy. The reason, the will, and the conscience, memory and hope, love, reverence, awe, joy, and gratitude, are all of them blended in a great and perfect faith. To raise the soul to this height and to keep it there, it is necessary that we should "*be strengthened with power through* [God's] *Spirit in the inward man.*"

On the other hand it is equally true that apart from Christ we have no strength at all. To suppose that until we are strong we cannot have access to the life and righteousness and peace which are ours in Him is contrary to the whole current of Christian thought and Christian experience. God has blessed us with all spiritual blessings in Christ, and only as we are in Christ can any of these blessings be ours. The power and grace of the Spirit cannot come to us while we are "apart" from Him.

But when Paul prayed that Christ might "*dwell*" in the hearts of the Christians at Ephesus he was thinking of something far greater than that kind of union with Christ which is the condition of even the lowest forms of spiritual life. The whole emphasis of the clause is thrown on the word "*dwell*." There is an abiding presence of Christ in the heart which is a perpetual manifestation of the infinite love of God, and brings with it the very righteousness and blessedness of heaven, a presence which fills the whole life with a glory unbroken by clouds, and that does not change with rising and setting suns, but is like the glory of the city of God of which it is said that "there is no night there." This presence is possible only where there is a great faith, and for a great faith there must be a great strength, a strength which is given to the inward man through the power of the Divine Spirit.

The apostle has not yet touched the loftiest blessings which he desires for the Ephesian Christians;

As the result of the strength which he prays that they may receive through the Spirit, and of the permanent presence of Christ in their hearts, the root of their life will be in love, as the roots of a tree are in the soil, and the foundations on which their whole life is built will be laid in love; they will be "*rooted and grounded in love.*" Love will not be an intermittent impulse, or even a constant force struggling for its rightful supremacy over baser passions; its authority will be secure; it will be the law of their whole nature; it will be the very life of their life.

And then they will "*be strong to apprehend with all the saints what is the breadth and length and height and depth of the love of Christ which passeth knowledge.*" The words recall the question which we have just considered. For Christ to dwell in the heart we must be strengthened by the Spirit of God; and yet unless Christ dwells in the heart spiritual strength is impossible. And so, to apprehend the love of Christ, we must be filled with love; and yet it is the apprehension of Christ's love by which love is inspired and perfected.

The difficulty in the second case, as in the first, vanishes in the light thrown upon it by Christian experience. It is by the knowledge of Christ that we begin to love God; with the growing love we become capable of receiving a larger knowledge; and every fresh accession of knowledge enriches, invigorates, and expands the love. "He that loveth not knoweth not God; for God is love." "The Life is the Light of men." For that great knowledge of the love of Christ of which Paul is thinking, a great love is necessary.

This knowledge, though so wonderful, is not regarded by Paul as a privilege too lofty, a prerogative too Divine, for the commonalty of the church. The best and highest things in the kingdom of God are not reserved for a few elect and princely souls. There are gradations of power in the Christian church and varieties of service. But the knowledge of the love of Christ in its "*breadth and length and depth and height*" is accessible to "*all the saints.*" It is like the visible heavens which bend over the monotonous plains of human life as well as over its mountains, and flood with the same splendour the cottages of peasants and the palaces of kings. The heavens are always near, and they are equally near to all men, as near to the poor as to the rich, to barbarous as to civilized nations, to the obscurest as to the most illustrious of mankind. It is the same with the knowledge of the love of Christ. No genius or learning can give us any exclusive property in it. The open vision of its glory is not reserved for those who can leave the common paths of men and live in silence and solitude on mountain heights of contemplation. To no prophet or apostle was a knowledge of the love of Christ ever given that we ourselves may not receive. To apprehend "*what is the breadth and length and height and depth and to know the love of Christ*"—this was all that Paul could ask for himself; he asks it for the Christians at Ephesus; and he describes it as the common blessedness of "*all the saints.*"

And yet "*it passeth knowledge.*" When Paul speaks of the love of Christ the fire in his heart nearly always bursts into flame. Its "*breadth*" cannot be measured, nor its "*length*," nor its "*height*," nor its "*depth.*" Immensity is the only adequate symbol of its greatness.

But the energy of the love has been revealed. It has been revealed by Christ's infinite descent, for us sinners and our salvation, from His eternal glory to the limitations of man's earthly life; from eternal peace and eternal joy to hunger and thirst and weariness and pain; from the sanctity of heaven to contact with the evil passions and with the evil lives of men; from the immortal honours with which angels and archangels surrounded His throne to the kiss of Judas, to the slander and malice of the priests, to condemnation for blasphemy, to the death of a criminal on the cross; from His infinite blessedness with the Father to the desolation of that awful hour in which He cried, "My God, My God, why hast Thou forsaken Me!" Revealed? No! For the heights of Divine majesty from which He came rise far beyond the limits of our keenest vision, and we cannot sound the depths of darkness into which He descended to achieve our redemption. The love of Christ "*passeth knowledge.*"

It is to be measured not merely by what He endured for us, but by the energy of the eternal antagonism between good and evil. In His infinite righteousness He regarded our sin with an abhorrence which our thoughts can never measure, and yet the energy of His love transcended the energy of His righteousness, or, rather, blended with it, and transfigured just resentment into pity; and under the power of this glorious inspiration infinite righteousness, which abhors sin, became infinite mercy for the race that had been guilty of sin, and so restored us to life, to holiness, and to endless joy. The love of Christ "*passeth knowledge.*"

Nor was the revelation of His infinite love, which though revealed can never be known, exhausted in His incarnation, or in His earthly ministry, or in His death which atoned for the sin of the world. He has risen from the dead and ascended to glory, but He has not forsaken the race He came to save, nor has He withdrawn to Divine realms of untroubled peace remote from the darkness, the confusion, the storms of this present evil world. The kingdom of heaven is founded on earth, and He, its Prince, is here. Unseen He has been present with those in every generation who have asserted His authority over all nations and who have entreated men to receive from His love the remission of their sins and eternal life in God. Their sorrows and their joys, their reverses and their triumphs, have been His. The hostility which surrounded Him during His earthly life has been prolonged during the eighteen Christian centuries, has extended from country to country, from race to race, has assumed vaster proportions, and is still undiminished. The fierce and reckless cruelty of Herod has reappeared in the persecutions which have tried the faith and loyalty of innumerable saints. Secular governments, resenting His claims to a throne diviner than theirs, have flung His people to the lions and burnt them at the stake. At the bidding of corrupt priests and of popular fury, judges as base and cowardly as Pilate have condemned to death those whose only crime was loyalty to the truth and to Him. On one day the common people, stirred with a passion of enthusiasm by some great display of His power and goodness, have surrounded Him with shouts of Hosanna and have hailed Him as their King; on the next they have rejected Him as an impostor, covered Him with infamy, clamoured for His destruction. Within the church itself there has been wide and persistent neglect of His plainest laws; and its spirit has often seemed altogether alien from His own. There has been fierce contention as to who should be the greatest, keen personal ambition for the highest places in the kingdom of heaven. How often has self confidence as lofty as Peter's been followed by as deep and as shameful a fall! How often, in hours of darkness and danger, have many who really loved Christ forsaken Him and fled! How often have those who were elect to great responsibilities in the church, and great honours, betrayed Him for thirty pieces of silver! How often has the kiss of the traitor come from the lips of a friend! But there is no need to appeal to the gloomy history of Christendom. We ourselves can recall a vacillation in His service which at the beginning of our Christian life we should have regarded as impossible; high resolutions broken almost as soon as they were formed; hours when love for Him kindled into enthusiasm, followed by base disobedience to His commandments. Our own history, it is to be feared, has been the history of great multitudes besides. And the love of Christ has not only been unquenched; its fires have never sunk.

We cannot measure the awful vastness of human sin, but His mercy infinitely transcends it. His love, like His power, faints not neither is it weary. Through generation after generation He continues to appeal to the world with pathetic entreaty to receive eternal redemption. Through generation after generation He continues to confer upon the church, notwithstanding revolt, ingratitude, and treachery, blessings which are beyond the desert of a saintly perfection. His love "*passeth knowledge.*"

We are even now only in the early dawn of the supreme revelation; the Divine morning will become brighter and brighter through one millennium of splendour after another, and will never reach its noon. In the resurrection of Christ and His ascension to the throne of God He has illustrated the immense expansion and development possible to human nature, and His resurrection and glory are the prophecy of our own. Through ages without end, inspired with the life of Christ and sustained by the exceeding greatness of the Divine power which wrought in Him when God raised Him from the dead, we shall ascend from height to height of righteousness, of wisdom, and of joy. From age to age with unblenched vision we shall gaze upon new and dazzling manifestations of the light in which God dwells; with powers exalted and enlarged we shall discharge nobler and yet nobler forms of Divine service; with capacities expanding with our growing delight we shall be filled with diviner and yet diviner bliss; eternity will still lie before us, stretching beyond the farthest limits of vision and of hope; and through eternity the infinite love of Christ will continue to raise us from triumph to triumph, from blessedness to blessedness, from glory to glory. His love "*passeth knowledge.*"

And yet we are to know it, to know it by the illumination of the Spirit of God. And the knowledge, according to Paul, is to invigorate, enrich, and perfect our higher life, or, to use his own phrase, by the knowledge of "the love of Christ which passeth knowledge" we are to "*be filled unto all the fulness of God.*"

Perhaps it would be well to leave the phrase in its vague sublimity without any attempt to explain it. As it stands, it appeals to the imagination, touches lofty sentiment, and seems to suggest a grandeur belonging to worlds as yet unvisited by human thought. But though the phrase stands for an idea which passes beyond the limits of all definitions, the idea will be better apprehended if we attempt to get an exact conception of the phrase, and we may reach this conception by the aid of an illustration.

There are plants which we sometimes see in these northern latitudes, but which are native to the more generous soil and the warmer skies of southern lands. In their true home they grow to a greater height, their leaves are larger, their blossoms more luxuriant and of a colour more intense; the power of the life of the plant is more fully expressed. And as the visible plant is the more or less adequate translation into stem and leaf and flower of its invisible life, so the whole created universe is the more or less adequate translation of the invisible thought and power and goodness of God. He stands apart from it. His personal life is not involved in its immense processes of development; but the forces by which it moves through pain and conflict and tempest towards its consummate perfection are a revelation of " His eternal power and Godhead." For the Divine idea to reach its complete expression, an expression adequate to the energy of the Divine life, we ourselves must reach a large and harmonious perfection. As yet we are like plants growing in an alien soil and under alien skies. And the measures of strength and grace which are possible to us even in this mortal life are not attained. The Divine power which is working in us is obstructed. But a larger knowledge of the love of Christ will increase the fervour of every devout and generous affection; it will exalt every form of spiritual energy; it will deepen our spiritual joy; it will add strength to every element of righteousness; and will thus advance us towards that ideal perfection which will be the complete expression of the Divine power and grace, and which Paul describes as the "*fulness of God.*"

It might seem that after a prayer like this the apostle would have paused and wondered whether he had not been asking for what lay beyond all hope. But no. He began by invoking blessings on the Ephesian Christians "according to the riches of [God's] glory." From the first his prayer was measured, neither by the necessities nor the deserts of those for whom he was interceding, but by the infinite greatness of the Divine perfections. And now that the intercession is ended he acknowledges in a burst of glorious praise that the power of God immeasurably transcends the limits of his prayer. "*Now unto Him that is able to do exceeding abundantly above all that we ask or think, according to the power that worketh in us, unto Him be the glory in the church and in Christ Jesus*[1] *unto all generations for ever and ever.*"

---

[1] "For not outside of Christ, but *in Christ*, as the specific element of faith in which the pious life-activity of the Christian

moves—does he praise God."—*Meyer, in loc.* True and just as far as it goes, but does it go far enough? In Christ God is revealed to the universe, but in Christ—in a very true sense— the universe is revealed to God ; and the perfection of Christ is the final expression of that created perfection from which God receives glory.

XV.

THE UNITY OF THE CHURCH.

> "*I therefore, the prisoner in the Lord, beseech you to walk worthily of the calling wherewith ye were called, with all lowliness and meekness, with longsuffering, forbearing one another in love; giving diligence to keep the unity of the Spirit in the bond of peace. There is one body, and one Spirit, even as also ye were called in one hope of your calling; one Lord, one faith, one baptism, one God and Father of all, who is over all, and through all, and in all. But unto each one of us was the grace given according to the measure of the gift of Christ. Wherefore he saith, When He ascended on high, He led captivity captive, and gave gifts unto men. (Now this, He ascended, what is it but that He also descended into the lower parts of the earth? He that descended is the same also that ascended far above all the heavens, that He might fill all things.) And He gave some to be apostles; and some, prophets; and some, evangelists; and some, pastors and teachers; for the perfecting of the saints, unto the work of ministering, unto the building up of the body of Christ: till we all attain unto the unity of the faith, and of the knowledge of the Son of God, unto a fullgrown man, unto the measure of the stature of the fulness of Christ: that we may be no longer children, tossed to and fro and carried about with every wind of doctrine, by the sleight of men, in craftiness, after the wiles of error; but speaking truth in love, may grow up in all things into Him, which is the head, even Christ; from whom all the body fitly framed and knit together through that which every joint supplieth, according to the working in due measure of each several part, maketh the increase of the body unto the building up of itself in love.*"
> —EPH. iv. 1-16.

IT is with a faint shock of surprise, almost of disappointment, that we pass from the third chapter of this Epistle to the early verses of the fourth. The transition from Paul's lofty and impassioned account of the present glory of the church and of its infinite hopes to these exhortations to "*lowliness*," "*meekness*," "*longsuffering*," and mutual forbearance, is sudden and unexpected. Our imagination has been set on fire; the invisible and eternal world by which we are environed has been revealed to us; the clouds which conceal the infinite future from mortal vision have broken, and we have seen the endless ages which are our inheritance in Christ; our hearts are throbbing with fervent affection at the discovery of "the breadth and length and height and depth" of "the love of Christ which passeth knowledge"; and the apostle's prayer that we "may be filled unto all the fulness of God"—"dark with excess of light"—has made us tremble with wonder and joy at the greatness of our destiny. That he should charge us to "*walk worthily of the calling wherewith* [we] *were called*" is only natural. It was Paul's characteristic manner to connect faith and righteousness, to rest the obligations of human duty on the revelations of Divine love. But I think that we should hardly have expected him in this place to enforce virtues of so quiet and unambitious a kind as "*lowliness*," "*meekness*," "*longsuffering*," "*forbearance*."

I.

"*I therefore, the prisoner in the Lord, beseech you to walk worthily of the calling wherewith ye were called.*" These words, after all that has gone before, thrill us like the tones of a trumpet. If it had been left to ourselves to expand the general exhortation into practical details, we should have insisted perhaps on the duty of cultivating a magnanimity corresponding to the greatness of our position and the greatness of our hopes. We might have argued that those who have received such a "*calling*" should exhibit a certain stateliness of character, a lofty indifference not only to the baser pleasures of life but to power and fame. Or we might have urged that with such a "*calling*" Christian men should be inspired with a passionate zeal for the honour of Christ, should have strength for heroic tasks and fortitude for martyrdom. This would be to "*walk worthily of the calling wherewith* [we] *were called.*"

But instead of appealing to us in this lofty tone Paul exhorts us to humility, to meekness, and to long-suffering; and this suggests a principle of great value in the discipline of the spiritual life. There are certain forms of religious excitement with which imagination has more to do than faith. Beginning, as we think, with God, we soon lose sight of Him and of our dependence upon Him, and are occupied with dazzling dreams about the grandeur of our own spiritual life and its possibilities of power, of righteousness, of honour, and of glory. These unreal and transient delights it may, for a time, be hard to distinguish from a religious experience which is created by a real and immediate vision of God and of unseen and Divine things. The test, though we may be reluctant to apply it, is extremely simple. Religious excitement originated by direct contact with God will always enlarge and exalt our conception of God's greatness, and will deepen our sense of dependence on Him. The heart may be flooded with a shining sea of religious emotion; the imagination may be glowing like the heavens at sunset with purple and golden splendour; but as emotion becomes more intense and as our conceptions of the Christian life become more and more glorious, the infinite greatness of God's righteousness and power and grace will inspire us with deeper wonder and awe. On the other hand, religious excitement created by the imagination, though it may fill us with devout and beautiful sentiment, though it may suggest lofty ideas of moral and spiritual perfection, and inspire a vehement and chivalrous desire to translate these ideas into conduct, will leave us with a new sense of our own greatness rather than with a new sense of the greatness of God.

The "*lowliness*," the *humility*, which Paul inculcates, is a characteristically Christian virtue. Only occasionally does it receive recognition from heathen moralists, but it has a large place in the Old Testament Scriptures and a still larger place in the New. Christ Himself was "lowly in heart." He had descended from Divine heights, and knew the immeasurable distance between God's infinite greatness and the limitations of human life. In "taking the form of a servant" He had also taken the spirit of a servant; He had come, not to do His own will or to seek His own glory, but to do the will of God and to seek the glory of God. Having become man, He was absolutely dependent on the Father; and lowliness of heart is the immediate result of the consciousness of dependence on God and of the vision of God's majesty. It is deepened, in our case, by the consciousness of sin.

That the representations of the dignity of the Christian calling and the glory of the Christian hope contained in the first three chapters of this Epistle should be immediately followed by an exhortation to humility is, therefore, in harmony with a deep philosophy of the spiritual life. We have received immeasurable blessings, we have been raised to wonderful honours, we are hoping to share with Christ Himself infinite blessedness and glory; but all that we have has come from the eternal thought and purpose and love of God; all that we hope for will be conferred by His grace and "the exceeding greatness of His power." The wealth is not ours; it is a Divine gift: the strength is not ours; it is the inspiration of the Divine life: the dignity is not ours; it is conferred on us by the free unpurchased love of God, because we are in Christ. We live in palaces of eternal light and righteousness, and among the principalities and powers of heaven; but our native home was in the dust, and this transfigured, eternal, and glorified life was not achieved by our own strength, it has come to us from God. We are nothing; God is all.

Humility, "*lowliness*," is disciplined by prayer, by communion with God, by the vision of Divine and eternal things; by meditation on God's righteousness and our own sin, on the greatness of God and the limitations of all created life, on the eternal fulness of God and our own dependence on Him; on the blessings which God has made our inheritance in Christ and the dark destiny which would have been the natural and just result of our indifference to God's authority and love.

Where there is "*lowliness*" there will be "*meekness*," the absence of the disposition to assert personal rights, either in the presence of God or of men. Meekness submits without a struggle to the losses, the sufferings, the dishonour which the providence of God permits to come upon us. It may look with agitation and distress upon the troubles of others, and the miseries of mankind may sometimes disturb the very foundations of faith; but in its own sorrows it finds no reason for distrusting either the Divine righteousness or the Divine goodness. It is conscious of possessing no merit, and therefore in the worst and darkest hours is conscious of suffering no injustice.

The same temper will show itself in relation to men. It has no personal claims to defend. It will therefore be slow to resent insult and injury. If it resents them at all, the resentment will be a protest against the violation of Divine laws rather than a protest against a refusal to acknowledge its personal rights. There will be no eagerness for great place or high honour, or for the recognition of personal merit; and therefore, if these are withheld, there will be no bitterness or mortification.

Where there is "*lowliness*" there will be "*meekness*"; and "*meekness*" is one of the elements of "*long-suffering.*" Paul is thinking of the mutual relations of those who are in Christ, and his words imply that there will be large occasions for the exercise of this grace in the conduct and spirit of our Christian brethren. We are not to assume that all those who are honestly loyal to Christ will keep His precepts perfectly, or that in all those who have received the Divine life the baser elements and passions of human nature have been extinguished. Our Christian brethren will sometimes treat us unjustly. They will judge us ignorantly and ungenerously. They will say harsh things about us. They will be inconsiderate and discourteous. They will be wilful, wayward, selfish. They will make us suffer from their arrogance, their ambition, their impatience, their stolid perversity. All this we have to anticipate. Christ bears with their imperfections and their sins; we too have to exercise forbearance. In forbearance, meekness and love are blended. We may say of either that it "suffereth long and is kind, . . envieth not . . . vaunteth not itself, is not puffed up, doth not behave itself unseemly, seeketh not its own, is not provoked, taketh not account of evil; . . . beareth all things, believeth all things, hopeth all things, endureth all things."

The apostle finds in the Divine idea of the church an additional obligation to the exercise of the graces on which he is insisting; for in requiring us to give "*diligence to keep the unity of the Spirit in the bond of peace*" he is simply urging a fresh reason for "*lowliness,*" "*meekness,*" "*longsuffering*" and mutual forbearance.

The church is one. When the apostle wrote this Epistle there were societies of Christians—churches—in Rome, in Corinth, in Thessalonica, in Philippi, in Colosse, in Ephesus, in the cities and towns of Galatia, in the Syrian Antioch, and in Jerusalem. There were less famous churches in other cities. They stood apart from each other; every separate church had authority over its own affairs, maintained its own discipline, elected its own bishops and deacons, organised its own worship. As yet there was no confederation of these independent societies under any central ecclesiastical authority. Their unity was not constituted by an external organisation but by their common possession of the Spirit of God, and it is therefore called by the apostle "*the unity of the Spirit.*" He has spoken of the unity of the church in the earlier part of the Epistle. The exclusion of the pagan races from "the commonwealth of Israel" had ceased; "the middle wall of partition" which separated them from the sacred court in which the elect nation had nearer access to God had been broken down. There was now one city of the saints, of which all Christian men of every nation were citizens; one household of God in which they were all children; one holy temple "built upon the foundation of the apostles and prophets, Jesus Christ Himself being the chief corner-stone," into the sacred walls of which they were all built "for a habitation of God in the Spirit." He has asserted this unity in a still bolder form; for after speaking of the glory of Christ, who sits at the right hand of God, "far above all rule and authority and power and dominion, and every name that is named not only in this world but also in that which is to come," he described the church as "the body" of Christ, the organ of His life and thought and will, "the fulness of Him that filleth all in all."

And now he returns to this great conception. The "*body*" of Christ, he says, is "*one*"; the "*Spirit*" of God who dwells in it is "*one*"; and in harmony with this unity of the "body" of Christ and this unity of the "Spirit" who dwells in it, the great "*hope*" of all Christian men, of all who have been called into the Divine kingdom and have obeyed the call, is "*one*."[1] There is "*one Lord*," only one—Christ Jesus the Prince and the Saviour of men; "*one faith*"—not a common creed, but a common trust in Christ for eternal righteousness and eternal glory; "*one baptism*" and only one, the same rite by which

---

[1] The hope according to Paul is a hope arising from the Divine calling (see chap. i. 18), and it was in the power of this hope that they were called.

Christ visibly claims men as belonging to the race for which He died and over which He reigns, is administered to all. There is "*one God and Father of all*," we all worship before the same eternal throne, and in Christ we are all the children of the same Divine Father; His sovereignty is absolute and supreme—He is "*over all*"; the power of His life penetrates the whole body of Christ—He is "*through all*"; and His home is in all Christians—He is "*in all.*"

What is true of the Holy Catholic Church, which consists of all that are in Christ, of all races, in all lands, is true of every separate society of Christians. According to the Divine idea—an idea which must in some measure be realized or else the society is not a church at all—every separate society of Christians is an organic unity: it is "*one body*," the temple of "*one Spirit*," and its members have "*one hope*"; they all have "*one Lord*," are united to Him by "*one faith*," have received "*one baptism*"; they worship "*one God and Father of all, who is over all, and through all, and in all.*"

But the Divine unity of the church is impaired, the Divine idea is not perfectly realized, if any of us by personal ambition, by arrogance, by a disposition to take offence, by yielding to a spirit of resentment, separate ourselves from other Christian men. Our quarrel is not a mere personal affair; it does not affect merely those whose anger we provoke by our wilfulness and self assertion, or whose wrongs against ourselves we refuse to forgive. We are committing an offence against the body of Christ; we are marring the perfection of its unity. Give diligence therefore "*to keep the unity of the Spirit in the bond of peace.*"

II.

The obligations of this duty are strengthened by a second conception of the church. It is the body of Christ, and each member has its own appointed functions; each member not only receives life and vigour for itself, but has to serve the whole body and to contribute to its vigour and perfection. "*Unto each one of us was the grace given according to the measure of the gift of Christ.*" The grace was given, as the apostle shows in subsequent verses, that we may each do our part towards "*the building up of the body of Christ*"; and our function is measured and determined by the light and power we receive from Christ for discharging it.

The development of this truth is interrupted by a quotation from Psalm lxviii. 18: "*Wherefore he saith*"—or the psalm saith—"*when He ascended on high He led captivity captive, and gave gifts unto men.*" The psalm was a war song, written and sung in celebration of some great victory; whether won by David as suggested by the traditional heading of the psalm, or by some later hero, is not certain.

The conqueror is represented as returning in triumph to the hill of God, to Mount Zion, the strong fortress of the elect race, and leading in procession a train of captives. There, on the secure and consecrated heights, the psalm describes him as receiving gifts, the tribute which expresses the homage and allegiance of the vanquished, and the submission of those who had rebelled against his authority.[1] But Paul gives another turn to the description: Christ, he says, who ascended to glory, "*gave gifts unto men*" instead of *receiving* gifts from men. The original historical meaning of the passage hardly admits of question; and that meaning is very obviously not the meaning which Paul attributes to it. Nor do we gain any help by appealing to the Septuagint; for the Septuagint is faithful to the grammatical sense of the Hebrew and represents the conqueror as receiving instead of conferring gifts. Are we to suppose that Paul intentionally varied the words in order to adapt them to his purpose, just as we sometimes vary the terms of a quotation from a well known poet, and by the very variation give it fresh point and force? Or is the variation to be attributed to a lapse of memory? Neither of these explanations is quite satisfactory. It is only when the words which we are quoting are familiar that we give them fresh point and force by a startling change intended to adapt them to our purpose; and as most of the Ephesian Christians were Gentiles they would not be very familiar with the Jewish Scriptures. That Paul's

---

[1] See Delitzsch, *in loc.*

memory failed him is also unlikely; the conception of the conqueror receiving tribute from his vanquished enemies is so vividly represented by the psalmist that it is extremely improbable that Paul could have forgotten it and supposed that the conqueror was represented as conferring gifts. Curiously enough the Chaldee Targum on the Psalms—a Jewish expository paraphrase—gives the same sense to the words that Paul gives. But the earliest of the Targums was not written and published till about two hundred years after Christ. It therefore seems probable that in this quotation Paul has preserved a remembrance of his student life in the schools of Jerusalem. The rabbinical tradition, which was fixed in the Targum long after Paul's death, may have represented an earlier form of the Hebrew text than that which we possess in our present Hebrew Bible or than that which was used by the translators of the Septuagint. Or perhaps rabbinical exposition had assigned to the passage the sense in which Paul used it.[1] But as the quotation was simply intended to enrich the illustration of the apostle's thought, and as it may be removed altogether without lessening the real force of his appeal, the decision of the question is of no practical importance.

If we are to suppose that all the imagery of the quotation had an exact and definite meaning for Paul when he applied it to the resurrection and ascension

---

[1] See Meyer, *in loc.*

of the Lord Jesus Christ, then it is probable that by the captives whom the conqueror is represented as leading captive, Paul meant all those evil and hostile powers that Christ overcame for us by His death and His return to life and glory.

The comment on the quotation is quite in Paul's manner. He "goes off at a word." He had spoken of Christ as ascending; but when Christ ascended He returned to His true home; to have ascended He must have previously descended; and Paul says that He "*descended*" into "*the lower parts of the earth*," to those dark regions of mystery beneath the earth which the Jews supposed were the regions of the dead; "He that descended" to those deepest depths "is the same that also ascended" to heights beyond all height, "*far above all the heavens*"; He touched the lowest deep of humiliation, and rose to the loftiest height of glory, "*that He might fill all things*."

And now Paul returns to his main thought which he had expressed in ver. 7: "*unto each one of us was the grace given according to the measure of the gift of Christ.*"

To himself, although in his own judgment he was "less than the least of all saints, was *this grace given, to preach unto the Gentiles the unsearchable riches of Christ.*" "*The grace*" given to Paul was his apostolic commission and authority to preach Christ to heathen nations. It was his habit to describe his apostolic ministry as "*the grace*" which God had given him.

In his account of his famous conference with the apostles at Jerusalem he says: "when they saw that I had been entrusted with the gospel of the uncircumcision, even as Peter with the gospel of the circumcision, . . . when they perceived *the grace that was given to me*, James and Cephas and John . . . gave to me and Barnabas the right hands of fellowship, that we should go unto the Gentiles."[1] In writing to the Romans he appeals to his apostolic authority and office as "*the grace that was given*" to him: "For I say, through the grace that was given to me, to every man that is among you, not to think of himself more highly than he ought to think."[2] He was speaking, not as one Christian man to another, but with the authority of an apostle of Christ. He tells the Corinthian Christians that it was as an apostle that he had laid the foundation of their Christian life and faith. He came to them not as an unofficial preacher of the gospel, animated by personal zeal, but with the authority of a special commission: "according *to the grace of God which was given* unto me, as a wise master-builder, I laid a foundation; and another buildeth thereupon."[3]

"*The grace*" was a form of service; the free love of God had appointed him to a function of transcendent honour. But not him alone: "For even as we have many members in one body, and all the

---

[1] Gal. ii. 7–9. [2] Rom. xii. 3.
[3] 1 Cor. iii. 10.

members have not the same office; so we who are many are one body in Christ, and severally members one of another. And *having gifts differing according to the grace that was given to us*, whether prophecy let us prophesy according to the proportion of faith; or ministry let us give ourselves to our ministry," etc.[1] The gifts differ according to "the grace," the $\chi\alpha\rho\iota\sigma\mu\alpha\tau\alpha$ according to the $\chi\acute{\alpha}\rho\iota\varsigma$, the powers according to the function. But it might also be said that the function is determined by the powers which are given, the particular office of service by the particular faculties for service, the $\chi\acute{\alpha}\rho\iota\varsigma$ by the $\chi\alpha\rho\iota\sigma\mu\alpha\tau\alpha$, "the grace" by the gifts. And this is what is actually said in this passage: "*unto each one of us was the grace given according to the measure of the gift of Christ.*" Our function, the kind of service we are able to render to the church, varies "*according to the measure*" of the wisdom and the strength of the Divine life and Divine inspiration given us by Christ.

There is something infinitely beautiful in this use which Paul made of the word "grace." To be appointed to render a special service to men was to receive a special favour from God. It is more blessed to give than to receive; the Son of man came not to be ministered unto but to minister.

And this description of office and service in the church as a grace given by God is in harmony with the whole representation of the church which appears

---

[1] Rom. xii. 4-7.

in the New Testament. The relations between every Christian man and the whole body of Christ are of such a kind that whatever light, or power, or righteousness comes to an individual comes to the whole church. If "one member is honoured, all the members rejoice with it." In Christ we have no separate and private rights. When Christ blesses any Christian man He blesses all Christians. Where the deepest wisdom is given, the clearest knowledge of God, the firmest faith, the most ardent love, the brightest hope, there Christ completes the blessing by appointing to the most responsible service. "HE," a strong emphasis is thrown upon the word, "HE *gave some to be apostles ; and some, prophets ; and some, evangelists ; and some, pastors and teachers.*" Paul begins with the ministry which is highest in rank, and descends by regular gradations to the ordinary ministry of the church.

It is usually said that "the chief characteristics of an apostle were an immediate call from Christ, a destination for all lands, and a special power of working miracles"[1]; but this is an incomplete account of the essential elements of apostolic authority and service. These characteristics might have belonged to the ministry of men who, during the earthly life of the Lord Jesus Christ, had acknowledged His Divine mission, but who never saw Him after His resurrection from the dead. It was the special func-

---

[1] Ellicott, *in loc.*

tion of apostles to bear witness to the authority of the Lord Jesus Christ over all nations, and to the actual establishment of the kingdom of God upon earth. It was therefore necessary that they should have seen the risen and glorified Christ; should be able to declare, on evidence of an exceptional and supernatural kind, that though unseen He is always near. It was necessary that they should have seen in Christ the translation of human nature into new and higher conditions of life. It was necessary that for them the gates which separate the earthly from the heavenly life should be unclosed, the veil which conceals from mortal vision the Divine and eternal world by which we are environed drawn aside. There were others, no doubt, to whom this wonderful apocalypse was granted and who received no apostolic commission, but apart from this the qualifications of Peter, James and John for delivering their apostolic testimony would have been incomplete. They were apostles not merely because they had been Christ's nearest friends and elect servants during His earthly life, but because He "showed Himself alive [to them] after His passion by many proofs, appearing unto them by the space of forty days, and speaking the things concerning the kingdom of God."[1] Paul, who had not been among the disciples of Christ before the crucifixion and who persecuted the church after Christ had ascended into heaven, declared that he

---

[1] Acts i. 3.

was "not a whit behind the very chiefest apostles." The essential thing was to have known, not the earthly, but the heavenly Christ; and he too had seen the Lord."

"*Prophets*" were men who, under the special inspiration of the Holy Spirit, had a keen insight into the things of God. Their higher reason received exceptional illumination, so that they saw, as ordinary Christian men could not see, the Divine ideas which had been revealed in Christ, and which were still being revealed in the relations of the Christian life to God, and in the Divine government of the church.

"*Evangelists*" were, in our modern phrase, "missionaries." Their work was to effect the conversion of men by preaching the gospel, and so to bring them into the fellowship of existing churches, or to found new churches where no churches already existed.

The ministry of "*pastors and teachers*" was then as now a ministry to the church itself. There were teachers who were not pastors, but all pastors were required to be "apt to teach." As pastors they had a real but undefined authority over the church; they had control over the conduct of worship; they were exceptionally responsible, both for the purity of the faith of the church and the purity of its morals. They discharged their principal pastoral duties by the instruction they gave to the church in its ordinary assemblies; and as this function of teaching was so important a part of their ministry, Paul describes them here as "pastors and teachers," giving a double title to the same office.

Paul then describes the object for which Christ has given to the church these various ministries. Apostles, prophets, evangelists, pastors and teachers, are given for "*the perfecting of the saints*"; they are given to render to the church all kinds of service, "*unto the work of ministering*"; they are given for "*the building up of the body of Christ.*" Their work is to be consummated when all Christian men reach the same perfect faith in the Son of God and the same full and sure knowledge of Him; when they touch the ideal maturity of the Christian life, and every one of them becomes a "*full-grown man*," and in the complete development of Christian righteousness attains "*unto the measure of the stature of the fulness of Christ,*"[1] illustrates the energy of the life of Christ in his own personal perfection.

Paul says that as yet Christian men are very far from this great ideal. They have not reached manly maturity, or perfect faith in Christ, or a full and sure knowledge of Him; but apostles, prophets, evangelists, pastors and teachers have been given to them by Christ that they "*may be no longer children, tossed to and fro*" as by stormy waves, "*and*

---

[1] The meaning of the phrase "the fulness of Christ" receives illustration from the discussion, page 257, of the similar phrase, "the fulness of God."

carried about" like a rudderless ship driving helplessly away from her true course, swept now in this way and now in that "*with every wind of doctrine.*" That is a representation of the Christian thought and life of many of the members of the early churches; it is also a representation of the Christian thought and life of too many of those who are in the membership of the churches of our own times. To control and to correct this inconstancy of opinion, to develop this immaturity of character into manly vigour, was the object of all the ministries of the church in apostolic days, and it is still the object of every ministry given to the church by Christ Himself. Not brilliant declamation but solid instruction is the chief business of every man that has received "grace" to be a minister to the church; and his end will be, not to excite transient religious sentiment, however beautiful, or to stir vehement passion, but to discipline men to moral and spiritual strength. And the true "pastors and teachers" of the church will not be content to limit themselves within the province of the evangelist. It is not enough to extend the area of the church and to multiply converts; "pastors and teachers" are called to "the perfecting of the saints" in the knowledge of Christ and in the practice of righteousness.

Paul then describes in new terms the object of the ministries which Christ has given to the church. It is that Christian men "*speaking the truth in love may grow up in all things into Him which is the Head, even Christ.*" It was not in the power of the revisers of our translation to represent in a single English phrase the full force of the word which they have rendered "*speaking the truth.*" Both this and the alternative rendering, "dealing truly," which they have given in the margin, are inadequate. The current of Paul's thought makes it certain, I think, that he attached to the word a great intensity of meaning. Truth was to be the life of the life of all Christian men. The revelation of God in Christ was to penetrate and inspire their whole activity. Truth was to become incarnate, personal, in them; they were not only to hold fast to it, they were not only to speak it, they were to live it. And they were to live it "*in love.*" Truth was to be the central and vital force, "love" its atmosphere and environment. And then the whole development of their life, its development in thought, in moral conduct, in the varied activity of emotional energy, in religious endeavour, in worship, would be a continuous approach to the ideal perfection of Christ, and would make their union with Christ more and more intimate. They would "*grow up in all things into Him which is the Head, even Christ.*"

There has been a great deal of discussion as to what Paul meant by our *growing up into* Christ. How, it has been asked, can the body be described as *growing up* into the head? The conception has appeared to some commentators so impossible that they have put very violent pressure on Paul's language in order to modify it. The explanation appears very obvious. Paul was much more anxious about conveying his meaning than about preserving the consistency of his metaphor. All Christian growth is a growth towards the transcendent perfection of Christ and a growth into union with Him. That the body does not "grow up into" the head Paul knew quite well; but Christian men do grow up into Christ, and, as he wanted to say this, he dropped his metaphor and said it. And so, in the next verse, he describes Christ as the centre and source of all the activity and growth of the church. No such relation as this can be strictly said to exist between the head and the rest of the body; but Paul uses his metaphor to convey his meaning, and when the metaphor will not help him he lays it aside.

At this point Paul passes from his account of the object for which Christ has given to the church its official ministries; and in the next verse announces the truth that not only the official ministers of the church but all its members have to contribute to the growth and perfection of the body of Christ. From Christ "*all the body, fitly framed and knit together through that which every joint supplieth according to the working in due measure of each several part, maketh the increase of the body unto the building up of itself in love.*"

This is the final illustration of what Paul meant when he said "unto each one of us was the grace given according to the measure of the gift of Christ." Every Christian man, however narrow the range of his knowledge, however inconsiderable his powers, however obscure his position in society or the church, receives life and light and strength from Christ, not merely for himself, but for others. He may have no office in the church, but he has his function, which he cannot leave undischarged without injuring the growth of the body of Christ. He may have neither the capacity nor the opportunity for undertaking what we specifically call "Christian work," but he may fulfil his function with admirable fidelity and may, according to the measure of the power given to him, augment the moral and spiritual force, elevate the righteousness, and enrich the Divine joy of all his Christian brethren.

III.

And now we are in a better position to understand the strength of the motives with which Paul sustains his exhortation to give " diligence to keep the unity of the Spirit in the bond of peace." We are ministers, every one of us, to the perfection of the body of Christ. We are all necessary to each other. " The eye cannot say to the hand, I have no need of thee : or again the head to the feet, I have no need of you." Even " those members of the body which seem to be more feeble are necessary." Every man receives service ; every man renders service. It is only by " the working in due measure of each several part " that the body of Christ can be built up to its full stature and full vigour.

I—as the minister of this church—hold my own place and discharge my own functions. By solitary thought and prayer, by meditation on whatever God has revealed of Himself and of His invisible and eternal kingdom, I have to discover, not for my own sake merely but for yours, the greatness of the Christian redemption, the fountains of Christian joy and Christian righteousness, the unchanging laws of the Divine kingdom for the government of Christian conduct. By contact with the life of men, by familiarity with private and public affairs, I have to discover what are the moral and religious perils which menace your Christian integrity, and what are the special forms of virtue and of grace which in your actual circumstances will most adequately illustrate your fidelity to Christ. The deacons of the church and the deaconesses have also their places and their functions; the teachers in the schools have theirs; those who are engaged in mission work have theirs. But, as I have said already, those who occupy no office and who cannot undertake any definite tasks in connection with any of the organisations of the church are also "necessary" to the life and power of the whole of this Christian community. By their devoutness, their uprightness, their charity, their zeal, they may add immeasurably to the force of the church and have a large share in its triumphs.

In a life otherwise commonplace there is sometimes illustrated in a very impressive form the full meaning of some precept of Christ, to which the common ethics of the church have given no adequate recognition; and such a life may, within the range of its influence, effect a most real and substantial ethical reformation. An integrity and an industry which have nothing heroic in them may sometimes act like a tonic on men whose moral nature is deficient in original vigour, and whose moral environment has been unfriendly even to the common virtues. Cheerfulness in poverty, in physical infirmity, in a life destitute of all the common sources of happiness, has sometimes rebuked the discontent of those who with a thousand reasons for joy suffer themselves to be vexed by trivial annoyances and worried by trivial cares. When the faith of the scholar falters it sometimes receives a sudden inspiration of vigour by the discovery in some poor and narrow life of a beauty and splendour which could have come only from heaven. In times when great trouble has embittered the heart both against God and man, the rude sympathy of a nature with no grace or beauty in it except that which it has derived from fellowship with Christ, sympathy roughly expressed or hardly expressed at all, will sometimes give wonderful vividness and reality to the tenderness of the Divine compassion. We come to understand God's laws by seeing how other men obey them, and God's promises by seeing how other men trust them. In the great struggle between God and the sin of the world, every man that stands firm in the ranks of the army of light gives other men courage to stand firm too. Be righteous, and you make righteousness easier to some other Christian man, perhaps to many other Christian men. Let your faith be strong, and even though you may say little about it you will make the faith of other men stronger. Be devout, and in ways that you cannot trace you will check irreverence and deepen the awe with which your Christian brethren worship God. Love men, and you will diffuse within the limits of your influence the spirit of Christian charity, and how far that spirit may extend who can tell? Fire kindles fire, and when fire is once kindled it burns and spreads. Care for the salvation of men, and you will do something towards maintaining and strengthening the evangelistic zeal of the whole church.

That we may render and receive this mutual service it is plainly necessary that we should all cultivate that temper which will "keep the unity of the Spirit in the bond of peace." What benefit, for example, would it be possible for you to receive from my ministry if you and I were separated from each other by distrust and hostility, either on your side or on mine? Suppose that I had the impression, true or false, that I was being treated unjustly and unkindly, either by the church generally or by any of its members; suppose that I refused to forget or to forgive this treatment; it is certain that there would be an element of bitterness in my preaching which would poison the blood of the church; and instead of contributing to your health and vigour I should be inflicting on you immeasurable harm. Suppose, on the other hand, that the resentment were on your side; that you were provoked by my arrogance, ambition, vanity, wilfulness, or obstinacy; or that when you were listening to me within these walls you were always recalling with a sense of injury, harsh, ungenerous, reckless words I had spoken about you elsewhere; it is equally certain that while this condition of mind lasted you would be incapable of receiving any good from my ministry.

The same principle governs your relations to each other. The "unity of the Spirit" must be kept "in the bond of peace," if all the body of Christ "fitly framed and knit together through that which every joint supplieth, according to the working in due measure of each several part," is to grow in righteousness, in the knowledge of Christ, and in Divine joy. You can receive no good from your Christian brethren, you can confer no good upon your Christian brethren, if you are separated from them by real or imaginary wrongs. There must be cordial mutual affection and mutual trust, if the members of a church are to increase in moral strength and in religious fervour. You cannot yield to a spirit of hostility against any individual Christian without lessening the intimacy and happiness of your relations to the whole church. Among the many profound and noble words of Marcus Aurelius the following have always seemed to me exceptionally deserving of being constantly remembered: "A branch cut off from the adjacent branch must of

necessity be cut off from the whole tree also. So
too a man, when he is separated from another man,
has fallen off from the whole social community.
Now as to a branch, another cuts it off; but a man
by his own act separates himself from his neighbour
when he hates him and turns away from him, and
he does not know that he has at the same time cut
himself off from the whole social system. Yet he
has this privilege certainly from Zeus who framed
society, for it is in our power to grow again to that
which is near to us, and again to become a part
which helps to make up the whole." [1]

The principle is more strikingly illustrated in our
relations to the church than even in our relations
to society. A Christian man has received injury
from another, a real injury; he gives way to his
resentment; he maintains that his resentment is
just; he refuses to forgive. All this may be true;
but his separation from the man who has wronged
him ends commonly in most tragic results. For a
time his moral and religious character seems to have

---

[1] "M. Aurelius Antoninus": George Long's translation, p. 187. The rest of the paragraph is very worthy of being quoted: "However, if it often happens, this kind of separation, it makes it difficult for that which detaches itself to be brought to unity and to be restored to its former condition. Finally, the branch, which from the first grew together with the tree, and has continued to have one life with it, is not like that which after being cut off is then engrafted, for this is something like what the gardeners mean when they say that it grows with the rest of the tree, but that it has not the same mind with it."

received no harm; the leaves on the branch are still fresh and bright, and the fruit is sound and wholesome. But gradually the leaves fade and the fruit loses its freshness. He is a branch "cut off" not only "from the adjacent branch," but "from the whole tree." In separating himself from his Christian brother he has separated himself from Christ; and "if a man abide not in [Christ] he is cast forth as a branch and is withered; and they gather them and cast them into the fire, and they are burned."

You imperil your own life by yielding to the moral resentment provoked by injustice or unkindness. Do you say that the injury is real and intolerable? If the injury were not real you would have nothing to forgive; if it were not a grave injury your forgiveness would be worth very little as a proof of your loyalty to Christ. Give "diligence to keep the unity of the Spirit in the bond of peace." "Be ye kind one to another, tender hearted, forgiving each other, even as God also in Christ forgave you." "If ye forgive men their trespasses, your heavenly Father will also forgive you. But if ye forgive not men their trespasses neither will your Father forgive your trespasses." "Blessed are the peacemakers, for they shall be called sons of God."

In the presence of the divisions and controversies of Christendom the representation of the Unity of the church contained in this chapter suggests the gravest and most anxious questions. Is the Unity a Divine idea which has never yet been realized?

Or has it been lost? If lost, who was responsible for the catastrophe? Has the responsibility been inherited by modern churches? Should there be an endeavour, a serious, earnest endeavour, made with "all lowliness and meekness, with longsuffering" and with mutual forbearance, to bring to an end the theological and ecclesiastical strife by which great religious communities are separated from each other? Should Nonconformists and Anglicans consider how they can include all the Christian life of England in one undivided church? Should Protestants and Romanists confer on the measures which are necessary for healing the schism of the Reformation and restoring unity to Western Christendom? And, after more than a thousand years of hostility, ought there to be an attempt to bring together the east and the west in one great and august confederation?

These questions raise a false issue. The unity of the church, according to Paul's conception of it, is a unity of life not of external organisation. It is the creation of the Spirit of God, not of ecclesiastical statesmanship. It actually exists, notwithstanding differences of polity and differences of creed. Christian men belong to different churches, but "the body" of Christ is "one"; "one Spirit" dwells in them; they have "one hope" of eternal righteousness and glory; they acknowledge and serve "one Lord"; their "faith" in Him is "one"; they have received "one baptism"; they worship "one

God and Father of all, who is over all, and through all, and in all."

The unity does not merely exist; it has been manifested through all the Christian centuries; it is manifested still. It has been manifested and is manifested still in a remarkable unity of doctrine. The immense majority of those who have called themselves Christians have believed that the Father, the Son, and the Holy Ghost are one God; that in Christ the Eternal Word became flesh; that Christ died for the sins of men, and that we receive remission of sins through Him; that to enter the kingdom of God it is necessary to receive the life of God; that holiness is a fruit of the Spirit; that there is a judgment to come; that the doom of the impenitent is irrevocable; that those who are in Christ will inherit eternal righteousness and eternal joy in God.

The unity of the church has been manifested in a common ideal of ethical perfection. In all churches the gentler virtues—humility, meekness, patience —have been rescued from neglect or dishonour; and in all churches an active compassion for poverty, pain, misery, and sin has been made a large part of the service which man owes to God.

The unity of the church has been manifested in a new and original type of the religious life, which notwithstanding local, temporary, and accidental variations, has been the same in all Christian countries from the earliest Christian centuries down to our own time. The prayers of the church, its hymns, its devotional manuals, the sorrows and the joys of saints, are all penetrated by the same spirit, and bear witness to a unity which is unbroken by differences of race, of language, of civilization, by differences of theological creed and differences of ecclesiastical connection. The saints of all lands and of all generations are akin.

This is the unity which we should endeavour to "keep" "in the bond of peace." The obligations of charity, the obligations to mutual service, which are created by common membership of the body of Christ, may sometimes require us to protest and to protest vehemently against the errors into which great churches have been betrayed, the superstitions which great churches have sanctioned. The hand would be disloyal to the foot if it shrank from extracting a thorn, though the very effort to extract it might cause the foot to throb with sharp pain. And for the Protestant to be silent concerning the errors which impair the religious strength of Roman Catholicism would be treachery—not to truth merely, nor to Christ merely—but also to his Roman Catholic brother. The truth which has been revealed to me is no private estate of mine; it has been revealed to me for the sake of all my Christian brethren.

But I can render no service to those for whom I feel no love. Controversy should be one of the highest and fairest expressions of charity. I must speak—not to wound but to heal; to rescue from error, not to cover with ridicule and contempt. I must speak—not with the desire to win a personal triumph but with the hope of bringing my brother into the light in which I am already living, into the same freedom and the same joy. If in controversy there is no hostility against those from whom we differ; if, instead of hostility, there is deep and fervent affection for them, controversy, instead of provoking strife and schism, will contribute to that "unity of the faith and of the knowledge of the Son of God" in which the unity of the church will be finally perfected.

XVI.

THE IMMORALITY OF THE HEATHEN.

"This I say therefore, and testify in the Lord, that ye no longer walk as the Gentiles also walk, in the vanity of their mind, being darkened in their understanding, alienated from the life of God because of the ignorance that is in them, because of the hardening of their heart; who being past feeling gave themselves up to lasciviousness to work all uncleanness with greediness."

—EPH. iv. 17-19.

THERE is a startling contrast between the earlier and the later chapters of this Epistle. In the earlier chapters Paul describes the Christians at Ephesus as "saints," as "the faithful in Christ Jesus," as having been raised from the dead with Christ, as sitting with Christ "in the heavenly places," as God's "workmanship created in Christ Jesus for good works which God afore prepared that we should walk in them." They are "of the household of God," a temple "built upon the foundation of the apostles and prophets . . . for a habitation of God in the Spirit."

As if they were already familiar with all the elementary principles of the Christian gospel, he speaks to them of the eternal thoughts of God which are gradually being fulfilled in the history of the human race, and which are to reach their final accomplishment in the ascent of the whole universe —heaven and earth, angels and men—to perfect and eternal union with God in Christ.

And now to the persons whom he has described by these sacred titles, and to whom he has spoken of these Divine mysteries, he gives a succession of precepts relating to the most elementary moral duties. He thinks it necessary to warn them against the basest and the coarsest vices—against lying and thieving, against foul speech, against drunkenness, against gross sensual sins.

The difficulty is not to be evaded by the suggestion that, while many of the members of the church at Ephesus were devout and saintly, some of them were still mere heathen, having no real faith in Christ and no spiritual life. It is clear that these precepts, which imply the possibility and the existence of such gross immoralities in the character and conduct of those to whom they are addressed, were meant for the very same persons that Paul had described as "saints," as "the faithful in Christ Jesus"; for the considerations by which the precepts are enforced imply that persons who were guilty of these immoralities really believed in Christ as the Son of God and Saviour of men, had received the remission of sins and the inspiration of the Holy Spirit.

The access of the Divine life does not at once and in a moment change a man's moral temper and habits.

The ethical laws which had a real obligation for him before his conversion, though he may have kept them imperfectly, are re-enforced by motives of immense power, and he receives the aid of the Spirit of God in obeying them; what he knew and felt to be wrong before he discovered the righteousness and love of God he will avoid; but the urgency and pressure of the Divine authority will not be felt immediately in every province of the moral life. Moral distinctions which were faint will not at once become vivid. Moral distinctions which were not recognised at all will not at once become apparent.

The Christians at Ephesus had been breathing from their childhood the foul atmosphere of a most corrupt form of heathenism; they were breathing it still. In the community which surrounded them the grossest vices were unrebuked by public sentiment. Many of them had been guilty of these vices before their conversion, and were conscious neither of guilt nor of shame. When they came into the church they did not escape at once from their old heathen habits; there was not a sudden elevation of their whole moral life to a higher level.

We surely need not be astonished at this. We constantly see the same thing among ourselves. When a man becomes a Christian he becomes a better man, but the ethical change is not immediate, is not complete. A rough and violent temper is not at once softened into gentleness. Selfishness does not at once expand into generosity. The suspicious man does not at once become trustful; or the vain man modest; or the proud man humble. If a man is covetous before his conversion the passion for money is not at once extinguished; and even after its fires have sunk, the evil habits which the passion had formed may remain for many years and may only gradually wear away. A man who has been accustomed to lie through cowardice does not at once become courageous enough to be always perfectly truthful; a man who has been accustomed to lie through vanity will be surprised, again and again, into boastful exaggeration which will sometimes pass into positive falsehood. Where there has been a habit of loose and reckless talking, a certain measure of intellectual as well as of moral discipline will be necessary in order to form a habit of exact truthfulness. The indolent workman will not become conspicuous at once for his uniform and unflagging industry. The clerk who before his conversion was often too late at his desk in the morning, and who was habitually careless at his work, will not become at once a model of punctuality and accuracy to the whole office. Masters that have been hard with their men will only gradually learn to be generous and kindly. Tradesmen that have not been very scrupulous in the conduct of their business will not at once discover that they have to carry on their business for the public benefit rather than for their own. Politicians that have engaged in public life at the impulse of personal ambition will not immediately suppress the desire for personal authority, for distinction while they live, and for enduring fame; it will take them time to accept political life as simply affording them great opportunities for serving Christ by serving the nation.

The Ephesian Christians, when they acknowledged the authority of God and trusted in His love and power for eternal redemption, did not at once escape from the spirit and habits of their old life; nor did we. Their old life was more gross and foul than ours, and their life in the church was therefore stained with grosser and fouler sins; but we too have brought the ethics of the world into the kingdom of God. Sometimes indeed, when the supreme revelation comes to a man, many of his vicious habits fall away from him at the touch of Christ, as the chains of Peter fell at the touch of the angel. And sometimes after a Christian man has been trying for years to rid himself of a disposition, a temper, a habit alien from the spirit of Christ, the gracious lightning of heaven falls on it suddenly and blasts it to the very roots. But, normally, Christian righteousness is achieved slowly. A Divine life is given to us, but the life has to grow. "Love, joy, peace, long-suffering, kindness, goodness, faithfulness, meekness, temperance" are "the fruit of the Spirit"; and the fruit is not ripened in an hour or a day.

There will however be real ethical progress wherever there is genuine loyalty to Christ. There will be a persistent effort to do the will of God as far as the will of God is known. With this fidelity there will be a steady increase of ethical knowledge. The ethical ideal will gradually become loftier. By influences which we cannot trace, the prevailing temper of a Christian man will become more like the temper of Christ. He will be drawn beyond the reach of many temptations by the new and nobler interests of the Divine kingdom; other temptations he will have the strength to master. The Divine life will perish if it is so obstructed by evil tempers and evil habits that it cannot grow. Its growth will gradually bring about a complete moral transformation.

But we must not assume that this transformation will come of itself, or as the result of the exclusive cultivation of the spiritual affections. Moral culture is necessary for moral perfection.[1] And Christian people who are troubled because, notwithstanding all their prayers and all their meditation on eternal things, their faith in God is infirm, their love for Him cold and inconstant, and their hope of eternal glory very dim, would do well to consider whether their spiritual failure may not be explained by their defective morality. Paul told the Ephesian Christians that unless they renounced their vices they would be eternally lost; "for because of these things cometh the wrath of God upon the sons of disobedience";

---

[1] On the grave defects, theoretical and practical, of evangelical Christianity in relation to ethics, see Sermons II., III., IV., V., and VI. in the "Evangelical Revival," by the author. (Hodder and Stoughton.) On the necessity of the education of the conscience see especially Sermon IV.

and our own moral offences, though less flagrant than theirs, may be equally pernicious to the growth of the Divine life and may expose us to equal peril.

Paul strengthens the authority and adds to the solemnity of his ethical exhortations by the manner in which he introduces them. He is not speaking for himself and in his own name, but "*in the Lord.*" In charging them to break with their old life he is vividly conscious of Christ's abhorrence of sin and Christ's delight in righteousness. He is conscious too of the strenuous urgency with which Christ authoritatively commands all that acknowledge Him as their Prince and Saviour to "depart from all iniquity." What he has to say is not a matter of mere personal conviction, which might be open to discussion and about which different men might have different opinions; he is a witness, and is delivering his testimony. He is speaking therefore with a grave sense of responsibility, and with a clear recognition of how much depends upon his speaking truthfully: "*This I say therefore and testify in the Lord, that* YE *no longer walk as the Gentiles also walk.*"

The brief account which follows of the ethical condition of the heathen world should be compared with the fuller and more elaborate passage in the second half of the first chapter of the Epistle to the Romans. In both descriptions the gross ethical corruption of heathen nations is attributed to their ignorance of God and of Divine and eternal things; and the ignorance is represented as the result of their moral unfaithfulness to the light which they had once had. The law which is constantly illustrated in the history of individual men is declared to have been illustrated in the history of those great races which had sunk into gross idolatry and gross vice. Where there is irreverence for the Divine majesty and disobedience to the Divine law the vision of God becomes fainter; as the vision of God becomes fainter the restraints of the Divine righteousness are lessened, irreverence and disobedience become more and more flagrant, and at last the vision of God is lost altogether.

The description of the heathen both here and in the Epistle to the Romans is to be taken as representing their general condition, and we must not suppose that Paul meant to affirm that the gross moral ignorance and the gross moral corruption were universal. There were heathen men that had not fallen so far. "The law written in their hearts" had been obeyed, and was therefore not effaced. There were heathen men of whom it could not be said that "they loved the darkness rather than the light, for their works were evil"; and therefore "the true light, even the light which lighteth every man," was shining in them still, though they did not know that it had come into the world in the person of the Lord Jesus Christ.

But, speaking broadly and generally, heathen men had lost the knowledge of God and had lost the knowledge of the steadfast and eternal laws of righteousness; and this is what Paul means when he says that they were walking "*in the vanity of their minds.*" We are environed by an invisible, Divine, and eternal world. It does not lie far away from us in the remote future, but surrounds us now as the starry heavens surround the common earth. There is a faculty in us which, when inspired and illuminated by the Spirit of God, enables us to see it. When once that world is revealed to us our whole conception of human duty and of human destiny is changed. We discover that the pleasures and pains of this brief and transitory life, its poverty and its wealth, its honours and its shame, are of secondary importance, that there is a kind of unreality in them all, that they are external to us, that they are rapidly passing away. In this life indeed it is impossible for us not to be affected by them; and they have their place in the discipline of our righteousness. But our horizon has widened, and we see beyond them. We discover that it is only the larger world which has been revealed to us by Christ that is real and enduring; and that compared with its august and glorious realities "things seen and temporal" are but passing shadows. We see that the true life of man is the eternal and Divine life by which he is related to what is eternal and Divine; that the true honour, the true wealth, the true wisdom, the true happiness of man are found in that eternal and Divine kingdom.

But Paul says that heathen races are living among

things seen and temporal, not among things unseen and eternal. The faculty by which they should be brought into contact with what is real and enduring is impaired, so that it mistakes shadows for substances, dreams for realities; they "*walk in the vanity of their mind.*" And as no light reaches them from the infinite and eternal world, they are "*darkened in their understanding.*"

Darkness and death go together. Man was so created that the root of his perfection is in God. His truest and highest life is a life that has its springs in the life of God. But where the knowledge of God is lost the life of God is lost. Heathen men are living in regions of moral darkness in which the life of God cannot be theirs. They are separated, estranged, "*alienated from the life of God because of the ignorance that is in them.*" But the ignorance is not a mere intellectual defect involving no moral fault; they are "*alienated from the life of God . . . because of the hardening of their heart.*" Their increasing moral insensibility was the real cause of their ignorance; and their ignorance and moral insensibility were the causes of their alienation from the life of God.

What kind of men they had become through this hardening of their heart Paul describes in words which it is not possible to read without a sense of horror. They were "*past feeling.*" They had ceased to be sensitive to the obligations of truth, of honesty, of kindness, of purity; and to the guilt of falsehood, of injustice, of cruelty, of sensual sin. They committed the grossest vices and were conscious of no shame. Their imagination was no longer fascinated by the beauty and nobleness of virtue. No sentiment of personal dignity checked the indulgence of the foulest and most disgraceful passions. They had no reverence for the purer and loftier traditions of better times. They were untouched by the censure and scorn of the wiser and nobler of their contemporaries. All the inducements that draw men to virtue and all the restraints that hold them back from vice were destroyed. They were "*past feeling.*"

Their sin was therefore gross and habitual. They were not betrayed into sin, against their better purposes; they were not merely overcome now and then by the violence of their passions; they were not mastered by some malignant power against which they struggled in vain; nor were their worst excesses followed by any remorse. They sinned deliberately, and without any protest from their reason or their conscience or any purer and more generous affections in their moral life. " *They gave THEMSELVES up*"—it was their own act, done with set purpose and with the consent of their whole nature—" *they gave THEMSELVES up to lasciviousness,*"—to a life in which there was a wilful, reckless, wanton defiance of all moral restraints. Vice, by their own choice and intention, was not to be an occasional incident in their life, it was to be their main business, the employment at which they were to "*work*"; and as some men have an insatiable desire for money, these men had an insatiable desire for every kind of impurity, "*they gave THEMSELVES up to lasciviousness, to work all uncleanness with greediness.*"

It is a horrible picture. But Paul was describing the men among whom he had lived and among whom the Christians at Ephesus were living still. The morality of the Greek cities of Asia Minor was so base and so foul that we wonder that the fires of God did not descend to destroy them. Is it surprising that with such a moral environment the Christians at Ephesus, who a few years before had been heathen men themselves, required the ethical teaching contained in the later chapters of this Epistle?

In the churches founded in heathen countries by modern missions we should expect to find the same moral corruptions that stained the life of the church at Ephesus. Heathen men who have been habitual liars will not discover the obligations of truth as soon as they are converted; nor will the sensual become pure, nor the cruel gentle, nor the indolent industrious. The terrible entail of the vices of many generations cannot be cut off at once; a new social life and a new social sentiment must be created, before a complete moral reformation can be expected.

To ourselves the ethical condition of the Ephesian Christians is profoundly suggestive; perhaps I ought to say that it is very alarming. English society is free from the gross, the sensual, the brutal vice which infected the great heathen cities of Asia Minor. There is a strong public sentiment on the side of truthfulness, honesty, temperance, purity, industry, self control, kindliness, and public spirit. We inherit these virtues from our parents; we have been disciplined to them by all the complex influences that have contributed to form our character. In a very true sense they are natural to us, and we practise them without effort.

And so it is assumed that when a man receives the life of God there is no reason for any great change in his moral habits. There may be defects of temper which have to be corrected, and in some of the details of moral conduct he may recognise the necessity for amendment; but if he has lived among good moral people he takes it for granted that in working out his own salvation he has to think almost exclusively of his spiritual life; his moral character is already what it should be. He attends public worship more frequently than before; secures more time for private prayer, for religious thought, for reading the Bible and other religious books; he tries to increase the fervour of his love for God and the steadfastness of his faith in God; he takes up some kind of religious work. About moral discipline he thinks very little. About the necessity of reconstructing his whole conception of moral duty, adding to it new elements, resting it on new foundations, he thinks still less. The results of this grave error are most disastrous. The ideal of the ethical life is no higher in the church than it is in the world.

But if the morals of the church, as a whole, are not distinctly in advance of the morals of society as a whole, if when a man becomes a Christian his moral life is not governed by nobler laws and inspired with a new generosity and force, the power of the church will be seriously impaired, and its triumphs will be only occasional and intermittent. At times a great passion of religious enthusiasm may enable it to count its converts by thousands; but the fires of enthusiasm soon sink, and for its permanent authority the church should rely on steadier forces.

In heathen countries, although the morality of Christian converts may be grossly defective, it is in advance of the morality of the mass of their fellow countrymen. The darkness of their old life is about them still, but their faces are towards the light. In countries described as Christian there should be the same difference between the morality of those that are in Christ and the morality of those that are not. The revelation of the Divine love and the Divine righteousness, of our kinship to God, of the glorious immortality which is the inheritance of all that have received the Divine life, should ennoble our ideal of every moral virtue, and should inspire us with a more ardent passion for moral perfection.

XVII.

THE CHRISTIAN METHOD OF MORAL REGENERATION.

"But ye did not so learn Christ; if so be that ye heard Him, and were taught in Him, even as truth is in Jesus: that ye put away, as concerning your former manner of life, the old man, which waxeth corrupt after the lusts of deceit; and that ye be renewed in the spirit of your mind, and put on the new man, which after God hath been created in righteousness and holiness of truth." EPH. iv. 20-24.

IN the preceding verses Paul has described the gross moral corruption of heathen society. To that society the Ephesian Christians had belonged. He might have said to them what he said to the Christians at Corinth: "neither fornicators, nor idolaters, nor adulterers, nor thieves, nor covetous, nor drunkards, nor revilers, nor extortioners shall inherit the kingdom of God. And *such were some of you.*" For wherever the gospel was preached, it not only gave new hope and courage, new light and strength, to those who were already trying to practise the virtues which the natural conscience honours and enforces; it found its way to the very worst and the most depraved of mankind. Indeed it is clear from the precepts which follow in the latter part of this chapter and in the next, that some of the Christians at Ephesus had not completely escaped from the common vices of heathenism. There were the most urgent practical reasons why the apostle should remind them of the Christian method of moral regeneration. That they should continue to live the life they had lived before they became Christians, the life which heathen men were living still, was impossible. "YE"—he places them in emphatic contrast with their fellow citizens who were outside the Christian church and who had not received the Christian Faith—"YE *did not so learn Christ.*" He means that they did not "learn Christ" in such a way as to suppose that they could continue to be guilty of lying, of theft, of drunkenness, of sensuality, and all the vices of heathenism. The knowledge of Christ which they had received might be imperfect, but it did not leave them ignorant of the necessity of righteousness. For, as the apostle hopes and believes, they had not merely listened to human teachers whose conception of Christian truth might be false and who might be unable to convey the truth they knew to others; Christ's own voice had reached them; when they became Christians they "*heard* HIM."

Truth, the highest truth, the truth it most concerns Christian men to know, is "*in Jesus.*" Truth can never be rightly known when separated from Him. All real and effective teaching must be in harmony with truth as truth is in Him. But this was precisely the teaching which the apostle trusts had been given to the Ephesian Christians. For they themselves *were* " in Him " and "*were taught . . . even as truth is in Jesus.*" The expression of the apostle's thought is very condensed. Here, as in many other passages in his epistles, he assumes that the minds of his readers are already charged with Christian ideas. Every phrase is a symbol that stands for a whole province of Christian doctrine.

Paul now proceeds to develop the truth which he assumes that the Christians at Ephesus had "heard" from Christ; the truth which as they were "in Christ" they had been "taught"; the truth which all Christians find in Him : " *that ye put away, as concerning your former life, the old man, which waxeth corrupt after the lusts of deceit ; and that ye be renewed in the spirit of your mind and put on the new man which after God hath been created in righteousness and holiness of truth.*" This is what I described just now as the Christian method of moral regeneration. It includes three distinct processes : (1) the renunciation of the previous moral life ; (2) the constant renewal of the higher and spiritual life by the power of the Spirit of God ; (3) the appropriation of the righteousness and holiness of that new and perfect humanity which God created in Christ.

There must be, first, the renunciation of the previous moral life. Paul told the Ephesian Christians that " *as concerning* [their] *former manner of life* " they had been taught that they must "*put away . . . the old man which waxeth corrupt after the lusts of deceit.*" The ethical change was not to be partial but complete. To amend some of the details of conduct was not enough; they had to part with all their previous moral habits and to retain nothing of their previous moral personality.[1]

But this complete moral revolution is not accomplished either by one supreme effort of our own will or by any momentary shock of Divine power. It must be carried through in detail by a long, laborious, and sometimes painful process of self discipline. The process lasts as long as life lasts. For with the changing years there is a change in the forms of moral evil which have to be resisted and put away from us. We may have won a complete victory over the sins to which we were liable in youth and early manhood; but in mature life and in old age we discover that fresh tendencies to sin emerge, tendencies the presence of which in our nature we had never suspected. The earlier triumphs make the later triumphs easier, but do not release us from the hard necessities of battle.

Self examination is necessary. Our moral habits must be compared, one by one, with the command-

---

[1] The "*former manner of life*" concerns the *whole* moral nature of man before his conversion, and the requirement to "*put away the old man*" affirms that the converted man is to retain nothing of his pre-Christian moral personality, but as concerns the pre-Christian conduct of life is utterly to do away with the old ethical individuality and to become the new man."
—*Meyer, in loc.*

ments of Christ, and their conformity with the genius and spirit of Christian ethics must be patiently and honestly tested. We must contrast our own manner of life, in its details, with the manner of life of other Christian men in whom we recognise a noble righteousness and charity. In the humblest and obscurest of our Christian brethren we may often discover virtues which bring home to us how incompletely we have mastered our inferior and baser self. The imperfections in other men which provoke our resentment may make more vivid to us our own imperfections. The resentment itself, by its bitterness and impatience, may reveal to us a vanity, a wilfulness, and an impatience which we thought we had subdued. By these and by other means we may learn how much of "*our former manner of life*" still remains in our spirit and conduct and what moral evils have still to be "*put away.*"

There must be self discipline as well as self examination. Self reproach, penitent confession, prayers for deliverance from an evil habit, are not enough. Repentance is incomplete where there is no reformation; and for moral reformation there must be personal effort as well as reliance on the Divine grace. We must "work out [our] own salvation." If we discover that we have fallen into habits of careless speaking, and that with no deliberate intention to deceive we are frequently conveying false impressions, we must call these habits by their right name; careless and inaccurate speaking is falsehood.

LECT. XVII.] MORAL REGENERATION. 313

We must watch our words so as to check the sin. We must speak less. We must think before we speak. We must submit to the humiliation of correcting the false impressions which we have created by our carelessness. If we find that we judge men hastily and harshly, condemn them on inadequate evidence, draw injurious conclusions from facts of which perhaps we have an imperfect knowledge, we must break the habit of rash judgment, must be silent about the conduct of other men till we are sure that we are right, and even when we are sure that we are right ask ourselves whether there is any obligation resting upon us to pronounce any judgment at all. If we find that we are disposed to indolence we must try to discover whether we are yielding to any forms of physical indulgence which are unfriendly to vigorous and persistent industry, and avoid them. If sometimes we are betrayed into excessive drinking we must consider whether our moral safety does not require us to abstain altogether from the kinds of drink that are perilous to us.

These are but illustrations of a general law. Habit after habit must be broken if we are to "*put away as concerning* [our] *former manner of life the old man which is corrupt according to the lusts of deceit.*" We have passed into a new world and we know things as they are; but there was a time when the eternal realities of the universe were not revealed to us and when our moral nature was under the control of false conceptions of human life and human destiny. These false conceptions exerted a pernicious influence on the desires and impulses of our moral life; and "*the lusts of deceit*," the passions which were developed into vigour before we knew the truth concerning ourselves, the world, and God, corrupted our whole moral nature, introduced into it the elements of disease, poisoned its blood, impaired its fibre. It is not in a single limb or a single organ that we are affected; the very springs of life are foul; corruption has already set in. We must "put away" our old self. The whole structure of our former moral character and habits must be demolished and the ruins cleared away, that the building may be recommenced from its very foundation. "*The old man is corrupt after the lusts of deceit.*"[1]

The Christian method of moral regeneration includes a second process, of another and a very different kind. The truth which the apostle assumes had been taught to the Ephesian Christians required them to "*be renewed in the spirit of* [their] *mind.*"

---

[1] Writing to those who had become Christians in manhood, the apostle naturally spoke to them of the necessity of renouncing their "former manner of life," the morality of their heathen days. The same exhortation would take a different form when addressed to persons who received the Christian faith and were "born of God" in their early life, and who are therefore happily free from the sad memory of many years of flagrant indifference to the Divine authority. But in them too there is an "old man," a baser nature, a morality formed by the current opinions and prevalent habits of the world; and they have to put it away.

In his representation of the moral ruin of the heathen he described them as walking "in the vanity of their mind." By the "*mind*" he meant what we sometimes describe as the higher reason, a faculty which is at once speculative and practical. It apprehends the higher forms of truth and so determines the laws of life and conduct. In heathen men this regal faculty had been so impaired by the ascendancy of the lower elements of their nature that it mistook shadows for substances, earthly clouds for the everlasting hills of the kingdom of God. Those eternal things which are the ultimate foundation of the laws of human conduct were unknown; and until they are known it is impossible to achieve a high and perfect form of morality.

The "*spirit*," which is that element of our life which comes to us direct from God and by which we are akin to God, restores to the "*mind*" its soundness and health, the clearness of its vision, and its practical force and authority. In this high region of our nature Paul finds the springs of moral regeneration. It is by the discovery of the invisible kingdom of God that we learn the laws by which we are to be governed in the external and accidental relations of this transitory world. In sailing across the troubled ocean of life, with its changing winds and unknown currents, we steer by the stars. Strength as well as light comes to us from invisible and eternal things; from the immeasurable love of God, from the glory of His perfection, from the knowledge that He is our comrade in every conflict with sin, that He is troubled by our defeats and rejoices in our victories, from the hope of dwelling for ever in His eternal peace and righteousness and joy.

But if we are to be under the constant control of that spiritual universe by which we are environed, there must be a constant renewal of the spiritual life. It is not enough that, once for all, we have been born of God. Paul assumes that the Ephesian Christians were regenerate of the Holy Spirit. Regeneration must be followed by renewal. The Divine life given in the new birth must be fed from its eternal springs, or the stream will soon run shallow, will cease to flow, will at last disappear altogether. We must "*be renewed in the spirit of* [*our*] *mind.*"

The constant renewal of the spiritual life is the work of the Spirit of God; but we are not the merely passive subjects of His grace. It is our *duty* to "*be renewed.*" We are required to form the moral and spiritual habits which render possible, and which secure, the fresh access from day to day of Divine inspiration. There should be an habitual remembrance of the power and goodness of the Spirit, whose coming has more than compensated for the loss of the earthly ministry and visible presence of Christ. There should be habitual trust in Him as the Giver of light, of strength, of joy, and of righteousness. There should be habitual prayer for His teaching and His strong support. We should think much of God, and our thoughts of Him should be determined and controlled by the revelation of Himself in Christ, who is the "Truth" as well as the "Way" and the "Life." Relying on the illumination of the Divine Spirit, our thoughts should dwell constantly on the relations of human life to God and on the thoughts of God concerning human duty and destiny. We should "mind"—not "earthly things"— but things heavenly and Divine; for our citizenship is in heaven, our riches, our honour, our blessedness, our home are there. By such means as these we shall secure for the Divine life given in regeneration constant freshness and the vigour of immortal youth; from day to day we shall "*be renewed in the spirit of* [*our*] *mind.*"

For the completion of our moral regeneration a third process is necessary; we have to "*put on the new man, which after God hath been created in righteousness and holiness of truth.*"

In the incarnation of the Eternal Word in Christ, in Christ's life, death, and resurrection, there was not merely a development of pre-existent powers and capacities of humanity which had been latent, but a new creation. Human nature felt once more the touch of the Divine hand, and was raised to new heights of spiritual energy and perfection by the Divine life and power. Humanity was created afresh in Christ, created "*after God,*" in the image of the Divine perfection; and that image consists in "*righteousness and holiness of truth.*"

"*Righteousness*" is the conformity of conduct to those eternal laws which have their glorious illustration in the moral perfection of the Divine nature. It covers our relations both to man and God. It includes the discharge of all the claims of an ideal law.

"*Holiness*," according to the ordinary use of the word, emphasises the religious element in righteousness, and describes human perfection as based upon Divine laws. But in this place I think that we are to conceive of a perfection determined by something higher than any laws, whether human or Divine; a perfection formed and inspired by the immediate vision of God, and by participation in the life of God.

The "righteousness" is a righteousness "*of truth*," and the "holiness" a holiness "*of truth.*" Heathen men were under the control of false and misleading conceptions of human life, of man's present condition, and of his eternal destiny. They had lost the vision of real and eternal things, and lived among shadows. Their moral life was corrupted by "the lusts of deceit." The perfect humanity which God has created in Christ is raised above the region of shadows, and is in direct contact with the universe of Divine and eternal realities. Its righteousness does not consist in conformity to the laws of an imperfect, a transient morality, but in conformity to the eternal laws of the Divine kingdom; its holiness is not an external and technical sanctity, but the reflection of the holiness of God Himself. The new humanity created in Christ bears the image of God in "*righteousness and holiness of truth.*"

This humanity we are required to "*put on.*" And the moral process by which we "*put on the new man*" corresponds closely to the moral process by which we "put off the old man." As we cannot disengage ourselves from all the moral habits of our old life by a supreme act of will, neither can we by a supreme act of will appropriate and make our own the righteousness and holiness of the humanity of Christ. To "put off the old man" there must be persistent and painful effort; and persistent if not painful effort is necessary to "*put on the new man.*"

We are to "*put on*" Christ. We are to make our own every separate element of His righteousness and holiness. We are to make His humility ours, and His courage, His gentleness, and His invincible integrity; His abhorrence of sin, and His mercy for the penitent; His delight in the righteousness of others, and His patience for their infirmities; the quiet submission with which He endured His own sufferings, and His compassion for the sufferings of others; His indifference to ease and wealth and honour, and His passion for the salvation of men from all their sins and all their sorrows. We are to make His perfect faith in the Father ours, and His perfect loyalty to the Father's authority; His delight in doing the Father's will; His zeal for the Father's glory. The perfection at which we have to aim is not a mere dream of the imagination, but the perfection which human nature has actually reached in Christ.

It is sometimes alleged that our faith in the

Divinity of Christ destroys the value of His example, and that it is only those who believe that He was a man and nothing more, who can attempt, with any hope of success, to imitate His perfections. But it is precisely because Christ is Divine that I have the courage to make His life the law of mine. His character so far transcends all the common measures of human righteousness that if He were only a man I should regard Him with wonder and admiration, but with despair. I should suppose that He had a unique genius for moral and spiritual perfection. For me to attempt to imitate "Hamlet" or "Paradise Lost" would be insane presumption, for I have not the intellectual genius of Shakspere or Milton, and since Shakspere and Milton were men like myself they cannot make their genius mine. And if Christ were only a man He would be unable to inspire me with that genius for righteousness which alone would account for His transcendent perfection. But He is Divine. His human perfection was really human, but it was the translation into a human character and history of the life of God. He is living still. The fountains of my life are in Him. It is the eternal purpose of the Father that as the branch receives and reveals the life which is in the vine I should receive and reveal the life which is in Christ. When therefore I attempt to "put on" Christ, or to make my own the perfect humanity which God created in Him, I am not attempting to imitate a perfection which in its spirit and form may be alien from my own moral temperament and character, and which may be altogether beyond my strength; I am but developing a life and energy which God has already given to me. If I am in Christ the spiritual forces which were illustrated in the righteousness and holiness of Christ's life are already active in my own life.

But these forces are not mere instincts which act blindly and unintelligently; they require the control and direction of the reason illuminated by the Spirit of God. They do not render moral effort unnecessary; they make moral effort in its most energetic form possible, and they achieve their triumph by sustaining a vigorous and unceasing endeavour after moral and spiritual perfection.

Christ is the prophecy of our righteousness as well as the Sacrifice for our sins—the prophecy, not merely the example or the law, of our righteousness; for He came down from heaven to give the very life of God to man, and in the power of that life all righteousness is possible. The prophecy has been fulfilled in every generation since He ascended to the Father, and in every country in which the Christian Faith has been preached. It has been the custom of Christian apologists to vindicate the Divine origin of the revelations contained in our sacred books, by recalling the ruin which fell upon mighty empires that were menaced with the judgments of God. The fallen temples and palaces of Nineveh and Babylon, of Karnac and of Thebes, are declared to be the enduring demonstration of the Divine commission of the prophets of the ancient Faith. I prefer to appeal to the fulfilment of a prophecy of a more gracious and wonderful kind. The Lord Jesus Christ announced that He had come to give to the human race a new and diviner life, and strength to achieve a diviner righteousness. And we see that these great words have been accomplished. He has originated a new and nobler type of moral character and a new and nobler religious Faith. He Himself has been the root of the new ethical and spiritual life which has revealed its strength and its grace in Christian nations. His own unique perfection has been repeated, in humbler forms, in the lives of innumerable saints. The Vine has sent forth its branches into all lands, and men of every variety of civilization and of culture, of every variety of moral temperament and moral character, have illustrated the characteristic qualities of Christ's own righteousness. In Him a new humanity was created. He is the Head of a new race. We ourselves are conscious that through Him we have passed into the kingdom of God, are under the authority of its august and eternal laws, and that if our union with Him were more intimate we should have strength to achieve an ideal perfection.

XVIII.

MISCELLANEOUS MORAL PRECEPTS.

" Wherefore, putting away falsehood, speak ye truth each one with his neighbour: for we are members one of another. Be ye angry, and sin not: let not the sun go down upon your wrath: neither give place to the devil. Let him that stole steal no more: but rather let him labour, working with his hands the thing that is good, that he may have whereof to give to him that hath need. Let no corrupt speech proceed out of your mouth, but such as is good for edifying as the need may be, that it may give grace to them that hear. And grieve not the Holy Spirit of God, in whom ye were sealed unto the day of redemption. Let all bitterness, and wrath, and anger, and clamour, and railing, be put away from you, with all malice: and be ye kind one to another, tender-hearted, forgiving each other, even as God also in Christ forgave you. Be ye therefore imitators of God, as beloved children ; and walk in love, even as Christ also loved you, and gave Himself up for us, an offering and a sacrifice to God for an odour of a sweet smell. But fornication, and all uncleanness, or covetousness, let it not even be named among you, as becometh saints; nor filthiness, nor foolish talking, or jesting, which are not befitting : but rather giving of thanks. For this ye know of a surety, that no fornicator, nor unclean person, nor covetous man, which is an idolater, hath any inheritance in the kingdom of Christ and God. Let no man deceive you with empty words : for because of these things cometh the wrath of God upon the sons of disobedience. Be not ye therefore partakers with them ; for ye were once darkness, but are now light in the Lord: walk as children of light (for the fruit of the light is in all goodness and righteousness and truth), proving what is well-pleasing unto the Lord ; and have no fellowship with the unfruitful works of darkness, but rather even reprove them ; for the things which are done by them in secret it is a shame even to speak of. But all things when they are reproved are made manifest by the light: for everything that is made manifest is light. Wherefore he saith, Awake, thou that sleepest, and arise from the dead, and Christ shall shine upon thee. Look therefore *carefully how ye walk, not as unwise, but as wise; redeeming the time, because the days are evil. Wherefore be ye not foolish, but understand what the will of the Lord is. And be not drunken with wine, wherein is riot, but be filled with the Spirit; speaking one to another in psalms and hymns and spiritual songs, singing and making melody with your heart to the Lord; giving thanks always for all things in the name of our Lord Jesus Christ to God, even the Father; subjecting yourselves one to another in the fear of Christ."* EPH. iv. 25—v. 21.

WHILE reading these precepts we seem to have descended very far from the great words about the eternal purposes of God in relation to the perfection and glory of the human race, and the ultimate restoration of the whole universe to perfect unity in Christ, with which the Epistle begins. We have passed from heaven to earth, from the serene heights of eternity to the confusions of time, from the sanctity of the life of God to the foulness and darkness of the worst forms of human sin.

But unless we retain a vivid impression of the earlier chapters of the Epistle, with their great discoveries of the Divine ideal of the righteousness, the honour, and the blessedness of human nature, we shall fail to apprehend the loftiness of these moral precepts and we shall miss the force of the appeals by which they are sustained. For although these precepts are directed against very gross vices, Paul is inculcating no common morality, and the motives with which he endeavours to inspire and strengthen obedience are drawn from sources lying far beyond the limits of ordinary moral teaching.

The "*wherefore*" (ver. 25) with which the series of

precepts begins attaches them immediately to the words we were considering in the last lecture. The Ephesian Christians had "heard" Christ; they were "in Him," and what they had been taught was truth "as truth is in Jesus." They had learnt that they must renounce their old moral life and their old moral habits; that from day to day their higher life must be renewed by the power and grace of God; and that they must make their own that new and perfect humanity which was the image of God "in righteousness and holiness of truth." But this—which I called the Christian method of moral regeneration—implies all that Paul had said about the great thoughts of God concerning the human race. The general precept requiring those who had sunk into the grossest vices to make the moral perfection of Christ their own is only the practical application of the truths which Paul has illustrated in the earlier part of the Epistle. God "hath blessed us with every spiritual blessing in the heavenly places in Christ; even as He chose us in Him before the foundation of the world that we should be holy and without blemish before Him in love: having foreordained us unto adoption as sons through Jesus Christ unto Himself, according to the good pleasure of His will, according to the glory of His grace, which He freely bestowed on us in the Beloved." In Christ we were made God's "heritage," in Christ we were "sealed with the Holy Spirit of promise which is an earnest of our inheritance." "The exceeding greatness of [God's] power to usward who believe" is "according to that working of the strength of His might which He wrought in Christ when He raised Him from the dead and made Him to sit at His right hand in the heavenly places." It was this Divine power that quickened us when we were dead through our trespasses and sins, and raised us up with Christ, and "made us to sit with Him in the heavenly places, in Christ." "We are [God's] workmanship created in Christ Jesus for good works which God afore prepared that we should walk in them." We must believe all these great and wonderful things, or else we shall have no courage to accept the Lord Jesus Christ as the law of ou rrighteousness and to attempt to rise to the height of His perfection.

Paul began with God's great purpose that the life and power and glory of Christ should be ours. Since this is God's purpose, he has reminded the Ephesian Christians that they must "put on the new man which after God hath been created in righteousness and holiness of truth." And now, descending to the details of conduct, he says:—

"*Wherefore, putting away falsehood, speak ye truth each one with his neighbour: for we are members one of another.*" We are "in Christ," members of the body of Christ, and therefore "*members one of another.*" To be guilty of falsehood is for the eye to deceive the hand, or for the ear to deceive the foot. The ground on which Paul rests the duty of truthfulness shows that he was thinking of the intercourse of Christian people with each other. But if the Ephesian Christians were restrained from falsehood in their intercourse with each other by a vivid remembrance of the fact that they were "members one of another"—if this element of their religious faith became an effective law of conduct in the church—it would be as impossible for them to lie to heathen men as to lie to their Christian brethren. For if they were "members one of another" it was because they were all members of the body of Christ. They were the visible revelation to men of the invisible life of Christ. They were the organs of His will. He was working through their hands, speaking through their lips. They were under grave obligations to each other; they were under graver obligations to Him. For them to lie, whether to heathen man or to Christian, would be to offer violence to Him who was the very life of their life; it would be to implicate Christ, who is the Truth, in the shame and dishonour of falsehood.

"*Be ye angry and sin not.*" Anger in itself is not sinful. Christ, whose perfection is the root and law of ours, was sometimes angry. It would be sinful not to be kindled to indignation by baseness, treachery, cruelty, and hypocrisy. But anger must not be suffered to break out into violence. It must be kept within the control of conscience and of reason. It must not be poisoned by malignity, or degenerate into revenge. And the heat, the agitation, of it must be soon repressed.

Anger itself, a deep, serious, moral resentment

against a grave moral offence, may continue. There are cases in which it ought to continue. If I ought to regard an offence with moral indignation to-day, it is quite clear that I ought not to meet the man who has been guilty of it to-morrow, as though he were blameless. The moral resentment will remain unless he has repented of the wrong. But in the first moments of great anger there is wrath; we are excited; the blood is hot; we are exasperated. And while this lasts we are especially accessible to the temptation of those evil spirits of whose malignant power Paul has more to say later on in the Epistle.[1] He therefore says, "*Let not the sun go down upon your wrath, neither*—by letting the passionate agitation continue—*give place to the devil.*" We are the body of Christ, a holy temple, and should fortify ourselves against every approach of the spirit of wickedness.

There were men in the Ephesian church who had lived by theft, and Paul's words show that he thought that some of them might be thieving still.[2] He is not satisfied with charging them to give up stealing, and to earn their own living by honest labour. If they worked for themselves merely, this would not be to "put on" Christ, for the law of Christ's life was charity. He therefore says: "*Let him that stole*—and

---

[1] Chap. vi. 12 *seq.*

[2] Why did the Revisers retain, "Let him that *stole*"? Ὁ κλέπτων is a man that is stealing *now.* They might at least have translated, "Let the thief thieve no more."

is stealing now—*steal no more; but rather let him labour, working with his hands*—those hands with which he stole—*the thing that is good, that he may have to give to him that needeth.*"

The conversation of some of them was unfriendly to a healthy, vigorous, and generous morality, and to a pure and energetic religious life. It was like meat which had begun to go bad. It did men harm instead of good; it did not invigorate health but occasioned disease. It was a hindrance to the purifying and ennobling work of the Spirit of God, and it grieved Him. Conversation of this kind was to be given up; and they were to take advantage of all the accidental circumstances of life to say things that would contribute to the strength and development of Christian character. "*Let no corrupt speech proceed out of your mouth, but such as is good for edifying as the need may be, that it may give grace to them that hear. And grieve not the Holy Spirit of God, in whom ye were sealed unto the day of redemption.*" If He is grieved, the assurance of their final redemption will be lost.

The remembrance of God's great mercy to themselves was to make them gentle and loving to others. "*Let all bitterness, and wrath, and anger, and clamour, and railing, be put away from you, with all malice.*" This will be to "put away the old man." But to "put on the new man," which after God is created in righteousness and holiness of truth, there must be something more: "*be ye kind one to another, tender-hearted, forgiving each other, even as God also in Christ forgave you. Be ye therefore imitators of God, and walk in love, even as Christ also loved you, and gave Himself up for us, an offering and a sacrifice to God for an odour of a sweet smell."*

Paul then places "*covetousness*," avarice, a lust for wealth, in the same rank as offences which come from lusts of a fouler kind: "*But fornication, and all uncleanness, or covetousness, let it not even be named among you, as becometh saints.*" The vices are so gross that they ought to disappear, to disappear so completely that their very names shall go out of use.

"*Filthiness*"—impurity of act or speech, "*foolish talking*," and "*jesting*," are also to disappear, and to disappear as completely as covetousness and the grosser vices. They are "*not befitting*"; they do not harmonize with the character, the prerogatives, and the destiny of saints. "*Foolish talking*" is the talk of a fool, of a man that is insensible to the graver aspects of human life. The great discoveries of God and of eternity, of our own present relations to God and of our future glory, which have come to us through Christ, exert their power on the mind as well as on the heart and on outward conduct. They give a certain intellectual nobleness even to uncultivated and simple men. They inspire self respect and dignity. As the pride of the Roman people was justly offended when they saw an emperor descend into the arena with charioteers and gladiators, so the finer feeling of the Christian church is justly offended when Christian men indulge in buffoonery and play the fool. This is "*not befitting*." It should have no place among Christian people, and to find pleasure in such folly is also below the dignity of those who live near to the throne of God.

In condemning "*jesting*" Paul does not mean to insist that the conversation of Christian men should be always grave and serious. The mind needs rest as well as the body. There is a time to play as well as to work. Amusement has its legitimate place in the intellectual life; and if the mind is subjected to an incessant strain its strength will be broken down. The bright flashes of wit and the pleasant gleams of a kindly humour may be as beautiful and as harmless as the play of the sunlight among the trees or on the ripples of a mountain stream. The "*jesting*" which Paul describes as "not befitting" is the kind of conversation that reaches its perfection in a civilized, luxurious, and brilliant society which has no faith in God, no reverence for moral law, no sense of the grandeur of human life, no awe in the presence of the mystery of death. In such a society, to which the world is the scene of a pleasant comedy in which all men are actors, a polished insincerity and a versatility which is never arrested by strong and immovable convictions are the objects of universal admiration. The foulest indecencies are applauded, if they are conveyed under the thin disguise of a graceful phrase, a remote allusion, an ingenious ambiguity. There is a refinement to which, not vice itself, but the coarseness of vice is distasteful, and which regards with equal resentment the ruggedness of virtue. This is the kind of "*jesting*" that Paul so sternly condemns. It is destructive both of faith and of morality. The tongue was made for nobler uses. Instead of "foolish talking" and "jesting" there should be "*giving of thanks.*"

The apostle warns his readers that these sins, if not forsaken, will end in the loss of all their glorious hopes; and again he places covetousness among gross sensual sins. Indeed he singles it out for emphatic condemnation. The Ephesian Christians had come out of heathenism, and to them the service of false gods was the one sin which represented the dark and evil life from which they had been delivered by the power and grace of God. Between themselves and their idolatrous fellow citizens they thought that there was an infinite distance. But Paul tells them that "the *covetous man*" is "*an idolater*" still; he is unredeemed from his old heathen life, and has no place in the Divine kingdom. "*For this ye know of a surety, that no fornicator, nor unclean person, nor covetous man which is an idolater, hath any inheritance in the kingdom of Christ and of God. Let no man deceive you with empty words, for because of these things cometh the wrath of God upon the sons of disobedience.*"

He charges them not to share the sins of those who are menaced with the Divine wrath; for if they share the sins they will share the doom. "*Be not ye therefore partakers with them. For ye were once darkness*—as they are still—*but are now light in the Lord: walk as children of light (for the fruit of the light is in all goodness and righteousness and truth) proving what is well pleasing to the Lord,*" learning by actual obedience to the precepts and Spirit of Christ what kind of a life Christ delights in.

Nor will it be enough if they themselves renounce heathen vices, and illustrate in their own character the "goodness and righteousness and truth" which are "the fruit of the light." The light which has transfigured their own life is to reach and transfigure the life of others. "*Have no fellowship with the unfruitful works of darkness*—works which yield no honour or blessing—*but rather even reprove them.*" There is an awful need for this reproof, for the secret vices of the heathen are so horrible that a pure minded man shrinks from naming them, "*for the things which are done by them in secret it is a shame even to speak of.*"

But to the men that commit these vices it is necessary to speak of them, though we may refuse to speak of them to others. If they are to be convicted of their guilt and brought to penitence, the enormity of their offences must be made plain and brought home to them; "*all things when they are reproved are made manifest by the light.*" And if they really discover the true character of their sin, if the light reaches them, they will cease to sin. Darkness when it is shone upon is darkness no longer; "*for everything that is made manifest is light.*"

And, quoting very freely the words of the prophet Isaiah (chap. lx., ver. 1), Paul reminds the Ephesian Christians that Christ Himself came to give us light. "*Wherefore he saith, Awake, thou that sleepest, and arise from the dead, and Christ shall shine upon thee.*" In carrying the light of God into the secrecy and darkness which concealed the grossest vices of heathenism, they would be doing the very work of their Lord.

Paul now returns to the laws which should regulate the conduct of the Ephesian Christians themselves. In ver. 8, 9, he had charged them to "walk as children of light, . . . proving what is well pleasing to the Lord." He now says that if they are to do this they must closely and accurately consider their moral habits, and must know how they are living. There must be active thought, not merely about speculative questions, but about conduct, and about their own conduct. Whatever other knowledge might be beyond their reach, they must not miss the knowledge of themselves and of their own moral life. In this lies the difference between wisdom and want of wisdom. "*Look therefore carefully how ye walk; not as unwise but as wise.*" With this vigilance directed to conduct there should be alertness of mind to recognise, in the constant flux and vicissitude of human affairs, varying opportunities for doing the will of God; and as these opportunities occurred they were to use them at whatever cost. They were to "*redeem the time.*"

There was the greater need for this alertness, and for this resoluteness to let slip no chance of doing God's will, because the moral corruption which surrounded them was unfriendly to Christian righteousness. This increased their obligation to live righteously: for by their righteousness they were to offer a continual protest on behalf of the Divine authority which other men had forgotten. They were to "[redeem] *the time because the days* [were] *evil.*" And again he insists on the duty of cultivating practical Christian wisdom: "*Wherefore be ye not foolish, but understand what the will of the Lord is.*"

Paul closes this series of miscellaneous moral precepts by a precept against drunkenness. This precept follows very naturally what he has said about the necessity of wisdom. For even a wise man when he is drunk becomes a fool; the light of reason and of conscience is quenched, and the blind impulses of his physical nature are left without control. Some men take drink in excess to deaden their sensibility to trouble, to lessen the pain of distressing memories or distressing fears. With them it acts as an opiate. But Paul was thinking of those who drink to excess because intoxication, at least in its early stages, gives them excitement. It exalts the activity both of their intellect and of their emotion. Thought becomes more vivid and more rapid. The colours of imagination become more brilliant. Their whole physical nature becomes more animated. The river of life, which had sunk low and had been moving sluggishly, suddenly rises, becomes a rushing flood, and overflows its banks. This is the kind of drinking which betrays men into violence and profligacy. "*Be not drunken with wine,*" for in drunkenness there is "*riot,*" dissoluteness, release from all moral restraint.

The craving for a fuller, richer life, for hours in which we rise above ourselves, and pass the normal and customary limitations of our powers, is a natural craving. Paul indicates how it should be satisfied: "Be not drunken with wine, wherein is riot, *but be filled with the Spirit.*" Forsake the sins which render it impossible for the pure and righteous Spirit of God to grant you the fulness of His inspiration; keep the channels open through which the streams that flow from Divine and eternal fountains may find their way into your nature; and then the dull monotony of life will be broken, and hours of generous excitement will come. The grey clouds will break, and the splendours of heaven will be revealed; the common earth will be filled for a little time with a great glory. Harmonies such as never fell on mortal ear will reach the soul. The limitations which are imposed upon us in this mortal condition will for a time seem to disappear. Your vision of eternal things will have a preternatural keenness. Your joy in God will be an anticipation of the blessed life beyond the grave. And, looking back upon these perfect hours, you will say, whether we were in the body or out of the body we cannot tell.

But some men drink, not so much for the sake of personal excitement, as for the sake of good fellowship. They never drink much when they are alone; and when they are in company they drink to excess because, as the heat of intoxication increases, it seems to thaw and dissolve all reserve; conversation flows more freely, and becomes more frank; mind touches mind more closely; lives which had been isolated from each other blend and flow in a common channel.

Perpetual isolation is as intolerable as perpetual monotony. We were not made to live a separate and lonely life. This is the secret of our delight in listening to a great orator addressing a great assembly. If it were possible for him to touch the same heights of eloquence when speaking to us alone we should be less moved. We like to lose our individuality in the crowd; sharing their thought, our own thought becomes more vivid; sharing their passions, our own passion becomes more intense. It is hard to explain the mystery; but we are conscious of it; the poor and narrow stream of our own life flows into the open sea, and the large horizon, and the free winds, and the mighty tides become ours. We have all known the same delight while listening in a crowd to a great singer or a great chorus. The craving for this larger life in the society of other men is as natural as the craving for excitement; and Paul tells the Ephesian Christians that instead of trying to satisfy it by drinking with other men they should satisfy it by common worship and by sacred song.

Z

The church was to have its festivals as well as its days of sorrowful humiliation and agonising prayer. They were to "*speak to one another in psalms and hymns,*" and in "*songs*" which came to them from the inspiration of the Spirit of God. The genius of the poet and of the singer was to be consecrated to the service of the church, as well as the genius of the orator.

Their singing was not always to be worship addressed to God; they were to sing to each other as well as to Him. As the preacher speaks to the church, so those who have the gift of song are to sing to the church: to sing pathetic songs about the Divine pity, to soothe sorrow; triumphant songs about the love of God, to fill the heart with joy; songs about God's power, to give new energy to courage; songs about the glory of heaven, to transfigure hope into rapture; songs about the infinite grace of Christ and His death for our salvation, to flood the soul with a passion of affection.

There is another kind of singing in which those who have not the rare and beautiful gift of song may take part; while they are silent they may be "singing and making *melody with* [their] *heart to the Lord.*"

Thirdly, the life of every member of the church is to flow into one great stream of thanksgiving to God for all His goodness and grace. Whether in prayer or in hymn, we are to celebrate His infinite love and to bless Him for the blessings which He has bestowed upon us all, "*giving thanks always for all things in the name of our Lord Jesus Christ to God, even the Father."*

For the full joy of the festival, for the perfection of this union with each other, there must be the suppression of self assertion, there must be the oblivion of personal interests and personal claims; we must lose our own life in the larger life of the church, our brethren must be more to us than ourselves—"*subjecting [ourselves] one to another in the fear of Christ.*"

The festivals of the church with their worship and sacred song are to give a noble satisfaction to that craving for a common life which men endeavour to satisfy in a base and ignoble form by drunkenness and riot.

In reviewing these precepts I think that our first impression must be one of surprise at the lofty forms of virtue which Paul requires from men who had sunk into the grossest vices. In precept after precept he illustrates the great principle with which he began. He charges them not only to put away the vices of a most corrupt heathenism but to put on the very perfections of Christ. The transition is to be from the deepest moral debasement to the very highest levels of righteousness. The existence or the possibility of any intermediate form of morality is not recognised.

They are to put away lying; but it is not enough that they should cease to be guilty of deliberately and intentionally conveying a false impression, they are to take great care that the impression their words convey is exact and true. Their truthfulness is to be the truthfulness of the eye and the ear to the hand and the foot. Men are members one of another. What I know, I know, not for my own sake but for the sake of other men, just as the eye sees or the ear hears, not for itself but for the whole body. The obligations of charity re-enforce the authority of truthfulness. We are not to think of our own honour or our own interest in what we say, but simply of the interest of our neighbour; and so neither vanity nor selfishness will be permitted to impair our precise accuracy. This will secure not only truthfulness but candour. A keen observer of human life has described a man as having "an innate love of reticence . . . a talent for it, which acted as other impulses do, without any conscious motive."[1] There are people who may not injure others by saying what is false, but who may inflict injury almost as grave by not saying anything. The same great consideration to which Paul appealed in order to discipline the Ephesians to truthfulness would discipline them to the highest form of that virtue, would not only deliver them from habits of falsehood but make them candid and frank. The eye conceals nothing which it sees, and which it is the interest of the body to know.

The man who is guilty of theft is of course to cease thieving. But this is not enough. There may be

---

[1] Description of Tito, in "Romola."

honesty with the most intense selfishness. Paul transfigures labour, and requires those who were stealing, to work that they may be able to give.

It is not enough that men whose conversation has been morally and religiously pernicious should avoid "corrupt" speech; their words are to build up the religious life and strength of other men, and are to be channels of Divine grace. Men who have been guilty of bitterness and malice against those who have wronged them, who have clamoured against them and railed against them, are to imitate the very mercy of God, to "*be kind to one another, tender hearted, forgiving each other, even as God also in Christ forgave*" [them]. Their lives are to be inspired with the love and gentleness of Christ. Instead of foolish talking and cynical heartless insincerity, there is to be the "giving of thanks." Those who were guilty of sensual sins were not only to forsake these sins but were to rescue other men from them, were to have that Divine purity which would enable them to reprove deeds which "it is a shame even to speak of," were to shine, as the light of God, on those who were committing the darkest and foulest vices, and so to change sinners into saints. Drunkards are not only to become sober but to be filled with the Holy Ghost, and from the lips which had sung wild and coarse songs of riotous excess are to come psalms and hymns and songs inspired by the Spirit of God.

Christian faith and Christian morals are inseparable.

The most wonderful mysteries of the Christian revelation have a direct relation to conduct. When the apostle charges the Ephesian Christians to "put away as concerning [their] former manner of life the old man which waxeth corrupt after the lusts of deceit . . . to be renewed in the spirit of [their] mind, and to put on the new man which after God hath been created in righteousness and holiness of truth," it is plain that he assumes that they knew and believed what he had said to them about their having been elected in Christ before the foundation of the world, about their having risen with Him in His resurrection to a new and Divine life, about their being God's workmanship created in Christ Jesus for good works. And the particular precepts which we have been considering in this lecture are sustained by sanctions and motives derived from the invisible and spiritual universe.

It is interesting and instructive to notice that these sanctions and motives are derived from the most gentle and gracious as well as from the most terrible aspects of the Christian revelation, and that truths which are regarded by some as belonging to the region of the most unpractical mysticism are invoked as a protection from coarse vices and a support to common virtues. To restrain and repress the malignant passions, and to encourage kindness and tenderness of heart, Paul reminds the Christians at Ephesus of the infinite mercy of God who had forgiven their sins, of the perfect love of Christ, and of His sacrifice for human redemption. To check their "corrupt speech" he warns them that it will "grieve . . . the Holy Spirit of God in whom [they] were sealed unto the day of redemption." To enforce the obligations of truthfulness he tells them that as they were members of the body of Christ they were "members one of another." To strengthen his precept against drunkenness he reminds them that it is possible for them to be filled with the Holy Ghost. To quench the flames of a sudden and violent anger a sharper and more peremptory motive was necessary, a motive that would act in a moment; and he therefore warns them that if they do not control and suppress their wrath they will "give place to the devil." Those who are guilty of the grosser sins which debase the whole moral nature and harden the conscience and make men insensible to motives which appeal to the loftier and more generous elements of the moral life have to be dealt with more sternly. Covetousness and sensual sins require to be cowed with terror. They will not yield to any nobler force. They are the vices of a slavish nature, and those who are guilty of them must be lashed by the Furies. They are told that unless these vices are forsaken they can have no "inheritance in the kingdom of Christ and of God . . . for because of these things cometh the wrath of God upon the sons of disobedience."

It may be objected that this exclusive appeal to religious motives to enforce moral duties is inadequate and even illegitimate; that, as I have myself said elsewhere, "for the education of the conscience we need moral teaching that is really moral, and not religious; teaching that appeals to the natural conscience by natural means; that trains the mind to recognise for itself the righteousness of right actions, right habits, and right dispositions; that insists on the obligation to do right because it is right, without appealing to the Divine authority and to the penalties and rewards of sin and righteousness."[1] "Corrupt speech" ought to be regarded with loathing, and we ought to recoil from it without remembering that it will grieve the Holy Spirit of God. Lying in itself ought to be regarded with stern moral condemnation; and in order to be loyal to truth it ought not to be necessary for us to remember that we are members of the body of Christ and therefore members one of another. And we should be restrained from gross sensual sins by our love of purity, not merely by dread of the wrath of God.

The principle on which this objection rests is sound, and deserves far more consideration in the Christian church than I fear it has received. But as an objection to Paul's method in this Epistle it cannot be sustained.

In the education of those whose moral life is not

---

[1] "The Evangelical Revival, and other Sermons." (Hodder and Stoughton.) Page 53.

already corrupt, and whose conscience is not already hardened, there should be a careful cultivation of "a genuine love of righteousness for its own sake, a deep hatred of wrong doing, a sense of the repulsiveness of moral evil and of the infinite loveliness of goodness, a dread of the moral shame and of the moral humiliation which must come from a neglect of duty, a strong passion for the honour of victory over temptation." The natural conscience should be "educated to see for itself the infinite and eternal gulf between right and wrong, and educated to see for itself the moral motives for right doing. The moral affections to which righteousness appeals should be trained to energetic activity."[1] Paul himself in writing to the Christians at Philippi followed this very course. Without enforcing the precept with any religious sanction he said to them: "Whatsoever things are true, whatsoever things are honourable, whatsoever things are just, whatsoever things are pure, whatsoever things are lovely, whatsoever things are of good report; if there be any virtue, and if there be any praise, think on these things."[2] But the fine moral discernment and the delicate moral sensitiveness to which words like these appeal had no existence among those Ephesian Christians for whom the precepts we have been considering were necessary. Paul had to speak to them in quite another tone.

---

[1] "Evangelical Revival," p. 54.   [2] Phil. iv. 8.

The vision of conscience becomes clear and its authority firm by the practice of virtue. But these men had been under no moral restraints. They had lived in vice, and did not recognise the wickedness and shamefulness of their evil life. But they had religious faith, and in their religious faith was the only security for their moral regeneration. If Paul could restrain them from gross sensual sins by menacing them with the Divine wrath, they would gradually come to regard these sins with loathing. Fear in itself has no moral quality; but it may shelter the soul from the access of those vices which make the growth of the moral life impossible. If Paul could restrain them from "corrupt speech" by the menace that it would "grieve the Holy Spirit of God," they would gradually come to regard "corrupt speech" with disgust. Some of the religious motives to which he appeals had a direct tendency to develop ethical perfection. The remembrance of the Divine mercy to ourselves softens the severity of revenge, sweetens the spirit of bitterness, and makes us merciful and kind to other men. And while these religious sanctions were of a kind to rescue from vice men in whom the nobler elements of the moral life had suffered appalling degradation, they also, as I have already shown, suggest an ideal of moral perfection fairer and diviner than the natural conscience ever discovers when not invigorated and exalted by religious faith.

About a hundred years after this Epistle was written the fortunes of the Roman empire were under the control of a man who represents the loftiest morality of paganism. In Marcus Aurelius the severe virtues of stoicism were softened with a humility, a gentleness, and a sadness which gave to them an ineffable beauty and charm. Those who held the highest offices in the state shared his noble and generous philosophy. The whole power of the Roman world was in the hands of men who professed a doctrine which required a very lofty moral perfection. Some of them at least—and among these the emperor was conspicuous—were zealous and patient in practising the precepts which they gave to other men. There had been for many years a movement for the reformation of manners and the elevation of the moral life of the empire. Under Marcus Aurelius the movement culminated. The emperor himself, before leaving for his great campaign in central Europe, delivered a succession of public addresses on morals to the Roman people.

But stoicism, with all the resources of the civilized world on its side—wealth, learning, genius, eloquence, supreme political power — was a failure. Christianity, with all the resources both of the civilized and the uncivilized world against it, won great and enduring triumphs, created a new epoch in the history of the human race. M. Renan, in contrasting these two movements, has touched the critical difference between them. Christianity attempted the reformation of morals by an appeal to the supernatural.[1]

And whenever the supernatural in the Christian revelation is suppressed or concealed, whenever it does not hold the chief place, the moral power of Christianity is broken. The earth is kept in her orbit by the attraction of the sun which rules her from heaven; and man is rescued from vice and disciplined to virtue by the righteousness and love of God. The laws of human duty come from those eternal and Divine things by which human life is environed; and the life and vigour for the noblest forms of human perfection come from Divine and eternal fountains. Human nature can never bear the image of the Divine righteousness until it is penetrated, inspired, and transfigured by the Divine Spirit. Christian faith is the root of Christian morality.

---

[1] *Marc.-Aurèle.* Preface, page 1.

XIX.

WIVES AND HUSBANDS.

"*Wives, be in subjection unto your own husbands, as unto the Lord. For the husband is the head of the wife, as Christ also is the head of the church, being himself the saviour of the body. But as the church is subject to Christ, so let the wives also be to their husbands in everything. Husbands, love your wives, even as Christ also loved the church, and gave Himself up for it; that He might sanctify it, having cleansed it by the washing of water with the word, that He might present the church to Himself a glorious church, not having spot or wrinkle or any such thing; but that it should be holy and without blemish. Even so ought husbands also to love their own wives as their own bodies. He that loveth his own wife loveth himself: for no man ever hated his own flesh; but nourisheth and cherisheth it, even as Christ also the church; because we are members of His body. For this cause shall a man leave his father and mother, and shall cleave to his wife; and the twain shall become one flesh. This mystery is great: but I speak in regard of Christ and of the church. Nevertheless do ye also severally love each one his own wife even as himself; and let the wife see that she fear her husband.*" EPH. v. 22–33.

A LARGE part of this Epistle is occupied with the duties which arise from membership of the Christian church, that Divine society which is the visible revelation of the invisible kingdom of God. The true Christian life is not an isolated life. To live always alone, among Divine and eternal things, is a false ideal of moral and religious perfection; and the attempt to reach this ideal impoverishes the development of righteousness and narrows the Divine commandment which is "exceeding broad." We belong to the city of God and are "fellow-citizens with the saints"; the noble duties of citizenship rest upon us. We have to discharge offices of affection and of service to those who have been received with ourselves into the Divine "household." We are "members of the body of Christ."

To Paul the Divine kingdom was more real as well as more enduring than the empire. He has been illustrating the duties which those who belong to it owe to each other, and has also shown how its laws are to purify and elevate individual morals. And now he passes to those institutions which existed before the Christian church was founded, and which, as they belonged to the Divine order of human life, it was no part of the object of the Christian church to suppress. Marriage, the family, the organisation of industry, are necessary not only to the physical existence of the race, but to the development of those social affections and the exercise of those social virtues which constitute a large part of human morality. In this Epistle Paul says nothing about the State; but elsewhere he recognises it as a Divine institution for the repression of violence and wrong; "the powers that be are ordained of God."[1]

He does not approach the consideration of any of these institutions as a Christian politician, or as a Christian jurist, or as a Christian social reformer. In

---

[1] Rom. xiii. 1.

Paul's time the church was not strong enough to reconstruct the framework of human life and to bring it into harmony with the eternal laws of righteousness and with the genius of the Christian Faith. As yet society was pagan, and a pagan society must have pagan institutions. The political, social and domestic organisation of a people can never be far in advance of their morality. As the Christian Faith extended its authority over individuals it gradually modified customs, laws, and institutions. Its influence was felt first in the family, which lies nearest to the life of the individual. It then began to act on the organisation of society; alleviating the severities of slavery and ultimately abolishing it; providing for the relief of human misery, by establishing homes for fatherless and motherless children, hospitals for the sick, retreats for the aged and the destitute, refuges for strangers. Charity to the poor was honoured as the most acceptable form of service that could be rendered to God. The laws of the empire, which had already lost something of their ancient rigour and austerity under the influence of a lofty and generous philosophy, were still further softened under the influence of the new Faith. They became more equitable and more humane. Personal rights were surrounded with new guarantees; the control of the state over individual life became less exorbitant, and the area of personal freedom was enlarged.

But the time for these changes had not yet come.

Paul accepted the institutions of society as they stood, and endeavoured to teach the Ephesian Christians how they were to inspire the existing forms of social organisation with a new and diviner life.

He begins with marriage. He has just said that we are all to subject ourselves "one to another in the fear of Christ"; a fear which has no terror in it but which restrains waywardness and subdues a hard and rugged nature to gentleness and courtesy. And the general law which should govern the conduct of all Christian people to each other in the church is declared to be the law which should govern the conduct of wives to their husbands in the family.

Miss Cobbe in her excellent lectures on the duties of women has an interesting discussion on the vow to "obey" which is required from the wife in the marriage service of the Church of England; she says that "some people tell us that it is incumbent on a woman to take and keep this vow, because she is exhorted by St. Paul to 'obey her husband in the Lord.'" Miss Cobbe objects to the vow; and as to Paul's authority she says that she is "too far outside the pale of orthodoxy to consider a moral problem to be solvable by a text";[1] but she reminds those who quote this passage to enforce the obedience of wives, that Paul also commands slaves to obey their masters; and she argues that if the apostle's authority

---

[1] "The Duties of Women." By Frances Power Cobbe. (Williams and Norgate: 1881.) Page 102.

cannot be quoted now to sustain the authority of masters over slaves it cannot be quoted to sustain the authority of husbands over wives.

About the direction which the apostle gives to slaves to obey their masters I shall have something to say in a future lecture. Meanwhile I can suggest to Miss Cobbe a far more satisfactory way of disposing of the direction which the apostle is supposed to have given to wives. He never said that they were to "obey."

It is quite true that there are passages in Paul's Epistles in which he recognises and does not condemn the social inferiority assigned to women by Greek civilization. It is equally true that he does not recommend women to break out into revolt against the injustice from which they suffered, but to think more of their duties than of their rights. It has been by reminding mankind of their duties rather than of their rights that the Christian Faith has gradually undermined some of the most iniquitous institutions and customs of ancient heathenism. But there was a delicacy and refinement of sentiment in Paul, and, notwithstanding the passages to which I have referred, there was a certain chivalrous feeling in him towards women, which prevented him from saying that a woman was to "obey her husband." He had discovered a mystery and a sacredness in marriage which prevented him from saying it. The relations between husband and wife seemed to him to be of a kind not to be represented by bare authority on the one side and mere obedience on the other.

He has said that all Christian people are to subject themselves one to another in the fear of Christ; and without changing the word, indeed without repeating it, he goes on to say that this precept should govern the conduct of wives to husbands.[1] To slaves he said "obey," "be obedient"; to wives he used a word which he had just employed to describe the conduct which we owe not merely to those who have a right to command, but to our equals in the church.

The precept forbids a spirit of self assertion and an anxious struggle for personal rights. It requires the exercise of that charity which "vaunteth not itself, is not puffed up, doth not behave itself unseemly, seeketh not its own, is not provoked, taketh not account of evil, . . . beareth all things, believeth all things, hopeth all things, endureth all things."[2]

Wives are to "*be in subjection unto* [their] *own*

---

[1] In Titus ii. 5 the Authorised Version reads that wives are to "be obedient to their own husbands," but the Revisers have rightly given the more gracious word "being in subjection to their own husbands." No doubt the word which Paul uses to describe the duty of wives might also be applied, and was actually applied by himself (Tit. ii. 9), to describe the duties of slaves; but it also admitted of the less severe use, and could be employed to enforce the spirit of courtesy and self suppression which we owe to our equals.

[2] 1 Cor. xiii. 4-7.

husbands[1] *as unto the Lord*"; they are to show their reverence for Christ by obeying this law; even when they may think that their husbands have forfeited all claims to their "subjection" they are to remember that Christ's claims are unimpaired. Just as servants are required to make their work for their earthly masters part of their service to Christ, so wives are to regard their "subjection" to their husbands as part of their subjection to Christ; to refuse this subjection is to revolt against Christ Himself.

And now Paul platonizes. To him all the duties of this transitory life rest upon eternal laws, earthly institutions are the shadows and symbols of heavenly things, and the constitution of the visible world is the revelation of an invisible and Divine order. Marriage is not the creation of an arbitrary law. It has its roots in the eternal and ideal relations between the Son of God and the human race, relations which are actually realized in the church. "*For the husband is the head of the wife, as Christ also is the Head of the church.*" The human institution indeed is an imperfect representation of the Divine mystery on which it is based. For Christ is not only the Head of the church, He is "*Himself the Saviour of the body*," and there is nothing analogous to this relationship in the relationship between the husband and the wife.

---

[1] "*Your own husbands:* those specially yours, whom feeling therefore as well as duty must prompt you to obey."—*Ellicott, in loc.* But Paul did not say "obey."

"*But*," Paul goes on to say, although there is this great difference, "*as the church is subject to Christ, so let the wives also be to their husbands in everything.*"

Marriage is transfigured. In the light which Paul throws upon the institution, everything that is base and servile in the "subjection" on which he is insisting passes away. The "subjection" is a subjection to Christ. It is the "subjection" of the church of Christ to its Head. It is a "subjection" which is unconscious of the demands of external law, because in the energy of a perfect love all the demands of law are exceeded. It is a "subjection" to which service is freedom and to which the refusal of the opportunities of service would be intolerable slavery, a forcible repression of all the most vigorous and most spontaneous impulses of the heart.

Upon husbands Paul imposes a greater obligation than upon wives. "*Husbands, love your wives, even as Christ also loved the church and gave Himself for it*"; the love is to be large, free, faithful, patient, and generous, like the love of Christ for those whom He has redeemed; and like the love of Christ it is to be ready to accept the last extremities of self sacrifice. The devotion of "subjection" which Paul requires from wives is a devotion corresponding to that of the church to Christ; the devotion of love which he requires from husbands is a devotion corresponding to that of Christ to the church, a devotion which did not shrink from the shame and sharp agonies of the cross.

In the presence of a devotion like this a wife will have no occasion to think of personal rights; she will receive more than she could claim. And even if the devotion is imperfect she will be content to receive less from love than she might demand from law; and she will wait for love to grow stronger. When there is an attempt on either side to define the duties of marriage in terms of justice instead of discharging them under the inspiration of affection, when the husband begins to fix the limits of the self sacrifice which the wife has a right to demand, when the wife begins to fix the limits of the subjection which the husband has a right to enforce, the institution has lost its ideal glory, it has fallen from its true place among the stars of heaven, and is already soiled with earthly dust. In a true and perfect marriage both husband and wife are "not under law but under grace."

Paul then describes the purpose for which Christ "gave Himself up" for the church; He "*gave Himself up, . . . that He might sanctify it, having cleansed it by the washing of water with the word, that He might present the church to Himself a glorious church, not having spot or wrinkle or any such thing, but that it should be holy and without blemish.*"

There are three distinct movements in Paul's account of the purpose for which Christ died. In the order of time baptism comes first. "He gave Himself up for [the church] that He might sanctify it, *having cleansed it by the washing of water with the word.*" Baptism is the visible symbol and assurance of our separation from this present evil world, from the sin and guilt of the race. It is a glorious gospel expressed in an impressive rite. It declares that we do not belong merely to the visible and temporal order, but to that Divine kingdom of which Christ is the Founder and King. Baptism is associated with the "*word*," which explains the symbol and expresses its meaning. But when "the word" has thrown light on the symbol and revealed what it stands for, there are some to whom the symbol itself is richer in meaning, more pathetic, more forcible, than "the *word*" which has illustrated it. Indeed a Divine "*Word*" is found in the symbol, and it is this which distinguishes the two sacraments of the Christian Faith from all ritual observances invented by the church itself and from all acts of worship. The sacraments are not divinely appointed forms for the expression of our faith in God or our love for Him; they are the expression of a Divine thought, they are the visible symbols of Divine acts. To add to their number is therefore impossible.

In early times, before baptism had been degraded into an incantation and a spell, it was natural and safe to speak of it as cleansing men from sin and regenerating them; for all Christian men knew that the rite was only the symbol of that Divine power which really cleanses and regenerates. They knew that all baptized persons were not regenerated and cleansed. The "word" of God, when spoken, may be spoken without producing any beneficent moral and spiritual results; and the "word" of God when associated with a sacramental act, when expressed by means of it, may be equally ineffective.

Baptism when administered to a child is a declaration that the sacrifice of the Lord Jesus Christ has atoned for its future sins, that apart from its own choice the child belongs to Him, and that by the purpose and will of God the child is blessed with all spiritual blessings in Christ Jesus. Baptism does not make these great things true; it declares that they are true; they are as true before baptism as afterwards. But the child in subsequent years may be disloyal to the Prince who has claimed it as His subject. It is not an alien from the Divine commonwealth, but it may be guilty of revolt and incur forfeiture of the wealth and grace conferred upon it in Christ, exile from the kingdom of life and light, and so may suffer eternal destruction. Baptism when administered to an adult, after a profession of personal faith, is a visible assurance of the same great blessings that it assures to a child. It does not confer on him the blessings of the Christian redemption, but declares that they are his.[1] If his faith is genuine he will receive the declaration with immeasurable joy. He will look back upon the day of his baptism as kings look back upon the day of their coronation. He will speak of the hour when he was

---

[1] Cornelius and his friends received the Holy Ghost before baptism.

cleansed "by the washing of water with the word." But kings are not made kings by being crowned; they are crowned because they are already kings; their coronation is only the assurance that the power and the greatness of sovereignty are theirs;[1] and it is not by baptism that we are made Christ's inheritance; it is because we are Christ's inheritance that we are baptized.

In the order of time, sanctification follows baptism. "Christ gave Himself up for [the church]; that *He might sanctify it*, having cleansed it by the washing of water with the word." Christ died that in His death human sin might die, and that He might give us perfect righteousness, purity and holiness.

And the ultimate end of His death was that He might receive us to the eternal blessedness and glory of His heavenly kingdom; "*that He might present the church to Himself a glorious church, not having spot or wrinkle or any such thing; but that it should be holy and without blemish.*"

This account of the ends for which Christ died

---

[1] The rite receives a great accession of interest when it is administered to infants, since they can have made no appeal to the Divine grace. The great facts that the sin of the world has been atoned for apart from our choice and irrespective of our penitence; that Christ is the King of men, not by their own consent but by Divine appointment; that the infinite blessings of the Christian redemption have their origin in God's eternal purpose and grace, not in our righteousness or faith; are then most emphatically and impressively asserted.

is usually treated as though it were a digression in which Paul had lost sight of his immediate practical purpose; but it really adds great force to the precept on which he is insisting, and it replies by anticipation to the reasons which might be urged for denying the obligation to obey it. For as wives might plead that it was unreasonable and unjust to require them to "be in subjection" to husbands who were rough, coarse, selfish and tyrannical, so husbands might plead that it was unreasonable and unjust to require them to love with a perfect and self sacrificing love wives who had grave faults which made them unlovable. With that exquisite delicacy which is so often illustrated in Paul's writings, he says nothing to wives about the possible faults of their husbands; that is a topic on which wives should rarely if ever consent to be spoken to; but by charging them to be in subjection to their husbands "*as unto the Lord*" he reminds them that in an ideal Christian marriage the measure of the wife's subjection is to be determined by the infinite claims of Christ on her devotion, and that these claims are not lessened by the husband's imperfections. And with an equally exquisite delicacy he says nothing to husbands about the possible faults of their wives; that is a topic about which a high-minded husband will rarely, if ever, permit a stranger to speak to him; to listen to the remotest allusion to it is to be guilty of a certain disloyalty. But, in describing the objects for which Christ gave Himself up for the church, Paul reminds husbands that it was not because the church was free from fault, was free from even gross sins, that Christ loved it so well; He saw its sins, they troubled Him, and yet He loved it. He died for the church, not because its perfection had inspired Him with an immeasurable love for it, and because He was willing to endure any suffering to avert from it undeserved calamity; but because His love for it was so strong that He did not recoil from any shame or anguish to deliver it from its sins and from the sorrows which were the just consequences of its sins. "*Even so ought husbands also to love their own wives*"; the imperfections of wives do not release husbands from the duty of loving them, but may develop the strength of love and give occasion for the noblest acts of self sacrificing devotion.

And now Paul gives another reason for this love. He has said that husbands ought to love their own wives even as Christ loved the church, and he adds that they ought to love their wives "*as their own bodies. He that loveth his own wife loveth himself: for no man ever hated his own flesh; but nourisheth and cherisheth it, even as Christ also the church; because we are members of His body.*" He quotes some remarkable words from the second chapter of Genesis to show that according to the Divine ideal of marriage the life of the husband and the life of the wife should be blended into a perfect unity;

and that a man must relax or dissolve whatever ties, and qualify or renounce whatever interests, prevent this ideal from being realized. Even the ties of blood and the nearest natural relationships must give place to this supreme and unique claim: "*For this cause shall a man leave his father and mother, and shall cleave to his wife, and the twain shall become one flesh.*" There is something wonderful in this ideal of the human relationship; and to Paul, with his strong and passionate imagination, with his ardent affections, and with his power of sympathy which made the sorrows and joys of strangers his own, this perfect blending of the currents of two separate lives into one channel, this enlargement of the personality of each by its inclusion of the personality of the other, must have seemed all the more wonderful because he had elected to live a solitary life.

But to him the human relationship was the symbol of something more wonderful still; and while the words of the quotation from Genesis are on his lips and he is dictating them to the friend who is writing the epistle for him, I think I see a look of dreamy abstraction come over his face, showing that his thoughts have passed from earthly to heavenly things. He is in the presence of the transcendent unity of Christ and the church. He is thinking of how Christ forsook all things that He might make us for ever one with Himself, that our earthly life might become His and that His Divine life might become ours. Forgetting that he was writing about marriage he exclaims "*the mystery*"—the open secret of the unity of Christ and His people, the Divine purpose which from all ages had been hid in God but was now revealed—"*the mystery is great.*" And then, suddenly descending from these heights and remembering that he was writing about marriage, he adds, to prevent the exclamation which had broken from him from being misunderstood: "*but I speak in regard of Christ and of the church. Nevertheless,*"—to leave that high topic and to return to the subject which had for a moment been forgotten, and to bring it to a close,—"*do ye also severally love each one his own wife even as himself; and let the wife see that she fear her husband.*"

I shall now consider very briefly one or two of the grave controversies about marriage which have agitated Christendom, and shall then discuss at greater length some of the more practical aspects of the subject as illustrated by the teaching of Paul.

It is clear, I think, that the exaltation of celibacy as though it were, in itself and always, the nobler and more Christian state of life is inconsistent with the Christian conception of marriage contained in this passage. For, according to Paul, marriage enriches the Christian life with new duties, and therefore affords new opportunities for illustrating devotion to Christ. In her "subjection" to her husband the wife can manifest a form of devotion to Christ which can have no place in the life of an unmarried woman; and the husband in his self sacrificing love for his wife has an opportunity for the imitation of Christ which never falls to an unmarried man. The Romish preference for celibacy rests upon a false ethical idea. The ethical perfection of celibacy is simpler; the ethical perfection of marriage richer and more complex.

On the other hand, it is not clear that those Protestant moralists can sustain their position who maintain that "marriage is a duty, and the most universal duty incumbent on us."[1] Dr. Luthardt is nearer the truth when he says that "marriage is a vocation."[2] But vocations vary. The special form of life in which a man is divinely called to render service to God, and to reach the characteristic type of moral and spiritual perfection for which he was "created in Christ Jesus," is determined for him by the circumstances of his country and his age, by the general condition of the church and of the world, by his social position, by his material resources, by the claims of his kindred, by his physical vigour and constitution, by his native intellectual power, by his intellectual discipline, by his moral temperament and those original qualities and forces of his moral life

---

[1] "Apologetic Lectures on the Moral Truths of Christianity." By Ch. Ernst Luthardt. (Edinburgh: T. & T. Clark.) Page 114.

[2] Ibid.

which are not suppressed but transfigured by the power of the Holy Spirit, by the ethical and spiritual influences which, apart from his own choice, have contributed to form his character.

Celibacy may be the vocation of some of us, not marriage. When the profession of the Christian faith exposed men to the loss of property, to social obloquy, to imprisonment, and to death, Christian men and women might conscientiously shrink from marriage, because it would add fresh impediments to courageous fidelity, and would strengthen inducements to apostasy. Paul, who in this epistle glorifies marriage, recommends celibacy in another epistle for these very reasons. In times which are not harassed by persecution both men and women may be conscious of having received a vocation which they would have to resist, or to which at least it would be impossible to surrender themselves with unqualified and unreserved devotion, if they assumed the responsibilities of marriage. A man, a woman, may be under imperative obligations to care for an infirm and lonely parent, or for a brother or a sister who is suffering from incurable disease; and to discharge these obligations it may be necessary to live a single life. Some of the most beautiful forms of self sacrifice the world has ever seen have been inspired by this devotion to duties created by the ties of natural kinship. A man that is conscious of possessing a genius for scientific discovery or for scholarship may see that if he marries he must spend a large part of his time and strength in earning an income for the support of his wife and children. His own wants are simple. He is content to live a hard life if only he can use his rare gift for the glory of God and the service of mankind. In his genius and poverty he recognises a Divine vocation to celibacy. A woman may have a noble literary faculty, and may shrink from the household cares which might prevent her from putting forth all her strength. She is content to lose much of the joy of life in order to be faithful to the trust she has received from Heaven, and she believes that her true vocation is to live alone. Both men and women may sometimes be called to forms of religious work which leave neither heart nor strength for the claims of marriage. They are consumed with a passionate enthusiasm which excludes the possibility of an intense personal affection, and complete devotion to their work is inconsistent with the large and constant claims of a home. Marriage may be "the most universal of all earthly vocations";[1] but it is a vocation, not a universal duty. Celibacy is not a sin. Most men and women are "called" to marriage, but not all.

Paul's representation of the Christian ideal of marriage implies that when Christian people marry they are bound to regard their mutual vows as irrevocable. Life is to blend so completely with life that

---

[1] Luthardt. Page 114.

to recover a separate personal existence must seem impossible. Christ declared that only the one supreme offence against its obligations can dissolve the relationship. The tendencies of modern legislation in England and elsewhere are unfriendly to this austere conception. The tendencies of some modern forms of speculation are still more unfriendly to it. But if marriage could be legally dissolved for any reasons short of the crime by which its bonds are violently broken, a large part of the moral discipline which it is intended to confer would be lost.

There is nothing however in this representation of marriage which precludes the lawfulness of separation in cases in which men and women discover that in their marriage they have committed a tragic mistake. If the ideal cannot be realized, if there can be no approach to it, then, whatever other reasons may properly prevent an open rupture, there is nothing in Paul's teaching to enforce a common life which is the occasion both of misery and of sin. If on the husband's part there is an abnormal brutality and selfishness which make it impossible for the wife to be "in subjection" to him "as unto the Lord"; if on the part of the wife there is a bitterness and hostility which make it impossible for the husband to love her "even as Christ also loved the church," to love her as he loves himself; then I do not see what remains for them but separation. They are really separated already. The two have not become one, cannot become one; the same roof may cover them, but the ideal of marriage has been finally abandoned. The moral interests of society require that even then the marriage should not be dissolved ; but the moral interests of the husband or of the wife or of both may require that they should be allowed to part.

It is to be hoped that the cases in which a violent and irreconcilable antagonism between husband and wife justifies separation are extremely rare ; and separation should never be thought of except as the desperate remedy of desperate evils. But there may be estrangement where there is no antagonism. The ideal unity of married life may be lost where there is no active conflict and no suppressed hostility. Husband and wife may fall apart from each other without knowing how. Their intellectual interests and their moral sympathies may come to flow in new channels. New circumstances may stimulate into vigorous activity moral elements which were latent when they were first married. That there should be great intellectual and moral changes, both in men and women, after marriage is in many cases inevitable. These changes add greatly to the charm and animation of married life when they do not impair its unity. They relieve it from the monotony which to many of us would be intolerable if husband and wife after living together for twenty years were just what they were on their wedding morning. I suppose indeed that there are dull people to whom the growing years bring no such changes, and who have no craving for freshness and variety. But where there is a free, energetic life on either side, these intellectual and ethical developments are certain to come, and in a happy marriage they strengthen mutual affection and confidence. They make life a succession of pleasant surprises. Year after year the husband discovers in the wife, the wife discovers in the husband, some new and unsuspected power and grace. As their knowledge of each other increases they have all the delight of travelling in a country which had never been explored before; there are new rivers to trace to their sources and new mountains to climb; there are new flowers and new trees.

But this vigorous, vivacious kind of life has its perils as well as its pleasures. Its changes may diminish mutual interest, even if at first they do not diminish mutual affection; but the diminution of mutual affection is likely sooner or later to follow the diminution of mutual interest. Against both these evils husband and wife should maintain constant vigilance. I suppose that men are in more danger than women. Women live a more quiet and monotonous life, and their intellectual and moral sympathies are likely to remain steady. Men, who are in freer contact with the excitements of the world, are likely to become absorbed in fresh interests which have no attraction for their wives, and by insensible degrees these alien interests may become so imperious as to destroy the mutual sympathies which are necessary to a perfect marriage. Friends who share the husband's passion for his new pursuits have a charm for him that he does not find at home. But women are not free from peril. I think I have sometimes seen the gradual transfer of interest from a husband to children ; the affection of the mother has been too strong for the affection of the wife ; and the birth of children, which should bind husband and wife together more closely than before, is sometimes the beginning of estrangement.

A still more serious cause of estrangement sometimes emerges when a woman, after her marriage, begins to live a Christian life. The discovery of God fills her heart. Her chief thoughts are drawn to Divine and eternal things. She is constantly wanting to attend religious services in which her husband feels no interest and to which he will not accompany her. Sometimes she makes new friends, who, her husband feels, are more to her than he is ; he thinks that she finds more pleasure in their society than in his own ; and he knows that there are whole provinces of her life about which she speaks with the freest confidence to them and about which she is silent to him.

The mischief ought to be arrested as soon as it is discovered. It is impossible for her to close her eyes or her heart to the new glories which have been revealed to her ; but she should resolve that in her new faith she will find new motives to perfect wifely loyalty. If she is conscious that by her frequent attendance at religious services she is being separated from her husband, she should attend religious services less frequently, and rely for religious strength and light upon her solitary communion with God. She should resolutely withdraw from the friends in whom she is beginning to feel a deeper interest than in her husband. Her religious faith does not release her from her duties as a wife, but surrounds them with new and more august sanctions. Her life has risen to heights to which her husband does not follow her; but she should resolve that except in those Divine regions his life and hers shall be divided by no rival interests.

Both for men and for women life may be made or marred by marriage. In many cases indeed it seems to lead neither to romantic joy nor to tragic misery; it neither exalts nor degrades the moral ideal. But in many it gives to life its noblest strength and its most perfect delight; in many it is the shipwreck both of happiness and of character. Some of the conditions which are necessary to its ideal perfection have been already suggested. Where neither husband nor wife has religious faith, though the divinest form of the relationship cannot be reached, their married life may have a great deal of beauty and a great deal of happiness. But there is grave peril if there is religious faith on one side and not on the other; for in the central elements and forces of life there is antagonism between them. They are not agreed about the supreme laws of conduct, about the chief ends of human existence; and this want of agreement is likely to lead sooner or later to grave practical difficulties.

Even before these difficulties emerge their union is incomplete. For what is of supreme interest to one is regarded by the other with indifference. On one subject, and that the most sacred, there will be no confidences between the one that has faith and the one that has not. Into the innermost sanctuary of the heart of the husband the wife will never enter; or into the innermost sanctuary of the heart of the wife the husband will never enter. There is a rent in the unseen foundations on which their common life is built, and the whole structure is insecure. Husband and wife live in separate worlds. The central estrangement may lead to disastrous results.

There is another obvious reason why for a perfect marriage a common faith in Christ is necessary. In the ideal which Paul describes, an ideal which kindles the imagination and makes the heart throb with delight, husband and wife contribute to the security, the perfection, and the happiness of each other's Christian life. They are one; and the faith of each is a defence to the faith of the other. They are one ; and the streams of Divine joy reach them through a double channel. When the heart of either is glowing with the fervour of devout affection, the heart of the other will catch fire. When the heart of one is filled with the light of God, the heart of the other will receive some of the glory. For the wife, the duty of "subjection" will become easy, it will cease to be thought of as a duty, if she recognises in her husband the likeness of Christ ; and the love of the husband for the wife will more nearly approach the love of Christ for the church, if he recognises in her the outlines of a saintly perfection. This glorious ideal cannot be approached unless both husband and wife are in Christ. The ideal is deliberately renounced by those who seek or accept a marriage where this condition is not satisfied. They consent to live on a lower level. They have caught sight of a heavenly vision, and are disobedient to it. They deliberately expose their own religious life to the gravest peril.

But there is an inconsiderate religious enthusiasm which supposes that where there is a common religious faith there is everything that is necessary for a perfect married life. This is a ruinous mistake. A common religious faith is the sure and strong and adequate foundation of the common life of the church, but not of the common life of the home. The common life of the church is a life among unseen and eternal things; and in those lofty regions intellectual and social differences vanish and are forgotten. In that Divine world, a world in which those who are in Christ are already living, "there can be neither Jew nor Gentile, there can be neither bond nor free, there can be no male and female";[1] for all are one in Christ. But in marriage the life of the husband and the life of the wife should be one from base to summit; life should blend with life through all the gradations of human interest,

---

[1] Gal. iii. 28.

power, affection, and hope, from the lowest earthly levels to the loftiest heights of heaven.

In an ideal marriage husband and wife should find in each other a unique personal charm, and should be drawn together by strong mutual attraction. There should be something in each to touch the imagination and to command the esteem, as well as to inspire the love, of the other.

They should have strong intellectual sympathies. I do not mean that an astronomer royal should marry no woman that is not a profound mathematician; or that an oriental scholar will be unhappy if his wife cannot read Sanscrit. Nor do I mean that a woman who has a genius for music should refuse a lover who does not share her passion for Beethoven or Wagner. The common life of husband and wife is extended and enriched if there are wide provinces of intellectual interest familiar to each, which are almost unknown to the other. But there should be some ground where they can meet as equals. There should be no great disparity in their culture, whatever disparity there may be in their knowledge. Or if in one there is inferior culture the inferiority should be more than compensated by native intellectual alertness and vigour.

There should be ethical as well as intellectual sympathy, and perfect ethical sympathy is not always secured by a common religious faith. Early associations, habits, and training usually leave permanent results in the moral habits; and there are differences in the original moral fibre of different people which do not disappear even under the influence of the most admirable moral discipline or the most intense religious earnestness. A marriage will be very remote from ideal perfection, if there is a delicate moral sensitiveness on one side and not on the other; a nice sense of honour on one side and not on the other; on one side great moral refinement, on the other great moral coarseness; on one side a poetic moral enthusiasm, on the other an unimaginative dulness. These wide ethical contrasts may exist even where there is genuine and earnest religious faith. They are fatal to that perfect blending of life with life which is necessary to an ideal marriage.

To some of you, what I have said may appear to bar the gates of marriage against large numbers of the best men and the best women. You may say that if they must not marry beneath their intellectual and moral rank many of them will not be able to marry at all. That may be true. And while I have no desire to encourage young men and women to sacrifice real and substantial happiness in the romantic pursuit of an ideal perfection rarely to be attained in human life, I am prepared to say that both for men and for women celibacy is better than a marriage to which their conscience, their judgment, and their heart do not completely consent. A marriage in which there is no ardour of mutual affection, in which there is no strong intellectual and moral sympathy, is a marriage only in name; and a marriage in which there is religious faith only on one side is far more likely to lead to the extinction of faith where it exists than to the creation of faith in the heart which is destitute of it.

It is said that for cultivated women of the middle classes the difficulties in the way of marriage have greatly increased during the last thirty years, and are still increasing. The fact should be frankly recognised. It constitutes a reason for endeavouring to arrest that excessive expense in the style of living which is one of its principal causes; and it also constitutes a reason for opening to educated women offices and professions which have been closed against them. No woman should be forced, for the sake of a home and a living, to accept a man who is intellectually and morally greatly her inferior. At whatever cost, she should be loyal to her conscience and preserve her personal dignity. Marriage is a vocation; for a woman to make it a mercenary contract is to degrade the institution, to degrade herself, and to inflict what may be an irreparable wrong on the man she marries. The loftiest path is not only the most honourable; it is also the safest; it is freest from base troubles, and freest from moral perils.

Marriage at its best is the nobler and the happier state. But if a woman cannot have it at its best, let her decline to have it at all. In her solitary life she may achieve a lofty personal perfection; she may confer immeasurable benefits upon others; she may win strong affection; and may enjoy a tranquil happiness.

XX.

CHILDREN AND PARENTS.

"Children, obey your parents in the Lord: for this is right. Honour thy father and mother (which is the first commandment with promise), that it may be well with thee, and thou mayest live long on the earth. And, ye fathers, provoke not your children to wrath: but nurture them in the chastening and admonition of the Lord." EPH. vi. 1-4.

IN the preceding lecture we considered the duties of wives and husbands; we have now to consider the duties of children and parents.

I.

Paul assumes that the life of children may be a life in Christ. Children are to "*obey*" their parents "*in the Lord*"; and parents are to "*nurture*" their children "*in the chastening and admonition of the Lord.*"

I sometimes meet with men and women who tell me that they cannot remember the time when they began to love and trust and obey Christ, just as they cannot remember the time when they began to love and trust and obey their parents. If we had a more vivid and a more devout faith in the truth that every Christian family is according to God's idea and purpose a part of the kingdom of heaven, this happy experience would be more common. The law of Christ is the rule of human conduct in childhood as well as in manhood; and as in Christ's kingdom grace precedes law, the grace of Christ is near to a child in its very earliest years to enable it to keep the law, and the child's earliest moral life may be a life in Christ. Christ's relationship to men cannot be a relationship of authority merely. His authority is the authority of One who has assumed our nature and died for our sins. He is our Prince that He may be our Saviour.

These truths are assumed in the precept that children are to "*obey*" their parents "*in the Lord*." Every child, apart from its choice and before it is capable of choice, is environed by the laws of Christ. It is equally true that every child, apart from its choice and before it is capable of choice, is environed by Christ's protection and grace in this life and is the heir of eternal blessings in the life to come. Christ died and rose again for the race.

Children may "*obey*" their parents "*in the Lord*," before they are able to understand any Christian doctrine; they may discharge every childish duty, under the inspiration of the Spirit of God, before they have so much as heard whether the Spirit of God has been given; they may live in the light of God before they know that the true light always comes from heaven. And as men and women, who are consciously relying on God to enable them to do His will, appropriate God's grace and make it more fully their own by keeping His commandments, so the almost unconscious virtues of devout children make the life of Christ more completely theirs. Like Christ Himself, who in His childhood was subject to Joseph and Mary, as they advance in stature they advance in wisdom and in favour with God and men.[1] This is the ideal Christian life.

The difficulties of obedience are usually greatest in the troubled years between childhood and manhood; and not unfrequently these difficulties are increased rather than diminished when during these years the religious life begins to be active. To a boy or girl of fifteen the discovery of God sometimes seems to dissolve all human relationships. The earthly order vanishes in the glory of the infinite and the Divine. There is also a sudden realization of the sacredness and dignity of the personal life, and whatever authority comes between the individual soul and God is felt to be a usurpation.

At this stage in the development of the higher life the first commandment is also the only commandment that has any real authority. "Thou shalt love the Lord thy God with all thy heart, and with all thy soul, and with all thy mind," seems to exhaust all human duty; and life has no place for any inferior obligations. I have a very deep sympathy with those young people who are trying,

---

[1] Luke ii. 51, 52.

and trying very unsuccessfully, to adjust what seem to them the conflicting claims of the seen and the unseen, of earth and heaven. They have to remember that we live in two worlds, that both belong to God; and that we do not escape from the inferior order when the glory of eternal and Divine things is revealed to us. We still have to plough and to sow and to reap; to build houses; to work in iron and brass and silver and gold. The old world with its day and night, its sunshine and its clouds, its rain and snow, its heat and cold, is still our home. In things seen and temporal we have to do the will of the invisible and eternal God, and to be disciplined for our final perfection and glory.

As God determined the laws of the physical universe, so He determined the limitations of human life and the conditions under which human duty is to be discharged. The family, the state, and the church are Divine institutions; and the obligations which they create are rooted in the will of God. The family and the state belong to the natural order, but they are not less Divine in their origin than the church, nor are their claims upon us less sacred.

In the family, the parents by Divine appointment exercise authority, and children are under Divine obligations to obedience. The ends for which the family exists are defeated if authority is not exercised on the one side, if obedience is not conceded on the other; just as the ends for which the state exists are defeated if rulers do not assert and enforce the law, if subjects habitually violate it. Children are to obey their parents, "*for this is right*": right, according to the natural constitution and order of human affairs; right, according to the laws of natural morality; right, according to the natural conscience and apart from supernatural revelation. But in the discharge of this natural duty the supernatural life is to be revealed. Children are to obey their parents "*in the Lord*," in the Spirit and in the strength of Christ. Obedience to parents is part of the service which Christ claims from us; it is a large province of the Christian life.

It is not enough that children obey their parents in those things which would have obligation apart from parental authority. To be truthful, honest, kindly, temperate, courageous, industrious, are duties whether a parent enforces them or not. They may be sanctioned and sustained by parental authority, but to discharge duties of this kind may be no proof of filial obedience; a child may discharge them without any regard to the authority of his parents. It is when the parent requires obedience in things which are neither right nor wrong in themselves, or which appear to the child neither right nor wrong in themselves, that the authority of the parent is unambiguously recognised. A parent may require obedience in things of this kind for the good of the child himself; for the sake of his health; for the sake of his intellectual vigour and growth; for the sake of his moral safety; or for the sake of his future success in life. Before the parent's authority is exerted the child is free; but afterwards, whether the child sees the wisdom of the requirement or not, he is bound to obey.

Or parental authority may be exerted for the sake of the family generally. Regulations intended to secure the order of the household, to prevent confusion, to lessen trouble, and to lessen expense, are often felt by young people to be extremely irksome. The regulations appear to be unreasonable, and to have no other object than to place vexatious restraints on personal liberty. Sometimes, no doubt, they are really unwise and unnecessary. But children are not the most competent judges; and in any case it is the parents, not the children, that are responsible for making the rules. The parents may be unwise in imposing them; but the children are more than unwise if they are restive under them and wilfully break them. To submit to restraints which are seen to be expedient and reasonable is a poor test of obedience; the real proof of filial virtue is given when there is loyal submission to restraints which appear unnecessary.

There is less difficulty when a child is required to render personal service to a parent. The obligation is so obvious that unless the child is intensely selfish the claim will be met with cheerfulness as well as with submission. Affection, gratitude, and a certain pride in being able to contribute to a parent's ease or comfort, will make obedience a delight. To be of use satisfies one of the strongest cravings of a generous and noble nature, and the satisfaction is all the more complete if the act of service involves real labour and a real sacrifice of personal enjoyment.

The duty of obedience to parents, which is a natural duty, a duty arising out of the natural constitution of human life, was enforced in Jewish times by a Divine commandment. And this commandment had a place of special dignity in Jewish legislation; it was "*the first commandment with promise.*" Paul was not thinking of the Ten Commandments as if they stood apart from the rest of the laws which God gave to the Jewish people, or else he would have said that this was the *only* commandment that was strengthened by the assurance of a special reward to obedience. He meant that of all the Jewish laws this was the first that had a promise attached to it. The promise was a national promise. It was not an assurance that every child that obeyed his parents would escape sickness and poverty, would be prosperous, and would live to a good old age; it was a declaration that the prosperity, the stability, and the permanence of the nation depended upon the reverence of children for their parents. The discipline of the family was intimately related to the order, the security, and the greatness of the state. Bad children would make bad citizens. If there was a want of reverence for parental authority, there would be a want of reverence for public authority. If there was disorder in the home, there would be disorder in the nation; and national disorder would lead to the destruction of national life. But if children honoured their parents the elect nation would be prosperous, and would retain possession of the country which it had received from the hands of God.'

The greatness of the promise attached to this commandment, the fact that it was the first commandment that had any promise attached to it, revealed the Divine estimate of the obligations of filial duty. And although Jewish institutions have passed away, the revelation of God's judgment concerning the importance of this duty remains. And the promise with which it was sanctioned is the revelation of a universal law. The family is the germ cell of the nation. If children honour their parents, men and women will be trained to those habits of order and obedience which are the true security of the public peace and are among the most necessary elements of commercial and military supremacy; they will be disciplined to self control, and will have strength to resist many of the vices which are the cause of national corruption and ruin.

The commandment which Paul quotes requires children to "*honour*" their parents; "honour" includes obedience and something more. We may obey because we are afraid of the penalties of disobedience; and in that case the obedience though exact will be reluctant, without cheerfulness and without grace. We may obey under terror, or we may obey from motives of self interest. We may think that the man to whom we are compelled to submit is in no sense our superior, that he is at best our equal, and that it is mere accident that gives him authority over us. But children are required to remember that their parents are their superiors, not their equals; that they have to "*honour*" parental dignity as well as to obey parental commands, that honour is to blend with obedience and to make it free and beautiful.

To "*honour*," I repeat, is something more than to "obey." The child that honours his parents will yield a real deference to their judgment and wishes when there is no definite and authoritative command; will respect even their prejudices; will chivalrously conceal their infirmities and faults; will keenly resent any disparagement of their claims to consideration; will resent still more keenly any assault on their character.

In a family where this precept is obeyed, parents will be treated with uniform courtesy. There is a tradition that whenever Jonathan Edwards came into a room where his children were sitting they rose as they would have risen at the entrance of a visitor. Forms of respect of this kind are alien from modern manners; but the spirit of which they were the expression still survives in well-bred families, I mean in families which inherit and preserve good traditions, to whatever social rank they may belong. Nor is it to parents alone that children should show this spirit of consideration and respect; brothers and sisters should show it to each other; and both among the rich and the poor it may be taken as a sure sign of vulgarity, inherited or acquired, if courtesy is reserved for strangers and has no place in the life of the family. Children are to "*honour*" their parents, and if they honour their parents they are likely to be courteous to each other.

II.

But Paul had a sensitive sympathy with the wrongs which children sometimes suffer and a strong sense of their claims to consideration. Children are to "obey" and to "honour" even unreasonable, capricious, and unjust parents; but it is the duty of parents not to be unreasonable, capricious, or unjust. His precept is addressed to "*fathers*," because, I suppose, he held fathers specially responsible for the general government and discipline of the house. It applies of course to both parents. "*Fathers, provoke not your children to wrath.*"

Parents are sometimes wanting in courtesy to children as well as children to parents, speak to them roughly, violently, insultingly—and so inflict painful wounds on their self respect. Parents sometimes recur with cruel iteration to the faults and follies of their children, faults and follies of which the children are already ashamed, and which it would be not only kind but just to forget. Parents are sometimes guilty of a brutal want of consideration; they allude in jest to personal defects to which the children are keenly sensitive, remind them mockingly of failures by which they have been deeply humiliated, speak cynically of pursuits in which their children have a passionate or romantic interest, and contemptuously and scornfully of companions and friends that their children enthusiastically admire and love. Parents are sometimes tyrannical, wilfully thwarting their children's plans, needlessly interfering with their pleasures, and imposing on them unreasonable and fruitless sacrifices.

It sometimes happens that, through a fatal defect of temper or of sympathy, parents who have many noble qualities are guilty of this conduct. They have large and generous views for their children, and shrink from no labour or self denial in giving these views effect; and they wonder that their children have little love for them, treat them with disrespect, and regard home with fear and even with abhorrence. When the children are grown to manhood and womanhood they may remember with penitence their failure in filial duty; but they will also feel that the fault was not all on their side. In childhood and youth great and substantial services do not compensate for incessant irritation and annoyance. Parents who desire to be loved and honoured and cheerfully obeyed should lay to heart the apostle's warning: "*provoke not your children to wrath.*"

Then follows the positive precept, "*but nurture them in the chastening and admonition of the Lord.*" This covers the whole province of Christian education, and a full exposition of it would require a volume. I can only illustrate the general principles on which the precept rests.

1. The precept implies a real and serious faith on the part of the parents that their children belong to Christ and are under Christ's care. Christian education is not a mission to those who are in revolt against Christ. The "*nurture*" is to be "*in the chastening and admonition of the Lord.*" The children are Christ's subjects, and have to be trained to loyal obedience to His authority. The Christian redemption is theirs by their birth into this world, and the object of Christian education is to prevent them from forfeiting it. Their earliest impressions of God should assure them that God loves them with an infinite and eternal love, and that He has "blessed [them] with every spiritual blessing in the heavenly places in Christ." It is no part of the duty of parents to "dedicate their children to Christ," to use a common phrase, as though the children were not His already and before any act or wish of the parents; the parents have received the charge of their children from Christ, and have therefore to "*nurture them in the chastening and admonition of the Lord.*"

I sometimes fear that we have not yet wholly escaped from that appalling heresy which excludes children from the Divine kingdom and the Divine love until they have discovered for themselves the majesty of God's authority and have appealed to the Divine mercy for the remission of sins and the gift of eternal life. This terrible heresy teaches children that by their birth they are "children of wrath," that the awful fires of the Divine anger were burning around them during their infancy, and that the flames have become fiercer with their growing years. It teaches them that while the dearest human love came to them unsought and before they had the power to seek it, they have to win for themselves by penitence and faith a share in the love of God.

For ourselves we believe in a nobler gospel. We love God because God first loved us. "The living God . . . is the Saviour of all men," though "specially of them that believe."[1] It was because "God loved the world,"[2]—the whole world, little children as well as men and women,—that the Son of God became man and endured for us pain, sorrow, temptation, agony, and death. "Jesus Christ the Righteous . . . is the propitiation for our sins, and not for ours only but also for the whole world."[3] When a child is born it is born to an inheritance in the infinite love of God and in the infinite blessings of the Christian redemption. It comes under the sovereignty of Christ, for by Divine appointment Christ has "all

---

[1] 1 Tim. iv. 10. [2] John iii. 16.
[3] 1 John iii. 2.

authority" "in heaven and on earth."[1] The great truths which are affirmed in infant baptism are the true root of a Christian education.

2. The education of which the apostle is thinking is practical rather than speculative; it has to do with life and character rather than with knowledge.

Knowledge of religious truth has its value. It is the noblest kind of knowledge. It has a great place and function in the development of the higher life and in the control of conduct. The simplest, which are also the most august, religious truths should be learned by children in very early years from the lips of their mothers. But many Christian parents are not capable of giving systematic instruction in Christian doctrine and duty. Even where the knowledge exists there is not always the faculty for communicating it. For instruction of that kind provision should be made by the Sunday school and the church.

By "*the chastening . . . of the Lord*" the apostle means the Christian discipline and order of the family, which will form the children to the habits of a Christian life. "*Chastening*" is not chastisement, though chastisement may sometimes be a necessary part of it. The order of a child's life is determined by its parents, and is to be determined under Christ's authority, so that the child may be trained to all Christian virtues.

---

[1] Matt. xxviii. 18.

In the earlier years of childhood this training will be, in a sense, mechanical. The child will not know why certain acts and habits are required of it, or why other acts and habits are forbidden. There will be no appeal to the child's conscience or reason; the parent's conscience and the parent's reason will assume the responsibility of guiding the child's conduct. Indeed the training should begin before the child is capable of understanding the grounds on which the discipline rests. And even when the capacity begins to show itself a wise parent will not desire to hasten its development. A child of six or seven ought not to be worried by questions of conscience; and it is probably a healthy thing if for several years later the moral virtues are practised without reflection and self consciousness. In most Christian families what has been described as "the pre-ethical state" ends far too soon. Naturalness and freedom of character are lost; joyousness, which is a virtue of childhood, is clouded; and the strong foundations of morality are loosened by the premature activity of conscience. The burden and mystery of life should not be laid on a child's heart too soon.

But during these years the child should be disciplined to habits of obedience, industry, courage, temperance, self control, truthfulness, and kindness, so that when the grave temptations of life begin the child may find that the victory has been half won.

3. If it is the duty of a child to obey, it is the duty of parents to rule. There can be no obedience

where there is no authority; and if a child is not disciplined to obedience it suffers a moral loss which can hardly ever be completely remedied in later years. There are men and women of excellent native disposition and whose general character is admirable, but who are like horses or dogs that were not well broken in when they were young. You are never quite sure of them. They cannot work well with others. They are wilful and wayward. They are restive and impatient under the most necessary restraints. They are carried away by their impulses. Nothing holds them. They were not well governed by their parents, and are now unable to govern themselves.

The religious as well as the moral life is injured by the relaxation of parental rule. Obedience to the personal authority of parents disciplines us to obey the personal authority of God.

4. Children should be trained to the surrender of their own pleasure and comfort to the pleasure and comfort of others. Parents who have sacrificed themselves without reserve to their children's gratification are sometimes bitterly disappointed that their children grow up selfish. They wonder and feel aggrieved that their devotion receives no response, that their children are not as eager to serve them as they have been to serve their children. On the other hand, parents who with equal affection have made *themselves*, not their children, the centre of the family life, seem to have been more fortunate. Not self-

ishly, harshly, or tyrannically, but firmly and consistently, they have required their children to take a secondary position. The comfort of the children and their pleasures were amply provided for, but the children were not led to think that everything in the house must give way to them, that all the sacrifices were to be made by their parents, none by themselves. They were trained to serve, and not merely to receive service. This seems to be the truer discipline of the Christian spirit and character.

5. In relation to the higher elements of the Christian life, to those elements which are distinctively Christian and spiritual, more depends upon the real character of the parents than upon everything besides. In relation to these the power of personal influence is supreme.

If the parents really obey the will of Christ as their supreme law, if they accept His judgments about human affairs and about the ends of human life, if they live under the control of the invisible and eternal world, the children will know it and are likely to yield to the influence of it. But if the parents, though animated by religious faith, are not completely Christian, if some of their most conspicuous habits of thought and conduct are not penetrated by the force of Christ's spirit and teaching, the children are in great danger; they are as likely to yield to what is base and worldly in the life of their parents as to what is Divine.

The real religious discipline of a family, I repeat,

depends mainly upon the religious character and spirit of the parents. If, notwithstanding their Christian faith, they care too much for wealth, for pleasure, for social success, they will not discipline their children to be loyal to Christ and to care for things eternal and Divine.

The "*admonition*" of the Lord completes the "*chastening*." To quote Archbishop Trench's excellent definition, "it is the training by word, by the word of encouragement when no more is wanted, but also by the word of remonstrance, of reproof, of blame, where these may be required; as set over against the training by act and by discipline."[1]

I suppose that, under God, the primary condition of a successful Christian education is that *the parents should care more for the loyalty of their children to Christ than for anything besides*, more for this than for their health, their intellectual vigour and brilliance, their material prosperity, their social position, their exemption from great sorrows and great misfortunes. Their loyalty to Christ must be cared for, not because it will be a defence and guarantee of the moral virtues and a protection against vices which might end in disgrace and ruin, but for its own sake and for Christ's sake. Only when our children have found eternal righteousness and eternal life in Him,

---

[1] "Synonyms of the New Testament."

has the trust we have received from Him been successfully discharged; only then have our children discharged their supreme duty and achieved their supreme blessedness.

But there is a second condition of success. *Parents should expect their children to be loyal to Christ.* The children are the subjects of Christ by birth, and it should never be assumed that when they reach the years of moral freedom and moral responsibility they will be certain to revolt against Christ's authority. Why should they? They are born into the Divine household,—why should it be taken for granted that they are certain to leave home and go into a far country and there waste their substance in riotous living? The true ideal of human nature is something fairer and better than this. The Spirit of God may control and direct the whole stream of human life, from the moment it leaves its source until it reaches the ocean.

We should expect our children to be loyal to Christ. We expect them to be truthful and honest, and this expectation is one of the principal causes of their truthfulness and honesty; if in our words and conduct we implied that we were very doubtful whether they would be honest and tell the truth, we should do very much to make them thieves and liars. Children, even more than men and women, respond instinctively to a generous confidence and rise to the expectations which are formed of them.

We have the strongest grounds for expecting that

their hearts will be touched by Christ's infinite love and that the will of Christ will have supreme authority over their conduct. Everything is in favour of it. This is the eternal purpose of God, and for the fulfilment of that purpose we may rely upon "the exceeding greatness" of His "power," and on "the unsearchable riches of His grace." We ourselves are but the ministers of a higher Will; if we are loyal to Christ and dwell in Him, the discipline of the home is not ours, it is the "chastening and admonition of the Lord,"—and Christ Himself is with us to give it effect.

God forbid that I should say a word to add bitterness to the sorrow of those whose children have broken away from the control of Christ. The will of a child is free, and cannot be absolutely determined by any earthly authority or even by the light and power of the Spirit of God. But when parental affection, parental example, and the atmosphere and discipline of the home are on the side of Christ —when the strongest and tenderest human influences are blended with the gracious energy of the Divine Spirit—when earth is confederate with Heaven—we ought not to fear defeat. We ought to expect that children who are brought up in "the chastening and admonition of the Lord" will illustrate in their childhood the beauty and grace of the Christian life, and that when they reach the strength and joy of Christian manhood they will be unable to recall a time when they were not living in the light of God.

XXI.

SERVANTS AND MASTERS.

"Servants, be obedient unto them that according to the flesh are your masters, with fear and trembling, in singleness of your heart, as unto Christ; not in the way of eye-service, as men-pleasers; but as servants of Christ, doing the will of God from the heart; with good will doing service, as unto the Lord, and not unto men: knowing that whatsoever good thing each one doeth, the same shall he receive again from the Lord, whether he be bond or free. And, ye masters, do the same things unto them, and forbear threatening: knowing that both their Master and yours is in heaven, and there is no respect of persons with Him."

—Eph. vi. 5-9.

THERE are many indications in the New Testament of the extreme anxiety of the apostles to prevent any collision between the Christian church and the secular order of society. Peter charges Christian people to "be subject to every ordinance of man, for the Lord's sake: whether it be to the king as supreme; or unto governors, as sent by him for vengeance on evil-doers, and for praise to them that do well. For so is the will of God, that by well-doing ye should put to silence the ignorance of foolish men : as free, and not using your freedom for a cloke of wickedness but as bondservants of God. Honour all men. Love the brotherhood. Fear God. Honour the king."[1] Paul, in several of his epistles, insists with equal energy on the same duty. Writing to the Christians in Rome he says: "Let every soul be in subjection to the higher powers; for there is no power but of God; and the powers that be are ordained of God."[2] To obey the law, to pay all taxes and tolls, to concede to public authorities customary courtesy and respect, are moral duties which must be discharged "for conscience sake," and not merely to avoid punishment.[3] He tells Timothy that "supplications, prayers, intercessions, thanksgivings," are to be made for all men; for kings and all that are in high place.[4] He charges Titus to remind Christian people that they are "to be in subjection to rulers, to authorities, to be obedient."[5] The urgency and frequency of these precepts indicate that the apostles were alarmed at the temper with which some of their converts regarded the political order and institutions of society. In the church Christ was honoured as the true King of men, and it was not unnatural that Christian people should suppose that since they were in Christ's kingdom they were released from the obligations of secular law and owed no allegiance to secular rulers. What authority had the legislation of heathen governments for men who were under the laws of Christ, and who were to

---

[1] 1 Pet. ii. 13-17. [2] Rom. xiii. 1.
[3] Rom. xiii. 5-7. [4] 1 Tim. ii. 1, 2.
[5] Tit. iii. 1.

give account to Him of the deeds done in the body? How could men who were loyal to Christ be also loyal to heathen rulers who regarded the claims of Christ with derision? Questions of this kind were likely to be discussed at church meetings with a great deal of animation and vigour, and they might have produced the most disastrous results.

Slavery was a still more dangerous topic. There were large numbers of slaves among those who had received the new Faith, and they had learnt from Christ that all men are brethren. They were slaves, but they were the sons of God; they had received the life of God, they were hoping for everlasting glory. It was intolerable that they should be the property of heathen masters; and in some respects it was still more intolerable that they should be the property of Christian masters. We can imagine that Christian slaves when they met each other were likely to discuss their wrongs in the light of the Christian gospel; and we can also imagine that the authority of masters as well as the authority of heathen rulers would be debated with great heat and excitement in the meetings of the church.

Paul takes the institutions of society as they stand, and defines the duties of those who acknowledge the authority of Christ. He teaches that the state is a Divine institution as well as the church. Political government is necessary to the existence of human society; a bad government is better than no government at all. Governors might be unjust; but Christian people, with no political authority or power, are not responsible for the injustice, nor are they able to remedy it. Government itself is sanctioned by God, and submission is part of the duty which Christian people owe to Him.

Domestic and industrial institutions are also necessary for the existence of society. By the Divine constitution of human life we have to serve each other in many ways, and if the service is to be effective it must be organised. In apostolic times slavery existed in every part of the Roman empire. It was a form of domestic and industrial organisation created by the social condition of the ancient world. It was the growth of the history and mutual relations of the races under the Roman authority. To practical statesmen in those days it would have seemed impossible to organise the domestic and industrial life of nations in any other way, as impossible as it seems to modern statesmen to organise commerce on any other principle than that of competition. Christian people were not responsible for its existence, and had no power to abolish it. Their true duty was to consider how, as masters and slaves, they were to do the will of Christ.

Paul transfigures the institution. He applies to it the great principle which underlies all Christian ethics; Christ is the true Lord of human life; whatever we do we are to do for Him; we are all His servants. Slaves live in the eye of God. They are to do their work for Him. All that is hard, all that

D D

is ignominious, in their earthly condition is suddenly lit up with the glory of Divine and eternal things. "*Servants, be obedient unto them that according to the flesh are your masters, with fear and trembling*"—"with that zeal which is ever keenly apprehensive of not doing enough"[1]—"*in singleness of your heart,*" with no double purpose, but with an honest and earnest desire to do your work well, "*as unto Christ.*" This will redeem them from the common vice of slaves; if they accept their tasks as from Christ, and try to be faithful to Him, they will not be diligent and careful only when their masters are watching them, "*in the way of eye-service, as men-pleasers,*" but will be always faithful "*as servants of Christ, doing the will of God from the heart.*" They will cherish no resentment against their earthly masters, and will not serve them merely to avoid punishment, but, regarding their work as work for Christ, will do it cheerfully with real kindliness for those whom they have to serve, "*with good will doing service, as unto the Lord and not unto men.*" Their earthly masters may deny them the just rewards of their labour, may fail to recognise their integrity and their zeal, may treat them harshly and cruelly; but as Christ's servants they will not miss their recompence; they are to work, "*knowing that whatsoever good thing each one doeth,*" that very thing "*shall he receive again from the Lord, whether he be bond or free.*" No good works

---

[1] Meyer, *in loc.*

will be forgotten; the rewards which are withheld on earth will be conferred in heaven.

Masters are to act towards their servants in the same spirit, and under the government of the same Divine laws. "*Ye masters, do the same things unto them.*" As slaves are warned against the special vices of their order, and charged to do their work not reluctantly but "with good will," "not in the way of eye-service, as men-pleasers," but "from the heart," so masters are warned against the special vice of which masters were habitually guilty; they are not to be rough, violent, and abusive, but are to "*forbear threatening.*" They are reminded that their authority is only subordinate and temporary; the true Master of their slaves is Christ, and Christ is *their* Master too; He will leave no wrong unredressed. Before earthly tribunals a slave might appeal in vain for justice, but "*there is no respect of persons with Him.*"

These precepts may be met with the objection that slavery was a cruel tyranny, and that no moral duties could be created by social relations which were an outrage at once on human rights and on Divine laws: the masters had one duty, and only one—to emancipate their slaves; the slaves were grossly oppressed, and were under no moral obligations to their masters. But the objection is untenable. The worst injuries may be inflicted upon me by an individual or by the state, but it does not follow that I am released from obligations either to the man or to the community that wrongs me. I may be unjustly imprisoned, imprisoned by an iniquitous law or by a corrupt judge; but it may be my duty to observe the regulations of the jail; I ought not to be in prison at all, but being there it may be my duty neither to try to escape nor to disturb the order of the place. And though a man ought not to be a slave at all, he may be under moral obligations to those who hold him in slavery. So, on the other hand, I may be a jailer, and may have prisoners under my care who, in my belief, have committed no crime, and yet it may be my duty to keep them safely. To take an extreme case: the governor of a jail may be fully convinced that a man in his charge who has been condemned to be hung for murder is innocent of the crime, but if he were to let the man escape he would be guilty of a grave breach of trust.

We may say of slavery what John Wesley said of the slave trade, that it "is the sum of all villanies," and yet a servile revolt may be a great and flagrant crime. While the institution exists and a real and permanent improvement in the organisation of society is impossible, it is the duty of the slave to bear his wrongs patiently.

Circumstances may be easily imagined in which the position of a master, if he be a Christian, would be in some respects more difficult than that of a slave. Some of the miserable creatures whom he owns may have lost, or never possessed, the energy, the forethought, the self reliance, the self control, necessary for a life of freedom. In the organisation of society there may be no place for them among free citizens. To emancipate them would be to deprive them of a home, to give them up to starvation, to drive them to a life of crime. In such circumstances a Christian master might think it his duty to retain his authority for the sake of society, and for the sake of the slaves themselves; but would resolve to use his power with as much gentleness and kindness as the hateful institution permitted.

But it may be further objected that there are no indications in the New Testament that the apostles saw the hatefulness of the institution or desired its disappearance. They certainly did not denounce it. I suppose that if Paul had been asked for his judgment on it he would have said that slavery was part of the order of this present evil world. If he had been pressed more closely and asked to say whether he thought it just or not, he would probably have answered that, in a world which had forgotten God, and was in open revolt against Him, all the relations between man and man were necessarily thrown into disorder. It was not slavery alone that violated the true and ideal organisation of human society; the whole constitution of the world was evil; and no great and real reform was possible apart from the moral and religious regeneration of the race. When the golden age came, and the love and power of Christ had won a final victory over human sin, the order of the world would be changed. Under the reign of Christ tyranny, slavery, war, and poverty would be unknown. Meanwhile and in the actual condition of mankind the work of the Christian church was not to assault institutions, but to try to make individual men loyal to Christ. It was not Christ's plan to effect an external revolution, but to change the moral and spiritual life of the race.

It is very probable that the apostles themselves did not estimate adequately the disintegrating and transforming power of the principles and spirit of the Christian Faith. It soon became apparent that Christian men cannot regard with indifference institutions which are flagrantly cruel and unjust. With the changing spirit of nations, Christianity has changed their institutions too. The new principles it has promulgated and the new dispositions it has inspired have revealed themselves in civil and criminal legislation, in the usages of war, in new forms of national life. At what moment it may become a duty to insist on the readjustment of the political and social institutions of a people—when, for example, a nation which has been civilized by the influence of Christian missions should abolish arbitrary government and slavery and other forms of injustice—is a question of political ethics and political philosophy. There may be evil in delay as well as in precipitancy, for though no real moral progress is secured by the mere destruction of bad institutions while the spirit of a people remains unchanged, bad institutions perpetuate the injustice and cruelty in which they originated.

How Paul was likely to deal with slavery in individual cases is shown in his graceful and beautiful letter to Philemon. We know too little of the circumstances to be able to form a judgment upon the reasons which led Paul to send Onesimus back to his master, but there is not the slightest ground to suppose that the apostle would have required every fugitive slave to return to slavery. From the contents of the letter it may be inferred that Onesimus had been guilty of very bad conduct towards Philemon,[1] and had probably robbed him. Onesimus was conscious of grave fault, and desired to return to his master, and Paul sent him back with a letter in which affectionate courtesy to the master is blended with overflowing love for the slave. Paul speaks of the comfort which he had received from the voluntary attentions of Onesimus, describes him as his "child," as his "very heart"; is confident that Philemon will receive back the fugitive, not merely "as a servant, but more than a servant, a brother beloved," specially dear to Paul, still more dear to Philemon himself. For whatever loss Philemon had suffered from the misconduct of Onesimus Paul makes himself responsible—" if he hath wronged thee at all, or oweth thee ought, put that to mine account; I Paul write it with mine own hand, I will repay it." But the apostle, remembering Philemon's obligations to him, felt certain that the

---

[1] "Who was aforetime unprofitable to thee." (Ver. 11.)

fulfilment of the promise would never be claimed: "I say not unto thee how that thou owest to me thine own self besides." He does not mention emancipation, but suggests it in a way so gracious that Philemon could not have missed his meaning or resisted his appeal. "Having confidence in thine obedience I write to thee, knowing that thou wilt do even beyond what I say." And then he adds, "prepare me also a lodging; for I hope that through your prayers I shall be granted unto you." The prospect of seeing Paul in Colosse, and of receiving him as a guest, would make Philemon so happy that I think we may take it for granted that he resolved at once to give Onesimus his liberty. Perhaps too, as Dr. Lightfoot suggests, "there is a gentle compulsion in this mention of a personal visit to Colosse. The apostle would thus be able to see for himself that Philemon had not disappointed his expectations."[1]

That letter illustrates perfectly the spirit and attitude of the Christian Faith in relation to the institution of slavery. Great as were the wrongs of the slave, he must not avenge them by wronging his master. Onesimus went back to Philemon voluntarily, and went back, as is clear from the letter, with the intention of compensating by faithful service for whatever injury and loss his master had suffered from his misconduct. But Philemon was to receive him as a

---

[1] "St. Paul's Epistles to the Colossians and Philemon." Page 411.

"brother beloved." The slave and the master were to sit together at the table of Christ; in the church they were equals; the slave as well as the master was a son of God; the same Divine life was in both; they had received the same supernatural illumination; they were heirs of the same eternal glory. When masters began to regard their slaves in this way the horrible cruelties of slavery would be at once arrested, and emancipation was only a question of time. The Christian gospel invested the slave with such dignity that the church soon discovered that if the will of God was to be done on earth as it is in heaven, if the secular order was to be brought into harmony with the Divine kingdom, slavery must cease to exist. It became an honourable Christian work for masters to emancipate their slaves, and for the church to raise funds to buy the freedom of those whom their owners refused to liberate. There has gradually been created in Christian countries an ethical sentiment which had no existence in the pagan world, and slavery has come to be regarded with indignation and abhorrence.

It may seem that this subject has no practical interest for ourselves; for we are not slaves and we do not own slaves. But the principles which are expressed in the precepts of the apostle are of enduring and universal authority; if they were remembered and loyally practised they would work a wonderful change in the lives of very many of us.

We are happily free from the curse and crime of slavery; but even the social order of England, which we are accustomed, very inconsiderately, to call a Christian country, does not perfectly realize the ideal of social justice. There are no slaves among us, but there are tens of thousands of Christian people who feel and have a right to feel that their lot is a very hard one. They are inadequately paid for their work; they are badly fed, badly clothed, badly housed. They are never free from anxiety, they are always on the edge of misery and of ruin. They are without any hope of improving their condition. If by self denial and forethought they are able in good times to save a little from their poor wages, illness, depression of trade, and loss of work soon sweep their little store away. They have to endure harsh and unkindly treatment from men whose control they cannot escape.

But their position is not worse than the condition of slaves in apostolic times, and they should resolve with the help of Christ to obey the apostolic law. Let them do their laborious and ill-paid work as work for Christ. Let them look above and beyond their earthly masters to Him; cherishing no resentment against the men who treat them roughly and tyrannically, but "with good will doing service as unto the Lord and not unto men." Let them never yield to the base temptation to work badly because they are paid badly; their true wages do not come to them on Friday night or Saturday morning; they are Christ's servants, and He will not forget their fidelity. How often I have heard men say that they would not mind hard work if they only got well paid for it! and they sometimes say that they would not mind hard work if they were treated with kindness and consideration, as men not as brutes. Let them remember that Christ is their true Master, that whoever else may fail to honour honest work He will not fail, and that "whatsoever good thing each one doeth, the same shall he receive again from the Lord."

Masters have not yet escaped from their old vice. Their position of power encourages an arbitrary and despotic temper, and those who employ a few men seem to be in just as much danger as those who employ hundreds and thousands. They are to be not only just but courteous. They are to remember that the relations between the master and his workmen, the merchant and his clerks, the tradesman and his assistants, are accidental and temporary. They have all one Master in heaven, and to Him the supreme question in reference to every man's life is not whether he is rich or poor, whether he rules or serves, but whether by justice, industry, temperance, and kindliness he is trying to do the will of God.

The great revelation which has come to us through Christ abolished slavery; it ought to lift up our whole social and industrial life into the very light of God, and to fill the works, the warehouses, and the shops of this great town with the very spirit which gives beauty and sanctity to the palaces of heaven.

XXII.

THE WAR AGAINST PRINCIPALITIES AND POWERS.

"*Finally, be strong in the Lord, and in the strength of His might. Put on the whole armour of God, that ye may be able to stand against the wiles of the devil. For our wrestling is not against flesh and blood, but against the principalities, against the powers, against the world-rulers of this darkness, against the spiritual hosts of wickedness in the heavenly places.*"
—EPH. vi. 10-12.

PAUL closes the long succession of precepts extending over the whole of the second half of this Epistle with a passage of vehement and magnificent rhetoric, the grandeur and fire of which are likely to be lessened by any attempt at exposition.

The Christian church, the kingdom of God on earth, is engaged in a great war. All Christian people are enrolled in the army and are called to active service. The conflict is not "*against flesh and blood,*" against visible and human foes, persecuting governments, unjust magistrates, violent mobs, but against invisible and superhuman powers, animated with a deep and irreconcilable hatred of God and of righteousness. God alone can give us the strength and the arms which are necessary to defend ourselves, to support our comrades, and to destroy the enemy. "*Be strong in the Lord and in the strength of His might. Put on the whole armour of God, that ye may be able to stand against the wiles of the devil.*"

Paul believed in the existence and the formidable power of evil spirits, the enemies of God and of the human race. He believed that the crimes of wicked men were not to be attributed exclusively to themselves, but in part to the temptations of the devil, and that the best and noblest men were accessible to his malignity. This belief retained its place in the creed of the Christian church till very recent times. I suppose that it retains its place in the creed of most of us still; but it has lost its old force and exerts no effective control over the ethical and spiritual life. It is among those beliefs which, as the result of the changes which, during the last two or three hundred years, have passed upon the intellectual and moral life of Europe, have become obsolete; beliefs which, to quote the accurate language of Mr. Lecky, have perished " by indifference not by controversy," have been "relegated to the dim twilight land that surrounds every living faith; the land not of death, but of the shadow of death; the land of the unrealized and the inoperative."[1]

Against the existence of evil spirits, against the

---

[1] Lecky's "History of Rationalism," page xxi.

possibility of their exerting a malignant influence on the moral and spiritual life of mankind, nothing has ever been alleged, as far as I am aware, that has any force in it. Some people appear to suppose that they have said enough to justify their disbelief when they have recited the grotesque and incredible legends, the monstrous and childish superstitions, about the devil, which laid so firm a hold on the imagination and the fears of Europe in the middle ages; or when they have illustrated the history and growth of analogous legends and superstitions among savage or half civilized races. But they could justify atheism by a precisely similar line of reasoning. The mythologies of Greece and of Scandinavia are incredible; their original and central elements are obviously nothing more than the product of the imagination under the excitement of the glories and the terrors, the majesty and the beauty, of the visible universe. But because these mythologies are incredible shall I refuse to believe in the living God, the Creator of the heavens and of the earth, the God that loveth righteousness and hateth iniquity? The attributes and deeds attributed to Kali, the black and blood-stained goddess, with her necklace of human skulls, fill me with horror and fierce disgust; but is this horror, this disgust, any reason for withholding my faith from the revelation of God's infinite love in the Lord Jesus Christ? Many false, childish, dreadful things have been imagined and believed about invisible and Divine powers; but this does not prove that there is no God. Many monstrous and absurd things have been imagined and believed about invisible and evil spirits; but this does not prove that there is no devil.

Three hundred years ago men received popular stories about grotesque and malicious appearances of evil spirits without evidence and without inquiry. It was the habit of the age to believe in such things; men believed, in the absence of all solid reasons for believing. And now we disbelieve, without evidence and without inquiry, what Christ Himself and His apostles have told us about the devil and his temptations. It is the habit of the age to disbelieve in such things; we disbelieve, in the absence of solid reasons for disbelieving. We do not care to investigate the question. We go with the crowd. We think that everybody cannot be wrong. We regard with great complacency the contrast between our own clear intelligence and the superstitions of our ancestors. But when we are challenged to state our reasons for refusing to accept what Christ has revealed on this subject, we have nothing to answer except that other people refuse to accept it; and our ancestors had just as good an apology for accepting the superstitions of their times, everybody accepted them. It is not quite clear that there is any good ground for our self complacency; the belief of our ancestors was as rational as our own disbelief.

The subject is confessedly difficult, obscure, and

mysterious; but there is nothing incredible in the existence of unseen and evil powers, from whose hostility we are in serious danger. We know too little of the invisible world to declare that the existence of such powers is impossible. To claim omniscience is, to say the least, a violation of modesty. Give the faculty of vision to the blind, and they see the sun and the clouds and the moon and the stars, of whose existence they had known nothing except by hearsay; give a new faculty to the human race, and we might discover that we are surrounded by "principalities" and "powers," some of them loyal to God and bright with a Divine glory, some of them in revolt against Him and scarred with the lightnings of the Divine anger.

The moral objections to the existence of evil spirits can hardly be sustained in the presence of the crimes of which our own race has been guilty. It is not a rare but a common thing for men to be impatient of any limitations of their freedom. To be controlled by a higher will is resented as a personal humiliation. There have been vast numbers, who have revolted against the law of righteousness revealed to the conscience, as well as against the Divine authority revealed to faith; and the revolt has sometimes become passionate and fierce. Men have hated righteousness as they ought to hate sin; they have been the zealous propagandists of vice; they have committed with insolent ostentation the foulest wickedness; they have had a horrible delight in dragging other men down into the same depths of moral infamy. They have hated God, and in their frenzy they have denounced His government of the universe—if indeed He governs it; they have declared that if He exists, He is a tyrant and no God; and that it is the duty of mankind to make open war against Him. If such enormous wickedness may exist among men, if men may commit crimes so gross and so violent, if wicked men may put forth their whole strength to induce others to become as wicked as themselves, why should we regard it as incredible that other races may have broken loose from the moral control of God, and may be eager and vehement in inciting universal revolt against Him? There may be other worlds in which the inhabitants are as wicked as the most wicked of ourselves; we cannot tell. We may be surrounded —we cannot tell—by creatures of God, who hate righteousness and hate God with a fiercer hatred than ever burned in the hearts of the most profligate and blasphemous of our race. And they may be endeavouring to accomplish our moral ruin, in this life and the life to come.

If there is any evidence that we are menaced by this peril it is our duty, instead of dismissing the subject with a light jest, to consider the evidence seriously.

The Lord Jesus Christ, who revealed God as He was never revealed before, and who brought life and immortality to light, was not silent on this awful subject. He Himself must have given to His disciples the account of His temptation in the wilderness, and He told them that He was "led up of the Spirit into the wilderness, to be tempted of the devil."[1] He warned Peter of his approaching danger: "Satan asked to have you, that he might sift you as wheat; but I made supplication for thee, that thy faith fail not; and do thou, when once thou hast turned again, stablish thy brethren."[2] In explaining the parable of the sower, Christ said that "when any one heareth the word of the kingdom and understandeth it not, then cometh the evil one and snatcheth away that which hath been sown in his heart."[3] In explaining the parable of the wheat and the tares He said that "the enemy" that sowed the tares is "the devil."[4] When His seventy disciples returned from their mission, the story of their success filled His heart with joy; it was the prophecy of the final triumph of the Divine kingdom, and He said, "I saw Satan fallen as lightning from heaven."[5] When His supreme hour was near, and a voice came from heaven to give Him strength and firmness to meet His agony and His death, He said: "Now is the judgment of this world; now shall the prince of this world be cast out, and I, if I be lifted up, will draw all men unto Myself";[6] the race was at last to have

---

[1] Matt. iv. 1.
[2] Luke xxii. 31.
[3] Matt. xiii. 19.
[4] Matt. xiii. 39.
[5] Luke x. 18.
[6] John xii. 31.

its true King. He describes the eternal fire, in which wicked men and their wickedness are to perish, as "the fire which is prepared for the devil and his angels."[1]

The teaching of the Lord Jesus Christ is sustained by the apostles, by all the apostles. James writes: "Be subject therefore unto God; but resist the devil, and he will flee from you."[2] Paul declares that "the god of this world hath blinded the minds of the unbelieving, that the light of the gospel of the glory of Christ, who is the image of God, should not dawn upon them."[3] In this Epistle he warns the Ephesian Christians that if they yield to the excitement and violence of uncontrolled passion they will "give place to the devil."[4] He tells the Christians at Corinth to beware of men who will come to them with false teaching and with false claims to be apostles of Christ; and to give urgency to his warning, he adds: "Even Satan fashioneth himself into an angel of light. It is no great thing therefore if his ministers also fashion themselves as ministers of righteousness."[5] Peter speaks of our "adversary the devil" whom we are to withstand, "stedfast in [our] faith."[6] In a brief epistle John has no less than six or seven references to this dark and evil power. "I write unto you, young men, because ye

---

[1] Matt. xxv. 41.
[2] James iii. 7.
[3] 2 Cor. iv. 4.
[4] Eph. iv. 26.
[5] 2 Cor. xi. 14.
[6] 1 Pet. v.

have overcome the evil one. . . . I have written unto you, young men, because ye are strong and the word of God abideth in you and ye have overcome the evil one."[1] "Cain was of the evil one, and slew his brother."[2] "We know that whosoever is begotten of God sinneth not; but He that was begotten of God keepeth him, and the evil one toucheth him not."[3] "The whole world lieth in the evil one."[4] "He that doeth sin is of the devil; for the devil sinneth from the beginning. To this end was the Son of God manifested, that He might destroy the works of the devil."[5] "In this the children of God are manifest, and the children of the devil: whosoever doeth not righteousness is not of God, neither he that loveth not his brother."[6]

To these passages I might add many others. Some of them, if they stood alone, might be regarded as mere rhetorical personifications of the contagious and destructive power of moral evil; but many of them will not submit to any such attenuation of their meaning; and taken together they seem to me to constitute a decisive proof that our Lord Jesus Christ warned men of the hostility of unseen and evil spirits who were His foes and the foes of all mankind. The warnings are contained in His own discourses; they are repeated in the epistles of those whom He com-

---

[1] 1 John ii. 13, 14. [2] 1 John iii. 12.
[3] 1 John v. 18. [4] 1 John v. 19.
[5] 1 John iii. 8. [6] 1 John iii. 10.

missioned to lay the foundations of the Christian church.

It may be suggested that as He spoke the language, He thought the thoughts, of His country and His time; that as His contemporaries believed in the existence of evil spirits, He also believed in their existence. But it was not for Him to mistake shadows for realities in that invisible and spiritual world which was His true home and which He had come to reveal to man. It was not for Him to imagine that His kingdom was menaced by enemies that had no existence except in the dreams of popular superstition. It was not for Him to suppose that by His death on the cross and His ascension into heaven He would dislodge and dethrone a prince whose power and malignity were only the fantastic product of a gloomy imagination. It was not for Him—the Judge whose lips are to pronounce the sentence which will secure eternal life and blessedness or doom to eternal death—it was not for Him to warn men that He will condemn them to eternal fire prepared for the devil and his angels, if there is no devil to destroy and if there are no evil angels to share his destruction.

Nor can we believe that Christ Himself knew that evil spirits had no existence and yet consciously and deliberately fell in with the common way of speaking about them. The subject was one of active controversy between rival Jewish sects. In using the popular language Christ took sides on this very question with the one sect against the other; that He should have supported controverted opinions which He knew to be false is inconceivable.

And, in addition to the immediate and polemical demand upon Him for revealing the truth on this subject, there was a stronger claim. He came to us with glad tidings, with tidings of God's infinite love and of the blessed and glorious life beyond death. He was eager to give us perfect freedom and perfect joy. It would have been a relief to the men of His own time, it would have been a still greater relief to men of subsequent ages, to have been told that when they had reckoned with "the world" and "the flesh" they had done with all their enemies. The shadow and the terror of the belief in evil spirits had already fallen on the mind and heart of the race; if the shadow had been projected by superstition, and if the terror had been imaginary, it surely belonged to Him to liberate us from our fears. But His teaching, instead of contradicting the common belief, gave it authority. Instead of assuring men that they had nothing to dread from "principalities" and "powers" and "the spiritual hosts of wickedness," He described the devil as the active foe of the Divine kingdom, warned the chief of the apostles of the approach of Satanic temptation, and told His disciples that He Himself had been tempted by the devil in the wilderness.

Our belief in the existence of evil spirits and in the danger to which their hostility to God and to righteousness exposes us, rests on the teaching of the Lord Jesus Christ; but it has been the common conviction of Christian men that the teaching of Christ is confirmed by our religious experience. Evil thoughts come to us which are alien from all our convictions and from all our sympathies. There is nothing to account for them in our external circumstances or in the laws of our intellectual life. We abhor them and repel them, but they are pressed upon us with cruel persistency. They come to us at times when their presence is most hateful; they cross and trouble the current of devotion ; they gather like thick clouds between our souls and God, and suddenly darken the glory of the Divine righteousness and love. We are sometimes pursued and harassed by doubts which we have deliberately confronted, examined, and concluded to be absolutely destitute of force, doubts about the very existence of God, or about the authority of Christ, or about the reality of our own redemption. Sometimes the assaults take another form. Evil fires which we thought we had quenched are suddenly rekindled by unseen hands; we have to renew the fight with forms of moral and spiritual evil which we thought we had completely destroyed.

There is a Power not ourselves that makes for righteousness; light falls upon us which we know is light from heaven; in times of weariness strength comes to us from inspiration which we know must be Divine; we are protected in times of danger by an invisible presence and grace; there are times when we are conscious that streams of life are flowing into us which must have their fountains in the life of God. And there are dark and evil days when we discover that there is also a power not ourselves that makes for sin. We are at war, the kingdom of God on earth is at war, with the kingdom of darkness. We have to fight "*against the principalities, against the powers, against the world-rulers of this darkness, against the spiritual hosts of wickedness in the heavenly places.*"[1] And therefore we need the strength of God and "the armour of God." The attacks of these formidable foes are not incessant; but as we can never tell when "*the evil day*" may come, we should be always prepared for it. After weeks and months of happy peace they fall upon us without warning, and without any apparent cause. If we are to "*withstand*" them, and if after one great battle in which we have left nothing unattempted or unaccomplished for our own defence and the destruction of the enemy[2] we are still "*to stand,*" to stand with our force un-

---

[1] It seems remarkable that Paul should describe evil spirits as being "in the heavenly places"; but as *we* are there, we should be inaccessible to them unless *they* were there too. But the time will come when "the Son of man shall send forth His angels and they shall gather out of His kingdom *all things* that cause stumbling, and them that do iniquity, and shall cast them into the furnace of fire." (Matt. xiii. 41.)

[2] This seems to be the meaning of the phrase "*having done all*"; the word which is represented by the phrase implies the great difficulty of the task which is perfectly accomplished.

exhausted and our resources undiminished, ready for another, and perhaps fiercer engagement, we must "be strong in the Lord and in the strength of His might," and we must "*take up the whole armour of God.*"

XXIII.

THE WHOLE ARMOUR OF GOD.

"*Wherefore take up the whole armour of God, that ye may be able to withstand in the evil day, and, having done all, to stand. Stand therefore, having girded your loins with truth, and having put on the breastplate of righteousness, and having shod your feet with the preparation of the gospel of peace; withal taking up the shield of faith, wherewith ye shall be able to quench all the fiery darts of the evil one. And take the helmet of salvation, and the sword of the Spirit, which is the word of God.*"

—EPH. vi. 13-17.

IN the illustration of Paul's description of the Divine armour, expositors have shown an inexhaustible, and perhaps a not unprofitable, ingenuity. For purposes of edification his account of every separate part of the armour deserves the closest and most careful consideration. But Calvin, when he puts aside with a certain touch of scorn the expository method of some commentators and preachers, shows the masculine good sense which nearly always distinguishes him. "Nothing," he says, "can be more idle than the extraordinary pains which some have taken to discover the reason why righteousness is made a *breastplate* instead of a *girdle*. Paul's design was to touch briefly on the most important points required in a Christian, and to adapt them to the [military] comparison which he had already used."[1]

But though the passage is rhetorical the rhetoric is the rhetoric of truth and not of mere imagination and passion. If we consider the sources of the strength and security of the Christian life we shall discover that there is not only strict propriety but profound truth in the description of "righteousness" as a "breastplate" and of "salvation" as a "helmet," of "the word of God" as a "sword," and of "faith" as a "shield."

It is very characteristic of Paul that he should give the first place to "*truth*." He is thinking of the truth concerning God and the will of God which comes to us from God Himself through His revelation in Christ and through the teaching of the Spirit; for all the elements of Christian strength are represented in this passage as Divine gifts. Truth appropriated and made our own gives energy, firmness, and decision to Christian life and action, relieves us from the entanglement and distraction which come from uncertainty and doubt, gives us a complete command of all our vigour. It is like the strong belt of the ancient soldier which braced him up, made him conscious of his force, kept his armour in its place,

---

[1] *Calvin, in loc.* In 1 Thess. v. 8. Paul describes "faith and love," not "righteousness," as the "breastplate" of the Christian.

and prevented it from interfering with the freedom of his action. "*Stand therefore, having girded your loins with truth.*"

He gives the second place to "*righteousness.*" In the conflicts of the Christian life we are safe, only while we practise every personal and private virtue, and discharge with fidelity every duty both to man and to God.

"*Righteousness*" is the defence and guarantee of righteousness. The honest man is not touched by temptations to dishonesty; the truthful man is not touched by temptations to falsehood; habits of industry are a firm defence against temptations to indolence; a pure heart resents with disgust and scorn the first approaches of temptation to impurity.

The separate virtues of a perfect character are necessary to each other, and through a single vicious habit or tendency we may be betrayed into many kinds of sin. Vanity and cowardice make us accessible to temptations to untruthfulness; covetousness on the one hand and reckless extravagance on the other may be the means of destroying our integrity; intemperance may lead to violence and licentiousness. The practical obedience to Christ which is possible to us through the power of His Spirit is a protection against temptations which might destroy our very life. It is like the "*breastplate*" which the soldier wore to protect the vital parts of the body. In anticipation of the fierce assault of the "*spiritual hosts of wickedness*" we are to arm ourselves with perfect conformity to all the precepts of Christ; we are to "*stand . , . having put on the breastplate of righteousness.*"

Paul gives the third place to what he describes as "*the preparation of the gospel of peace.*" When we have received with hearty faith the great assurance of the remission of sins through Christ, we are released from the gravest anxieties and fears. We have escaped from care about the past, and are free to give our whole strength to the duties of the present and of the future. The discovery that God is at peace with us gives us confidence and inspires us with alertness and elasticity of spirit. We are not merely ready, we are eager, for every good work. We are like men whose feet are well shod: they can stand firm and they can run; they are prepared to resist the shock of the enemy's assault and to attack and pursue him when the assault is repelled. We are to "*stand , . . having our feet shod with the preparation*"—the readiness—"*of the gospel of peace.*"

The fourth place is given to "*faith.*" There are a thousand perils against which faith in the righteousness and love and power of God is our only protection. The immense and awful gloom which has rested upon the human race through a long succession of dreary centuries sometimes provokes us to desperate resentment, and we are ready to curse God and die. There are hours when the gloom seems without relief. The traditions of a golden age in which men lived in innocence and happiness, under sunny skies which were never darkened by storms, reaping golden harvests which were never ruined by blight, unvexed by cares, unstained by crimes, are idle dreams. The past was full of misery. The hopes which men cherish of a golden age to come seem to us nothing more than the illusions of a sanguine imagination which, finding the present misery of the world intolerable, endeavours to solace itself with the vision of a remote and impossible future. Through age after age hunger, weariness, wasting disease, racking pain and unconsoled sorrow are the doom of millions of mankind. Brutal ignorance and degrading vices are transmitted from generation to generation. Here and there in the universal darkness a few elect souls are fired with an enthusiasm of compassion for human wretchedness and of indignation for human wrongs; the fires kindle in thousands and tens of thousands of hearts; it seems as if the hour of retribution and of deliverance had come. But the fires are soon burnt out; the light is extinguished; the blackness of night returns; infinite hope sinks into infinite despair.

Sometimes fierce thoughts of God are forced upon us by the cruel disappointments and protracted troubles of our personal life. If we could see that our calamities were "the chastening of the Lord," and were likely to subdue our sins and to invigorate our righteousness, we might be patient and trustful. But many of our sorrows seem aimless. They are not discipline but torture. They seem to make us worse rather than better; they are of a kind, so we are ready to think, which might have been purposely selected to destroy whatever germs of goodness are in us, and to excite to unnatural activity every latent tendency to evil. We lose the child, the wife, whose love softened our heart and was the chief earthly support of the virtues which we find it hardest to practise. We are treated harshly and basely by the friends whom we had perfectly trusted, and their treatment of us makes it impossible for us ever to trust the affection or the honour of men again. The results of years of hard industry, of thrift, of self denial, are destroyed, just when we were hoping for some relief from the strain of anxiety and incessant labour, and when we were meaning to use our ripened experience in the service of society or the church. Or perhaps our distress comes from other causes. We have set our hearts upon knowing God's will and doing it; we have had a large, an unmeasured confidence in the power of God's grace. We thought that heaven would come down to earth, and that we should anticipate in this mortal life the blessedness of our immortality. The Divine promises seemed to assure us of this perfect holiness and joy. But every hope has been disappointed. There has been neither peace nor righteousness. We have found that "the spiritual hosts of wickedness" have assaulted us in "the heavenly places," and wounded us cruelly. We were not safe, so it seemed to us, even in God. Instead of the peace we hoped for, there has been agitation and war; instead of the uniform victory over sin, frequent and shameful defeat.

Or the Christian work into which we have put our whole strength has been a dreary failure. Instead of reaping the harvests which others have sowed—and this was what the words of Christ, as we interpreted them, encouraged us to expect—our own harvests have had no sun to ripen them, or have been spoiled by destructive floods, or have been set on fire by relentless foes. Everything has gone against us.

When the misery of the world oppresses us, or we are crushed by the misery of our personal life, terrible thoughts about God pierce through every defence and fasten themselves in our very flesh, torturing us, and filling our veins with burning fever. We writhe in our agony. If by any chance we hear about "the unsearchable riches" of God's grace, we listen, not only uncomforted, but sometimes with a passion of unbelief. "Grace!" we exclaim, "where is the proof of it? Is there any pity in Him, any justice, any truth?"

In these hours of anguish we are like soldiers wounded by the "*darts*," with burning tow fastened to them, or with their iron points made red hot, which were used in ancient warfare.

We should have been safe if, when "the evil day" came, it had found us with a strong and invincible faith in God; this would have been a perfect defence; and apart from this we can have no secure protection. Take up "*the shield of faith, wherewith ye shall be able to quench all the fiery darts of the evil one.*"

The fifth place is given to "*salvation.*" We are insecure, unless we make completely our own the great redemption which God has achieved for us in Christ. Our thoughts are to extend over the whole range of the blessings which God has conferred upon us in Christ's incarnation, death, resurrection, and ascension into heaven. These blessings include not only the remission of sins, but victory over all the powers of evil, and eternal blessedness and glory. They are to be accepted with courageous trust, though there are times when they seem to transcend all the measures of hope. They are to be regarded as our certain inheritance by the free gift of the Divine grace, an inheritance which can never be alienated and can never be impoverished. If we have mean and narrow conceptions of the Divine redemption, or if we think that it lies mainly with ourselves whether we shall secure "glory, honour, and immortality," we shall be like a soldier without a "*helmet,*" unprotected against blows which may be mortal. But if we have a vivid apprehension of the greatness of the Christian redemption, and if our hope of achieving a glorious future is rooted in our consciousness of the infinite power and grace of God, we shall be safe. We are to "*take the helmet of salvation.*"

But all these are arms of defence. Have we no weapons for attacking and destroying the enemy? Are the same temptations and the same doubts to return incessantly and to return with their force undiminished? The helmet, the shield, the breastplate, the belt, may be a protection for ourselves; but we belong to an army and are fighting for the victory of the Divine kingdom and for the complete destruction of the authority and power of the "spiritual hosts of wickedness" over other men; it is not enough that our personal safety is provided for.

We are to fight the enemy with "*the word of God.*" Divine promises are not only to repel doubts but to destroy them. Divine precepts are not only to be a protection against temptations, but to inflict on them a mortal wound and so to prevent them from troubling us again. The revelation of God's infinite pity for human sorrow and of His infinite mercy for human sin, of the infinite blessings conferred upon men by Christ in this world and of the endless righteousness and glory which He confers in the world to come— the Divine "word" to the human race—is the solitary power by which we can hope to win any real and enduring victory over the sins and miseries of mankind. We are to take "*the sword*" which the Spirit has given us, "*the sword of the Spirit, which is the word of God.*"

And now Paul drops his metaphor. Unless God personally stands by us we can hope for neither personal safety nor for any victories over the powers of evil. We are therefore to pray both for ourselves and for others. But the consideration of this subject must be reserved for the next lecture.

XXIV.

PRAYER; INTERCESSORY PRAYER; CONCLUSION.

> "*With all prayer and supplication praying at all seasons in the Spirit, and watching thereunto in all perseverance and supplication for all the saints, and on my behalf, that utterance may be given unto me in opening my mouth, to make known with boldness the mystery of the gospel, for which I am an ambassador in chains; that in it I may speak boldly, as I ought to speak. But that ye also may know my affairs, how I do, Tychicus, the beloved brother and faithful minister in the Lord, shall make known to you all things: whom I have sent unto you for this very purpose, that ye may know our state, and that he may comfort your hearts. Peace be to the brethren, and love with faith, from God the Father and the Lord Jesus Christ. Grace be with all them that love our Lord Jesus Christ in uncorruptness.*"   EPH. vi. 18–24.

PRAYER, which is of supreme necessity both for our own defence and for the destruction of the kingdom of darkness, cannot be properly described as part of the defensive armour which we are to wear or as one of the weapons which we are to wield. It is an appeal to the Divine strength and to Divine grace.

To speak of "the power of prayer," as though prayer itself were a spiritual force, is misleading. In prayer, human weakness invokes Divine protection and Divine support. We pray, because our position in relation to God is a position of absolute dependence. Apart from Him we can do nothing.

And in the spiritual life no system of secondary laws comes between Him and us. In the inferior provinces of our activity we are environed by the unchanging order of the physical universe; the Divine energy is voluntarily limited by natural laws; without any direct appeal to God we can command physical forces by a knowledge of the fixed methods of their action. But the higher life is a perpetual miracle. In the spiritual universe the Divine will works freely, and we have to do, not with forces which act under the restraint of fixed laws, but with a personal Will. God is the Fountain of our life and of our strength; but the streams flow, not under the compulsion of necessity, but according to His free volitions. We therefore pray that the life and the strength may be ours.

Our dependence upon God is constant, and therefore our prayers should be constant. With the chances and changes of life our necessities are infinitely varied, and our prayers should be equally varied. Our opportunities for prayer are not always the same; sometimes we must pray alone, sometimes we can pray with others; sometimes our prayers must be brief, sometimes they may be prolonged.

And we shall never pray with a true knowledge of our own wants or of the wants of others, and with a clear apprehension of the great power and love of God, unless we have the illumination and gracious aid of the Divine Spirit.

We are therefore to "stand" ready for the great

conflict, not only armed with the whole armour of God, but "*with all prayer and supplication,*[1] *praying at all seasons in the Spirit.*"

We are to be constantly cherishing the consciousness of our dependence on God, and constantly on our guard against whatever would destroy or enfeeble the spirit of prayer, "*watching thereunto in all perseverance.*"

With this persistency and vigilance on our own behalf there is to be solicitude for our comrades in the great army of God. We are to pray for them as constantly as for ourselves, "watching thereunto *in all perseverance and supplication for all the saints.*"

Paul adds a special request that the Ephesian Christians would pray for himself, that a Divine word might be given to him when he might have to make his defence as an apostle of Christ and to declare the truths and facts of the Christian Faith. I suppose that even Paul's vision of Divine and eternal things was clearer at some times than at others, and that the "*boldness,*"—the confidence, the vigour, the freedom—with which he was able to state what he saw and knew, varied. Great opportunities might be coming to him for bearing testimony to Christ; and he was anxious that when they came he might speak under the inspiration of Divine wisdom and Divine

---

[1] "Prayer" is the generic word, and includes every kind of address to God; "supplication" is more specifically a petition or request, and is used of petitions and requests addressed to men as well as to God.

strength : "*that utterance may be given unto me, in opening my mouth,[1] to make known with boldness the mystery of the gospel, for which I am an ambassador in chains, that therein I may speak boldly as I ought to speak.*"

Habitual intercession for others is one of the surest correctives of the tendency to regard prayer as deriving its chief value and importance—not from the fact that God listens to us when we pray and gives us what we ask for—but from the influence which devotional thought, the confession of sin and of weakness, the grateful acknowledgment of God's goodness, and the contemplation of God's eternal majesty and glory, exert on our own spiritual life.

None of us can escape altogether from the prevailing temper of our time. Those of us who think that we are least affected by the currents of contemporary thought feel their power. The tendency to eliminate the supernatural element from the spiritual as well as the physical universe is affecting the whole life of the church. Christian people can understand that when they pray their devotional acts exert a reflex influence on their own minds and hearts; but to expect a direct answer from God requires a vigorous faith; and to this faith I fear that many of us are

---

[1] "*In opening my mouth*," *i.e.* when I have to speak; and the phrase suggests that he was thinking of having to speak on occasions of special gravity.

unequal. If Christian men are in trouble they are conscious that their hearts are lighter after they have spoken to God about it, just as their hearts are lighter when they have spoken about it to a friend; and they suppose that this kind of relief is all that they have a right to look for. They pray for stronger faith, and they suppose that it is by their own thoughts about God and His great goodness, thoughts which are made more vivid by the act of prayer, that their faith is to be strengthened. Or if they pray that their love for God may become more ardent, they imagine that it is by the very excitement of praying for it that the result is to be obtained. They think that their prayer will be ineffective if, while they pray, their hearts are not flooded with emotion; they are satisfied if the emotion comes, and if, to use their own words, they "feel better" when the prayer is over.

It is no doubt true that religious thought and communion with God purify, invigorate, and ennoble the soul; but if when we pray we think only or chiefly of the effect of prayer upon ourselves, instead of thinking of its effect in inducing God to grant us what we pray for, we misapprehend the nature of the act. When your child comes to you hungry or thirsty, and asks for food or drink, the child expects you to do something in answer to its request. It does not suppose that the mere act of asking will satisfy its hunger or quench its thirst; and so when we ask God for spiritual wisdom and strength we are not to imagine that the mere asking will make us wiser and stronger. God teaches us and God strengthens us, in answer to our prayer.

While this defective theory must impair the reality and lessen the earnestness of prayer for ourselves, it is likely to prevent us altogether from praying for others. If we suppose that the great object of prayer is to soothe or excite the soul by its reflex influence, we shall see no use in praying for other people, unless they are present to hear us pray; and then we shall think more of the immediate effect on their hearts of what we say to God than of the blessings which God will give them in answer to our intercessions.

The habit of praying for others will discipline us to pray for ourselves in a right way; it will train us to believe that blessings come direct from God in answer to our prayers.

The duty of praying for others is frequently inculcated in the New Testament. It is one of the obligations arising from that great law which makes it impossible for any of us to live an independent and an isolated life. We are members of one body; if one member suffers all the members suffer with it; if one member is strong and healthy all the members share the health and strength. We are not fighting a solitary battle. We belong to a great army, and the fortunes of a regiment in a remote part of the field may give us an easy victory or increase the chances of our defeat. We are to offer supplication for "all the saints." Paul himself asked for the intercessions of the Ephesian Christians. He knew that by their prayers they might secure for him a clearness and a vigour of thought and a fearlessness of spirit which apart from their prayers he might not possess; and we cannot tell how much of his energy, fire, and courage, came to him in answer to the prayers of unknown and forgotten saints.

We often deplore the want of vigour and zeal in the work of the church. Why is it not more vigorous and more zealous? If there are times when Sunday school teachers are conscious that they have no heart for teaching, whose fault is it? If there are times when those who visit the homes of the poor are troubled that they have no Divine "word" on their lips likely to quicken the conscience of the irreligious or to console the misery of the wretched, whose fault is it? Is it their fault alone? No; it is ours as well as theirs.

You come to listen to me on Sunday and I have nothing to say that adds vigour to faith, or fervour to love, or that enlarges your knowledge of duty or of God. It is plain that during the week I have had no clear vision of spiritual truth, or that, if I have, the vision has faded away. You are naturally disappointed, perhaps discontented. It is partly my fault. But is it not possible that the fault is as much yours as mine? If you had prayed for me with earnestness and faith, might not the vision of God have come to me and the revelation of spiritual truth and the baptism of fire? In the absence of your intercessions God may have given me truth for myself but not for you. Suppose that in the course of a few weeks after the Ephesian Christians received this epistle Paul had been called to appear before the Roman emperor and that his courage had failed; or that if his courage had not failed, no wise and vigorous and penetrating words had occurred to him in defence of the honour of Christ and in illustration of the glory of the Christian redemption. The Ephesian Christians when they heard of his failure would have wondered how it could have happened that the great apostle had even momentarily lost his fearlessness and his power. But if they had forgotten to pray that "utterance" might be given to him "to make known with boldness the mystery of the gospel" the apostle's failure might have been the result of their neglect.

There are Christian people whose life is so far removed from excitement, agitation, and peril, that they seem to have no opportunities for winning great moral victories; their powers are very limited, and they are not appointed to tasks of great difficulty and honour. Let them resolve to have their part in the righteousness of their comrades who face the fiercest dangers, and in the fame of the very chiefs and heroes of the great army of God. Let them pray for "all the saints," and their prayers will give courage, endurance, and invincible fidelity to those who are struggling with incessant temptations. Some Christian brother, who under the stress of bad trade and unexpected losses is almost driven to dishonesty, will preserve his integrity. Some young man, who is no longer sheltered by the kindly defence of a religious home and who is surrounded by companions that are trying to drug his conscience, to excite his passions, and to drag him down into vice, will stand firm in his fidelity to Christ. Some poor woman, harassed by anxiety, worn down by unkindness, will receive strength to bear her sorrows with patience, and will rise to a lofty faith in the righteousness and love of God. The feverish passion for wealth will be cooled in some Christian merchant, and he will obey the words of Christ charging him to seek first God's kingdom and God's righteousness. Some Christian statesman will have a clearer vision of Divine and eternal things, and the vision will enable him to master the impulses of personal ambition and to care only for serving Christ by serving the state. Saintly souls will become more saintly. New fervour will kindle in many a heart already glowing with apostolic zeal for the glory of God and the salvation of men. New gifts of wisdom and of utterance will be conferred on some who are already conspicuous for their spiritual power and their spiritual achievements. By constant and earnest intercession for "all the saints," those who are living in quiet and obscure places may share the honours and victories of all their comrades, may have some part in the praise of their holiness, and some part in their final reward.

Paul knew that many of the Christians at Ephesus had a strong affection for him. For "three years" he had lived in the city and its neighbourhood, and during that time "ceased not to admonish every one night and day with tears." They would be anxious to know about his health, and about his prospects of release. He was an "*ambassador*" having in charge "*the mystery of the gospel*." Ambassadors are received with honour, and their persons are regarded as sacred; but he was an "*ambassador in chains*"; his friends at Ephesus would want to hear whether he was being treated harshly or with consideration. He had written to them about their duties; they also would want to know his "*affairs*";[1] and he says that Tychicus would tell them about him. "*But that ye also may know my affairs, how I do, Tychicus, the beloved brother and faithful minister in the Lord, shall make known to you all things: whom I have sent unto you for this very purpose, that he may comfort your hearts.*"

He closes, as he began, with a benediction. "*Peace be to the brethren*";—" the peace of God which passeth

---

[1] This seems to be the meaning of the words "that *ye also* may know our affairs." There is something unnatural, I think, in supposing Paul to have meant that he had sent Tychicus in order that the Ephesian Christians as well as Christians elsewhere might know about him. He had been thinking and writing about *them*; they in their turn would be anxious about *him*.

all understanding"[1]; the heavenly calm, the Divine rest, which results from a clear and unclouded consciousness of the Divine love, and from the restoration of perfect harmony between the soul and God. They have faith, and he invokes on them the Divine fire which will kindle in their hearts a most fervent love: "*Peace be to the brethren, and love with faith, from God the Father and the Lord Jesus Christ.*"

"*Grace be with all them that love our Lord Jesus Christ in uncorruptness.*" Love for Christ is the common life of all true Christians. In whatever else they differ from each other, in their creeds, in their modes of worship, in some of their conceptions of how the Divine life in man is originated, how it should be disciplined, and how it is manifested, they are alike in this; they all love the Lord Jesus Christ. The controversies and divisions of Christendom have gone a long way towards destroying the unity of the church; but in love for Christ all Christians are one.

And love for Christ is immortal. The religious passion which is created by sensuous excitements, whether those excitements are addressed to the eye or to the ear, whether they heat the blood or intoxicate the imagination, is transitory. It has in it the elements of corruption. But true love for Christ is rooted in all that is deepest and divinest in human nature. It is immortal, for it belongs to that im-

---

[1] Phil. iv. 6.

mortal life which comes to us by the inspiration of the Spirit of God. It will not decay with the decay of physical vigour. It will triumph over death; and will reveal the fulness of its strength and the intensity of its fervour in those endless ages which we hope to spend with Christ in glory. "*Grace be with all them that love our Lord Jesus Christ in uncorruptness.*"

www.ingramcontent.com/pod-product-compliance
Lightning Source LLC
Chambersburg PA
CBHW071138300426
44113CB00009B/1006